Cary Schmidt

Hook, Line & Sinker

How the enemy is dividing and destroying the Christian family

Striving Together Publications
4020 E. Lancaster Blvd.
Lancaster, CA 93535
800.201.7748

Cover design by Jeremy Lofgren
Layout by Craig Parker

ISBN 978-1-59894-067-1

Printed in the United States of America

Dedication

This book is dedicated first to my own parents who labored so diligently to make our family years so incredible! Thank you, Mom, for giving your life so fully to your boys. You are legendary, and I am most blessed to have grown up under your care. Thank you, Dad, for placing such emphasis on family fun and for always being a kid at heart and loving to play—even to this day! (A recent Coldwater Creek canoe trip comes to mind!)

Second, I dedicate this text to my wife and children. Dana, you are truly my best friend. A day with you is my favorite thing in life—nothing can even come close to comparing! Lance, Larry, and Haylee, my love for you cannot be described in words. I pray we can savor the daily joys of growing up together and then cherish the memories we made for the rest of our lives, and most of all I pray you will fall in love with your Heavenly Father and live for Him until you see Him.

Special Thanks To

Pastor Paul Chappell—Thank you for allowing me to serve in such a wonderful ministry. Thank you for exemplifying the truths of this book in your own family!

LBC Students and Families—My wife and I count it a great joy and privilege to help in some small way in the spiritual fight for your family! Thank you for entrusting us with influence in your lives.

The Early Readers and Proofreaders of This Book—A handful of teens, parents, friends, and co-laborers volunteered to read through this text as it was being written. These are busy people who chose to care! Thank you for prodding me on when I wasn't sure I should continue. Your insight, healthy feedback, and sometimes direct challenges were invaluable. Thank you for being willing to be brutally honest!

The Ministry Team I Serve With—The Lord has blessed me to work with such gifted, committed, and faithful servants of Christ in several areas of ministry! Thank you for sharing so diligently in a work that is far bigger than us. My respect for you is gargantuan!

A Personal Word from the Author

Dear Reader,

It's a scary thing to send a book to print. I'm grateful and humbled that you would take time to read it. I don't deserve any influence in your life, but I do thank you for picking up this book. I truly pray and hope that it will challenge you and equip you for the battle ahead.

The subjects addressed in this book are intricate, and the stakes are huge! For that reason I urge you to read the entire book, cover to cover as the material builds upon itself and the hooks that we will study weave together and work together. It will be difficult to pick and choose portions to read and still understand the entire message of the book. There is a thought flow from one page to the next that you must grasp and apply to your family life.

Much more could be written about these subjects. Hopefully the scriptural principles will spark your interest and move you to further study and greater understanding as you seek to please God in your family life.

As you read, I would truly love to hear your feedback. Please let me know what God does in your heart through this text. My email address is caryschmidt@pobox.com. Sincerely,

Cary Schmidt

Striving Together Publications
A Ministry of Lancaster Baptist Church
4020 E. Lancaster Blvd. • Lancaster, CA 93535
800.201.7748 • www.strivingtogether.com caryschmidt@pobox.com

Table of Contents

PART FIVE: BEFRIEND AND BEWILDER

PART SIX: CONCLUSION

Preface from Dr. Paul Chappell

There are many aspects of Brother Cary Schmidt's ministry that I have greatly appreciated, as a pastor and parent. One of the ways he has been a special blessing through the years here in the ministry of Lancaster Baptist Church and West Coast Baptist College has been through his ministry to parents. Through his quarterly teen-parent training meetings and his writing ministry, Brother Schmidt has encouraged and equipped not only teenagers, but also their parents in this exciting and important time of life.

Hook, Line & Sinker is the best material I have ever read for parents who want to glean wisdom in how to develop hearts for God in the lives of their teenagers. If you are serious about guiding your teenager away from the entanglements of the wicked one and into a life of devotion to Jesus Christ, you will want to read every page of this book.

May God grant you His grace as you apply the truths from His Word and this helpful book to your family life!

Dr. Paul Chappell
Pastor, Lancaster Baptist Church
President, West Coast Baptist College
Fall 2004

Introduction

Hook, Line & Sinker
Winning the Spiritual War Against Your Family

If you had a contract out on your life and a sniper was hunting you, what would you do? Other than panic, you might try to protect yourself. You would probably research the ways that this sniper has killed before and then try to defend yourself against his tactics. You would probably contact higher authorities and depend upon their help as well. Whatever the case, you wouldn't sit by and let it happen easily.

Well, you do have a contract out on your life—and on your family. This isn't a physical contract to kill—it is a spiritual contract to devour. Even now, as you read these words, an enemy that you cannot see is positioning and plotting against you and those you love. He never stops laying and springing traps. He never takes a break. He is the master of patience, and he is willing to wait years if he has to.

In the pages of this book, we will uncover a few of his tactics and gain some insight into how he is devouring families in our world today. We will expose his lies for what they are and share the truth of God's Word in contrast. Hopefully, as a result, your family can escape the snares and render your enemy's contract null and void.

What are the top four ways that teenagers and their parents are destroying their lives? Yes, I do mean teens and their parents. Quite often in counseling and teaching, it's not just the teen that is headed down the wrong path. Usually the parents are actively, albeit ignorantly, participating in the devouring of their own children. I don't mean that parents are doing the devouring—but that parents are participating in the process in some way that advances it or assists it.

In other words, quite often parents are unwittingly facilitating the attacks of the enemy as he devours young lives. They do this both by their actions and their inactions. The pages of this book detail the most common four "hooks" that the devil uses to ensnare and entangle young lives and young families. Along the journey, we will discuss both what parents and teens are doing to lose the battle and what they should be doing to win the battle.

This book is written to two groups of people—young people, and the "old" people who parent or work with them! Each chapter contains portions that are more directed to young people and portions that are more directed to parents. So, why put both in one book, and why blend them together? Because this book needs to be a journey—together. It's that simple. Parents need to understand their kids and kids need to understand their parents. That's the whole point. In a world that is desperately trying to pull you apart as a family, may this book help bring you together.

Parent, I hope you will take the lead in reading and then bring your teen in on pertinent portions of the book. I hope you will decide to make this a family effort—to take the journey together.

Also, this book is written from a Christian perspective. The principles contained herein are from the Word of God—the Bible, which should have absolute truth and authority in the life of a believer. If you are not a believer, I urge you to accept God's good news of salvation and place your life into the hands of Jesus Christ as your personal Saviour. There is no greater decision, and there is no other way to fully understand life's purpose and plan. Jesus Himself said, "I am the way, the truth, and the life: no man cometh unto the Father, but by me" (John 14:6b). We'll talk more about this later in the book.

In response to a questionnaire, a college-age young lady who grew up in our youth ministry recently wrote these words to me:

"When you are a teen, you get in trouble a lot. Sometimes it seems like the only time you get attention in your home is on your birthday or when you do something wrong."

I laughed when I read that, because it so concisely says what many teens feel. Often in a teen group I will ask for a raise of hands to the question, "How many of you feel like you are always in trouble with someone?" Usually every hand goes up! At first it's funny, but it's also sad, because this seems to sum up how many homes function. So long as things appear to be going all right on the surface, there's not much relationship. Yet, when suddenly there's trouble, we as parents tend to swoop in like a firefighting airplane to put out the blaze, and then our lives return to the "hangar" until the next forest fire.

My sincere hope is that the pages of this book will provoke you to be more like a forest ranger—nurturing and caring for the young trees in your household—rather than just a firefighter dumping retardant on them when they catch fire. Surely, there is great risk of "fire" in today's society, but there is also much that can be done to prevent spiritual "forest fires" in young lives. My prayer is that these pages will draw you together as teens and parents to build a loving, nurturing relationship that will both protect you from danger and prepare you for the wonderful future God has planned.

A few days ago, I walked into my office and discovered a hand-written letter taped to my computer screen. It was from my thirteen-year-old son Lance. He had come by while I was out. As I unfolded the letter, what I read was priceless. His words literally melted my heart and brought tears to my eyes. This is what he wrote:

> Dear Dad,
>
> I love you so, so, so much, and you are the best dad in the world! I know, I tell you that all the time, every night, I know, I know, but Dad you don't know what I really mean when I say you're the best. When I say you're the best each night, I mean it. I mean you're my friend no matter what tries to get in the way, we will always be true best friends.
>
> You know Dad, and this is the truth…nobody can ever get enough of you. I mean you're cool, you're smart (that's good, so you can help me with my math problems), you don't embarrass me in front of my friends, you pray with

me every night (I mean what dad does that!), and I like it. You can do it till I am 30 years old, and I still will love it.

Anyway…what I'm trying to get across to you is there is nobody ever in this universe that can replace you. I mean you are the ultimate! Love you Dad, I'm with you all the way!

Love, your best friend,
Lance D. Schmidt

That letter, in a few simple words from a young boy, seems to express so loudly the deepest needs of a teenager's heart. He expresses so simply how much he longs for and craves a strong relationship with me. The cry of my children's hearts—the cry of your children's hearts is what compelled the writing of these words. My heart's cry to God is that in ten or twenty years, Lance's words, "You're my friend, no matter what tries to get in the way…I'm with you all the way," will still be a spiritual reality with all of my children. I pray this will be true in your family as well.

Imagine that we're sitting in a restaurant—me, my wife, you, and yours—teens, parents, the youth pastor and his wife—all together. If you asked me, "What are the issues that are destroying teens and their parents today? What are the biggest problems and what are the Bible solutions?" this is what I would say…

Part One

The War We Cannot See

Exposing and Understanding Our Unseen Enemy

"While we look not at the things which are seen, but at the things which are not seen: for the things which are seen are temporal; but the things which are not seen are eternal."
—2 Corinthians 4:18

"Through faith we understand that the worlds were framed by the word of God, so that things which are seen were not made of things which do appear."
—Hebrews 11:3

"For we wrestle not against flesh and blood, but against principalities, against powers, against the rulers of the darkness of this world, against spiritual wickedness in high places."
—Ephesians 6:12

One

A Slaughter from Another World

My idea of fishing is pretty simple—find a spot, drop a line, and pull a fish in within ten seconds. Repeat the process until you've caught all the fish you want or until you are no longer having fun. Now that's fishing! After about ten seconds with no bites, I'm concluding that "if there are fish here, they aren't hungry," and I'm ready to move on to something fun. Yes—your typical "fair weather" fisherman!

In addition to this, I've always despised the mess. First you bait the hook with some slimy, squiggling, sub-life form, then you rip the hook (guts and all) out of the mouth of some nasty smelling fish—and then you eat a nicely packed tuna sandwich with the same hands! That never really appealed to me for some reason!

Oddly though, I come from a family of lifetime fishermen. My grandfather spent a good bit of his life on the Chesapeake Bay, landing some of the largest fish I have ever seen in my life! My uncle followed in those same steps. These men really knew their stuff! They took fishing to a whole new level. Fortunately for the fish, only my brother Matt inherited the "lifetime fishing" gene in the family. I've witnessed occasions where Matt would wait for hours for one bite, and loved every minute! That must be a genetic thing—how else could you explain it?

Some of my greatest childhood memories were captured at a pier on the Severn River, just off the Chesapeake Bay in Maryland. My brothers and I would spend hours catching anything that would bite the hook—and yes, it was usually every ten seconds that something would. Maybe I have "Fishing ADD" (Attention Deficit Disorder). Our grandfather was there most of the time—baiting hooks, pulling fish in, and making sure we were having a good time. Every now and then he would even decide to have a little fun himself—throwing a mis-hooked eel on the back of some unsuspecting six-year-old grandson!

One fishing trip sticks out unmistakably above all the rest, because it was the one time we finally went into deep waters on a charter vessel. Grandad, Dad, and all of us boys packed up and departed early in the morning from a port in southern Maryland—eager to catch some bigger fish for the first time. What happened that day has stayed with all of us for a long, long time.

After a two-hour trek into deep waters, the boat captain began to search for blue fish with his sonar equipment. In a matter of moments, he had found a school and told us to start dropping lines. My grandfather hurriedly began pulling rods off the wall, rigging them, and handing them out as fast as he possibly could. It was only a matter of seconds before six of us had our lines over the back of the boat—in the middle of a giant school of blue fish!

What happened next was unbelievable. We began pulling in blue fish in record numbers. My ten-second rule was obliterated! For the ensuing three hours, there was barely a five-second pause when someone wasn't wrestling another blue fish into the hull of that boat. My grandfather did nothing for three solid hours but rip hooks out of fish and pack the coolers on that boat. The rest of us did nothing but drop lines and wrestle fish in as fast as we possibly could. At any given moment, there were six or eight bloody blue fish flopping around the floor of that boat! It was fishing heaven!

We tracked that school of fish for three hours—and there wasn't a slow moment. It was such a successful day that we had to quit early. What would normally be a full day of fishing was over before 10 a.m. The boat was full, and there was no place left to put the fish!

The icing on the cake was the look on my grandmother's face when we unloaded what seemed like hundreds of blue fish onto the front lawn of her home shortly after noon that day. You see, she was the family fish-cleaner.

One thing I will never forget about that day is how well my grandfather and the boat captain knew those fish. For them, fishing was as much a science as it was a sport. The boat captain knew exactly where to look for fish; the boat was outfitted with equipment that could read the water below and detect fish; every rod was equipped with a lure that a blue fish would bite, fishing line that a blue fish couldn't break, and a pole that a blue fish couldn't snap. And of course, at the end of every lure, carefully hidden among the colorful, attractive bait were those razor sharp hooks. Once hooked, no blue fish got away. Once in the boat, no blue fish survived. Even the boat hull was equipped with freshly iced coolers—the final resting place of every blue fish—and a hose to wash away the blood from the slaughter.

Every catch was slightly different. Some fish fought harder than others. Some lived longer than others. Some swallowed the hook deeper than others. Some fought harder once they were in the boat. Some bled more than others. But none survived. Once hooked, they were reeled in, ripped up, and stacked neatly on ice.

I have often wondered in times like that, what was the last thing going through that fish's mind before he felt that hook? What did he think he was biting into before the pain struck and it was too late?

In recent years, I've witnessed an entirely different type of fishing blood bath. This one is no sport at all, and the product is certainly no family feast. The fisherman is Satan himself, the bait is a vast variety of deceptive tactics and worldly philosophies, and the fish are young lives and families. Over the years, I've watched the fish eye the bait— curiously, longingly, hungrily. I've watched them consider the pros and cons, weigh out the options, and ignore the warnings of God's Word. Then, I've seen them do the unthinkable—bite.

The bait differs from family to family, but the hook is always the same. The pattern is unmistakable. The product is amazingly predictable. Shortly after the bite comes the pain, the wound, the devastation—followed by the fight, the spiritual wrestling, the reeling in, and the ruination of another life or family.

Today, the devil isn't pulling in an occasional fish. He's hitting schools of fish by the thousands and hooking them faster than we can imagine. He's having more fishing success than ever before, and the slaughter is enormous, spiritually speaking.

In short, I'm weary of seeing the same decisions lead to the same bait, the same hook, and the same pain in life after life over the years. I'm weary of seeing whole families bite on the same hooks time after time. The devil's fishing trips always look the same, though the faces change. He is always out to destroy you, your family, and young lives. He is crafty and skillful with deception and trickery. He knows the "sport" well. He understands the fish, and he knows just how to bait a hook. His greatest pleasure is to see a bloody fish dying on the deck of his vessel.

In these pages, I hope to warn you and your family of the hooks that the devil is using—the lies that young people and their parents are swallowing in modern day culture—hook, line and sinker! I hope you will journey with me, as a family, into a close inspection of the devil's lies—his bait. Perhaps we can take a closer look together at this bait, and then through God's Word (the truth), perhaps we can pull back the facade to see the real hook and avoid the real danger that lies just under the surface. It is my prayer that these pages will enlighten and equip you to face the waters ahead with clarity, confidence, faith, and security in Jesus Christ.

Together, let's ask God to help us escape the slaughter that's happening all around us, from a world that we cannot see.

"A thousand shall fall at thy side,
and ten thousand at thy right hand;
but it shall not come nigh thee."
—Psalm 91:7

Two

Seeing the Other World

When it comes to fishing, there are really two worlds—the world of the fish and the world of the fishermen. "Life is the bubbles, under the sea"—as the song goes. Ignorant, rather unintelligent life forms of all kinds float, swim, feed, and otherwise exist with rather repetitive and mundane lives—you know, swim around, eat things smaller than you, hope something bigger than you doesn't come by—and life goes on.

Yet, just beyond the surface, just out of reach of fish senses exists a completely different world—the world of the predator. Little do these slick-bellied swimmers realize that they are being tracked, studied, followed, and targeted. Little do they know the great sport we have made out of hooking them and cooking them.

We have fishing derbies, fishing boats, fishing TV shows (yikes!), fishing magazines, and a seemingly endless list of fishing gear for any and all kinds of fishing environments. We have fish sandwiches, fish markets, fish filets, and fish gumbos. Every town has fish restaurants, every grocery store has fish counters, and every elementary school cafeteria has fish sticks! How shocked they would be if they could but see and understand our world!

Yet, they cannot. And for some reason, it gives us such pride that we can outsmart them, fight them out, and then gut them—all so we can grill them!

Can you imagine what kind of insane love I would have for the fish if, on that trip, I had jumped overboard in an effort to warn the fish of their impending doom? Can you imagine what kind of sacrifice I would have exhibited if I could have become a blue fish just to attempt to spare them from being hooked?

That's what Jesus did for humanity—for you and for me. This is the unimaginable love He displayed. When we were being tracked and hunted by a spiritual, unseen enemy—residing just beyond the "surface" of our world, He literally jumped into our world, put on a body, and became a man so that we could see and understand the world beyond our physical eyesight—the real, eternal world. He paid an amazing price to give us "intelligence into eternity." He laid down His life and shed His blood to expose our enemy and give us salvation. And to anyone who calls upon Him, He literally enters his heart, giving a new birth, making him a new creature.

As new creatures, we're not tied to our previously "water-bound" life and limited understanding. As new creatures, we have a new set of eyes—eyes that can see into the spiritual realm. These are the eyes of the heart—the eyes of our understanding. What a wonderful gift!

We no longer have to "swim" through life ignorantly biting on hooks and falling prey to an enemy that we cannot comprehend. We can now use our spiritual eyes to see the "other world"—the spiritual battle raging around us! We can, with God's enabling, literally see the spiritual implications—the other-world battles—that are hidden behind every circumstance, every trial, and every temptation of our lives.

We must realize that being a successful fisherman depends as much on the ignorance of the fish as it does on the skill of the fisherman! If fish ever had a "great awakening"—our tactics would be exposed and the fishing industry as we know it would fade away. What if they really "evolved" and the worlds were reversed? Imagine if suddenly fish started "humaning"! Wait a minute! Don't bite into that Big Mac—it might be the hook of a humanfisher humaning!

Suddenly, we are the prey and the fish are the predators! Flee! Run for your life or end up as a "man-stick" in some school of fish!

Okay, this is getting out of hand, I realize. The point is, when the human heart is reborn by the Spirit of God, suddenly the devil is exposed if we choose to believe and practice the Word of God. Suddenly, we can see, understand, and even resist him, and yes, he must flee.

As a Christian, you have the ability, if you choose to use it, to see and respond to the spiritual world. You have the ability to expose the fisherman and avoid his tricks. You have spiritual eyesight that you must use as you live your life!

In Ephesians 1, Paul wrote of his amazing heart's desire and prayer for the Ephesian Christians. He says in Ephesians 1:15–19, "Wherefore I also, after I heard of your faith in the Lord Jesus, and love unto all the saints, Cease not to give thanks for you, making mention of you in my prayers; That the God of our Lord Jesus Christ, the Father of glory, may give unto you the spirit of wisdom and revelation in the knowledge of him: The eyes of your understanding being enlightened; that ye may know what is the hope of his calling, and what the riches of the glory of his inheritance in the saints, And what is the exceeding greatness of his power to us-ward who believe, according to the working of his mighty power."

You have spiritual eyesight that you must use as you live your life!

Paul prayed that "the eyes of your understanding" would be enlightened. He desired for these Christians to see spiritual reality in what was happening around them and to understand the hope of God's calling. He prayed that they would have wisdom through the knowledge of Christ to see what otherwise could not be seen.

That is my prayer for you as you delve into these pages. I pray that God would use His Word to truly open your eyes to dangers, tactics, lies, and "hooks" that could destroy your life and your family. I pray that He will enlighten your spiritual understanding to see the hook rather than the bait, to see the end rather than the beginning, to see the devastation just beneath the attraction.

Paul said again in Ephesians 6:12, "For we wrestle not against flesh and blood, but against principalities, against powers, against the rulers of the darkness of this world, against spiritual wickedness in high places." Look again at his description of our spiritual warfare in 2 Corinthians 10:3–5 "For though we walk in the flesh, we do not war after the flesh: (For the weapons of our warfare are not carnal, but mighty through God to the pulling down of strong holds;) Casting down imaginations, and every high thing that exalteth itself against the knowledge of God, and bringing into captivity every thought to the obedience of Christ."

Friend, whether you see it or not, all around you there is a constant spiritual battle raging for your life and your family. This spiritual battle is more real and more significant than any part of your physical existence, and yet so often we focus only on physical, temporary priorities in our lives and families. We tend to minimize spiritual matters in our mind to our own detriment. We tend to focus only on what we can see with our eyes and what we can explain with our mind.

This warfare for your future and the future of young lives is real, it is intense, and it is bloody. Spiritual casualties are everywhere. You never have to look far to see the carnage of Satan's fishing follies. Let's find out how he operates…

"In whom the god of this world hath
blinded the minds of them
which believe not…"
—2 Corinthians 4:4

Three

Exposing the Enemy

As we uncover the lies of our enemy, it's important that you understand how he attacks you. Second Corinthians 10:3–5 gives us tremendous insight into his tactics. In verse three, Paul draws our attention to the existence of this "spiritual battle." In verse four, he explains that our weapons must also be spiritual. In other words, the attack will be against your spirit! The initial result of a successful attack will be a wounded, broken, hurt, closed, angry, or an otherwise "twisted" spirit! Your attitude, the spiritual condition of your heart is always the first to change in a spiritual attack! This is the very nature of the battle. If the devil can twist your spirit towards some key relationship in your life, or towards God Himself, then everything else will follow. The battle is won or lost in your spirit!

The Battlefield of Imagination

Then in verse five, he exposes the "battlefield." He uses the word "imagination." You must understand that the battleground of the spiritual war in your life is your imagination. Think about this for a moment.

Paul says in verse five that imaginations that exalt themselves against the knowledge of God must be "cast down." What does this mean functionally and practically? It can only mean one thing. First of all, think of imagination not as a function of your human brain, but rather as a given thought. In other words, while you may only have one heart, that heart can imagine many things or have many imaginations.

Second, in any given circumstance of your life there are two perspectives or two perceptions. On the one hand there is the TRUTH—the knowledge of God, or "what God knows to be true." Have you ever heard someone say "God knows my heart..." or "only God knows..."? In those common little phrases, we acknowledge that our human understanding is often limited. On the other hand you have "imaginations that exalt themselves against the knowledge of God"—or what the devil would have you imagine in a given situation to mislead your spirit, your attitude, and eventually your actions.

If these imaginations must be "cast down," they can only be from one source—our enemy, whose true desire is to "exalt himself against the knowledge of God" in our lives. This passage gives clear indication that Satan and his messengers use the battleground of our imagination to work against the truth—the knowledge of God—in our lives.

Now, this spiritual battle would be an easy thing if the devil would openly identify himself in our imaginations. Perhaps Satan would be easier to resist if he introduced himself as the author of these imaginations. "Hello, my name is Satan, and I'm about to mess with your mind..."

Obviously, this is not how he works. He's much more subtle and invisible than that. He poses as our old nature—which has been crucified with Christ. He comes to us in first person. He implants unfounded imaginations that run rampant in our hearts like wildfires across a dry plain—literally exalting themselves, flaring up into our lives against what is true—against what God knows! Our enemy's desire is that we would imagine a "false reality"—create a "false truth" and then begin acting in response to it!

Have you ever offended somebody completely unintentionally? Usually you said or did something that was taken completely out of context. What happened? Satan planted an imagination into the heart, and that imagination exalted itself until truth was strangled away in that person's life.

At some point, every pastor has thought while preaching, "This message is stupid, and no one wants to hear it!" Of course that imagination isn't true. The truth is somebody is probably being transformed by God's Word in that very moment! Yet if a pastor accepts this false imagination, it could quite literally cripple his ability to deliver the rest of the message effectively!

Every teenager has thought, "I can never please my parents! They are always on my case!" That imagination is planted in a moment, and then it begins to exalt itself, to grow in fury, until that teenager becomes angry, bitter, and even acts out in harshness because of imagination. In this situation, parents are shocked, caught completely off guard. "What's gotten into you?!" they wonder. Imagination is exalting itself against truth!

Every parent has thought, "My teenager doesn't need me as much now as they did when they were little. I guess this is all part of growing up—we'll spend less and less time together." The truth is, your teenager needs you more now than ever, but that imagination, once implanted and accepted, becomes the catalyst of all kinds of destructive family changes and lost opportunities.

Our enemy's desire is that we would imagine a "false reality" and then begin acting out in response to it!

Every wife has, at some point, imagined that she cannot please her husband. Every husband has, at some point, imagined that he cannot please his wife, even in the strongest of marriages. What is the source of these imaginations? Where is the thought coming from? The answer—your enemy. He is trying to convince you that these things are coming from within and that they are actually true.

From there, we tend to take over. Once the thought is accepted, we tend to run with it, and imagination begins to exalt itself against truth. It's amazing how we can imagine that someone is thinking something, that someone *meant* something, or that someone has impure motives or intentions—and then we give that imagination complete credence as if it's been validated entirely by fact! This is what these false imaginations do—they lift themselves up against God's truth, and all the while, the enemy is on the sideline laughing with glee.

Recently, in a church service while speaking on this subject, I asked our church family, "How many of you, at some point during one of our pastor's recent messages, have felt for certain that he was speaking directly to you?!" After a moment's hesitation, nearly every hand—literally hundreds of them—went up all around the auditorium! It was amazing and hilarious all at once! Amazing because the Holy Spirit can take a Bible message from God's Word and literally "divide the soul and spirit"—"discern the thoughts and intents of the heart"! Hilarious because in that moment, any human being would be tempted by the enemy to imagine that the pastor "has it out for him."

> *"Lord, before I run with this thought, before I accept this as truth—what is YOUR KNOWLEDGE..."*

It would be literally impossible for a pastor, no matter how "ingenious" he is, to know so many intricate details and circumstances of individual lives and be able to so perfectly and subtly address them during a preaching service! Yet, that's what your enemy would have you imagine. Then, that imagination brings resentment, offense, and anger—dividing your relationship. He would much rather have this than have you accept the truth as from the Word of God and the Holy Spirit's conviction, which would lead to spiritual transformation in your life!

Do you see how critical a battleground the imagination is? Do you see how subtly your enemy can mislead you into imaginations that exalt themselves against the knowledge of God?

Resting in the Knowledge of God

Ultimately, these false imaginations lead to wrong actions and broken relationships. You must realize how subtle and crafty the enemy is. He is the father of lies—he never tells the truth, ever! Every time he plants an imagination, it's false. Yet, as you become aware of his tactics, you can begin to pause at first arrival of these lies. You can stop them at the gate of your mind and simply say, "Lord, before I run with this thought, before I accept this as truth—what is YOUR KNOWLEDGE in this situation?"

In every case in my own life, I find that the Holy Spirit is quick to answer my heart with TRUTH! I'm embarrassed to admit how many lies I swallow and how frequently they come, yet spiritual resistance against these lies is a wonderful thing! It's a wonderful, enlightening, truthful experience! Before we accept the lie, we can give God the chance to expose it!

Before we accept the lie, we can give God the chance to expose it!

As you begin recognizing and responding to your "thought life"—your "heart life" in this way— you will be amazed at how all of the relationships in your life will take on a completely different perspective. You'll become amazed at how many lies you were swallowing—how many imaginations were exalting themselves in your life against God's truth. You'll be amazed at how the devil will flee—being exposed as the liar that he truly is!

Before you read on, I hope you will pause for a moment and deeply consider these few pages. It would be literally impossible for me to apply them to every detail and circumstance of your life, but God will shed some light if you will give Him a moment.

Start by looking at the most significant relationships in your life— the ones the devil is the most interested in destroying—your marriage, your family, your kids, your parents, your church, your pastor, your godly friendships. Imagination is the battleground, but key relationships are the target! Ask yourself, in what key relationships has the devil been planting lies? In what areas have I been allowing my imagination to run away with those lies? They *will* come to mind.

Then, ask God for His truth. If you could be so bold, go to that key relationship in your life and raise the issue with a "quest for truth" kind of spirit. I mean, ask your wife, your husband, your mom, your dad, or your pastor—"Is this thought I've been having towards our relationship true?" You'll be shocked at the deception you could have easily swallowed as truth, and you'll be amazed at how your key relationships will be strengthened as you "cast down" imaginations that exalt themselves against God's knowledge!

"I hate vain thoughts:
but thy law do I love."
—PSALM 119:113

Four

Living Preemptively

Over the past many years of working with teens and families, I see the same patterns of destruction emerge. These patterns come from a culture of unbiblical programming, humanistic thinking, and a constantly increasing liberal view of Christian living; and they always lead to confusion and spiritual disaster. May God give you the wisdom, the courage, and the strength to break the pattern in your life and in your family's life.

In the coming chapters, we will explore the most common lies that Satan is fishing with to destroy young lives. Consider these the bait (the hooks). Then we will explore the part that parents in modern culture are playing (or are not playing) in this process—sometimes for good and sometimes for bad. May God give you grace to see the danger and then to hide safely in His grace so that you don't get hooked and reeled in.

Psalm 91:7–9 says, "A thousand shall fall at thy side, and ten thousand at thy right hand; but it shall not come nigh thee. Only with thine eyes shalt thou behold and see the reward of the wicked. Because thou hast made the Lord, which is my refuge, even the most High, thy habitation."

Parent, you are the key to the spiritual health, nurture, and stability of your children. You are the link between the Christianity of the Bible and the Christianity of the next generation! While you cannot control adult choices of your children down the road, you most certainly can control your own choices while you are rearing them. To that end, we will study four very serious and dangerous issues in the life of your teenager, and also the wrong responses that parents commonly take to these issues.

More than anything else, your teen needs you.

More than anything else, your teen needs you. They don't need your money or your provision nearly as much as they need you. This book is geared toward encouraging you to take a proactive, preemptive approach to the spiritual health and well-being of your young person.

These chapters are more than theory—they are fact. Just look around, look back a few years, and look into God's Word. You will find that these four major lies are being used to destroy lives. I hope you will read with an open heart so that you can avoid the "hooks" of the devil.

Teenager, more than anything, you need God's truth, and you need your parents. You probably don't believe me, but wait 'til the end of the book. As we will see later, God has uniquely gifted your parents with a knowledge and spiritual understanding for your life that no one else has, and your future will depend greatly on your relationship with them. If you don't have parents, then you need the primary godly authorities that God has placed in your life. If God has allowed your family situation to be anything other than your dad and mom, together, helping you grow up in God's grace, then He has a plan for filling the void of parental authority with other godly influences, authorities— primarily through His grace and through a strong local church. You need to place yourself safely within the spiritual protection of those who can wisely see spiritual dangers that you cannot. Hopefully this book will help you do that.

The Truth Crisis in Our Culture

We live in a society that has completely eroded away the moral and biblical foundation upon which our nation, our freedoms, and our hope was established! For the most part, Bible truth is a foreign concept in our culture. In just a few short decades, our television sets have redefined the American family. In the fifties and sixties, Ozzie and Harriett Nelson, Ward and June Cleaver, and others portrayed a relatively clean and moral picture of the home. Yet in the new millennium, our kids learn what a family is from the dysfunctional living rooms of Ozzy Osbourne, Homer Simpson, and worse yet, increasingly pro-homosexual programs. Consider this: we live in a country where you can legally kill an unborn baby, yet also stand trial for murdering an unborn baby! Such conflicts in the moral fiber of our society abound!

Over the last century, the Bible has been slowly eroded away from society and even Christians. As a result, your generation, my generation, and those who come behind us have been gradually lured away from God's definition of absolute truth to a watered down, relativistic approach to truth.

In short, we are facing a truth crisis in America! My generation grew up with a culture that rejected Bible truth, and now, with little biblical foundation of our own, we are often at a complete loss in bringing up the next generation. We have become parents who are afraid to teach our kids any absolutes for fear they will reject us. We are busy building careers, paying for toys, and getting more things and all the while our children are growing up with things—but things don't nurture, train, or build them spiritually. Things don't address the most pressing issues of their hearts—the spiritual issues that will determine the outcome of their lives.

In the last ten years, in youth ministry, I have noticed a definite, disturbing trend. Rather than laboring to help teens believe the Bible and obey their parents, I find myself laboring to challenge parents to believe the Bible and obey their God.

All too often in youth ministry, I find myself in the uncomfortable position of challenging teens to pursue a God that their parents are not pursuing—to love a God supremely whom their parents love only casually—or perhaps, trying to lead a teen to a life of full commitment to Christ, when at home they are being taught more of a nonchalant commitment. In many "Christian" homes, God ranks right up there with little league practice, night classes, and music lessons—and often gets pushed aside at the whim of any of the above. He is more of a hobby that fits into the schedule than the central focus, passion and purpose of the schedule.

It is incredibly difficult to establish spiritual principles that are foreign in the home.

Though it is not impossible, it *is* incredibly difficult to establish spiritual principles that are foreign in the home. Usually, but not always, this kind of ministry is a losing battle—for a church can only reinforce what your kids are learning from you at home! No ministry can build a spiritual tower where there is no spiritual foundation. You, parent, are laying the foundation.

Consider this as you rear the next generation of Christians:

- The future of the family will be determined by how they define family, marriage, sex, and love;
- The future of our nation will be determined by how they define right, wrong, and character;
- The future of the church will be determined by their personal faith, convictions, and commitment;
- The future of their lives will be determined by who their God is and how committed they truly are to Him.

Living Preemptively in Spiritual Battle

Throughout the 1990s, a few wise men in our nation—men of clear understanding and well studied in the state of the world—urged those in government to take aggressive, preemptive action against terrorist networks around the world. Secretary of State Donald Rumsfeld was among them. In many public forums and private committees, men like Rumsfeld were warning of "a new kind of war" that was being waged against America. At the time, many in our nation wrote off these warnings and concerns as "extreme" and "needlessly aggressive." These men were somewhat of a "paranoid fringe" to many.

Time would prove otherwise. Indeed, these were men who had "enlightened understanding," much like what Paul referred to spiritually in Ephesians 1. They could see what others couldn't, and they were trying to engage proactive, preventative measures.

September 11, 2001, changed everyone's perspective. On that day, you could say that the entire nation had a collective "understanding enlightenment"! America experienced an unthinkable tragedy as terrorists attacked and thousands perished. In that moment, a sleeping nation was awakened for the first time in a long time to a very real and present threat.

Yet, it was too late to prevent the attack. Suddenly, the nation turned a listening ear to those who had, for years, been speaking of just such threats.

The leaders of our country began an immediate and aggressive military response in specific, target countries in an effort to fight terrorist aggression around the world. As our country rallied to this needed response, one word kept coming from the press conferences of our military leaders. In continually describing this "new kind of war" against terror, our leaders emphasized preemption. Preemption defined is: action that makes it pointless or impossible for somebody else to do what he or she intended.

Our national leaders knew that terror could not be fought at the site of an attack. Terrorists don't work that way. We all learned on September 11, 2001, that waiting for a terrorist to attack was no way to fight terrorism.

Our military leaders knew (because of keen understanding) that the war would be won and America would be protected through preemption. We would have to go to the enemies, find them, root them out, and destroy them before another attack was carried out. We would have to preemptively strike the enemies and destroy their ability to strike back.

Preemption. That's really a good word—especially when it comes to national security.

So, parent, here is my question. Are you content to live your life, go about your business, ignore the threat, and wait until your family or your teenager is attacked? It will be too late then. The damage will have been done. Are we so foolish as to think that our teens won't be attacked spiritually? Will it take a major setback, some devastating news, some major disturbance in your home to bring you to the point of spiritual renewal and preemptive action? Will you be like the sleeping nation, waiting for a spiritual wake up call?

God's Word calls us to preemptive Christian living in 1 Peter 5:8, "Be sober, be vigilant; because your adversary the devil, as a roaring lion, walketh about, seeking whom he may devour."

What we need in Christianity is "preemption." We need preemptive parents—those who will know the enemy is there, suspect his activity, have intelligence into his operations, and then strike preemptively at his base of operations—taking action that makes it pointless or impossible for the devil to do what he intended. We need parents who will research the enemy, develop a strategic defense against him, and literally wage a proactive warfare through the Word of God and prayer for the spiritual health of our children.

We need teens who will know that they are vulnerable and seek to protect themselves within the safe borders of parental authority and the Word of God. We need young people who are wise enough to see beyond today and to accept the preemptive efforts of those who love them more than life itself.

Are you willing to be thought of as extreme? Are you willing to have your "understanding enlightened" so that you can clearly see the spiritual threats that lurk and plot against your child and your life? Are you willing to be labeled as a part of a "lunatic fringe" that goes "too far" spiritually? That will be the price of winning this war. In seeing what most do not, you will be required to take your stand, fully commit to Christ, and chart the course upstream! You will be a cultural outcast. Yet, the rewards far outweigh the price! Only eternity will reveal the incredible benefits of helping your family avoid the snares of Satan.

You must be willing to be the eyes of understanding, the voice of clarity, the mind of biblical reason, and the definition of Christian commitment before your children. You must be willing to be aggressive against an unseen enemy. Yet, in time, your understanding will be validated, and God's truth will prove true! It always does!

In early 2004, our news media was reporting about a PDB (Presidential Daily Briefing) that warned of terrorist attacks prior to September 11, 2001. For the first time in recent history, a PDB was released to the media, and Americans were able to read for themselves a large portion of a highly classified document informing our president of America's potential vulnerability to terrorists.

Teenager, you are under surveillance. You are being stalked. Your enemy is after you and planning his attack. Parent, you are the primary source of spiritual protection for your family. Preventing the attack and surviving the war will require diligence and commitment. Consider this book your personal intelligence report—your very own PDB (Parental/ Personal Daily Briefing)—it's up to you to take preemptive action.

> *"Be sober, be vigilant; because your adversary*
> *the devil, as a roaring lion, walketh about,*
> *seeking whom he may devour:"*
> —1 PETER 5:8

Part Two

Hook #1
Divide and Conquer

Overcoming Family Fragmentation

The enemy's lie to a teenager...

"It's okay for me to not be as involved with my other family members as I once was. I am growing up…after all, I am not a child anymore. I have a life of my own to live…and my schedule is very full…"

"I should be more independent—I have earned it. I don't need Mom and Dad to make my decisions for me…or to control how I think—I can make my own choices. Dad and Mom have their own interests and pursuits, so should I…"

"Mom and Dad don't really have time for me…and what have I done that would make them proud of me? They probably don't want to spend time with me. I am just not really good at anything—I have no special ability or talent. I don't blame them for not wanting to hang out or do things with me…"

The enemy's lie to a parent...

"I have to provide for my family, their needs and expectations, or I am worse than an infidel the Scriptures say. So whatever it takes—I will work three jobs if I have to for their provision! Sacrifice is good! Whatever it takes…seven days a week, I'll work and make it happen."

"It's normal for my son to be distant at this age—he's growing up and becoming a man. He just needs his own space and some time to grow out of this phase that he is going through. His mom should be closer to him—that's normal, after all, she has had more time with him, raising him all these years. Plus, his youth pastor is keeping tabs on him, what more could I offer?"

"Other kids deal with broken homes! Leaving and starting over is normal these days—everyone is doing it. Sure, it will hurt my kids, but kids are resilient, they will adjust. And besides, it's not like I don't love my kids—it's just that my marriage isn't working out the way I expected it would! I deserve better…"

"My life is just too busy to spend more time with my kids! They have sports, youth group, school, and so many good things—what more could I offer them? I'm spending my life to provide these things—that should be more than enough…"

Five

The Threat of Family Fragmentation

I made a huge mistake this past Christmas! On our way home from a family day at Knott's Berry Farm, just a few days prior to Christmas, I had the brainy idea of stopping by one of the largest malls in southern California—the Glendale Galleria. You know—see the décor, experience the shopping frenzy, exhilarate in the spirit of the season with my wife, my three-year-old daughter, Haylee, and our two boys, Lance and Larry—a family trip to a famous mall. This was going to be FUN!

Wrong! This was insanity of gigantic proportions! I honestly don't know what I was thinking, and to make matters worse, I had mentioned the idea to the family—which only built up the excitement for the kids—before I realized the error of my ways. This left me trapped—no opportunity to "change my mind."

The first clue of my grave mistake was the half-mile line of cars waiting for a parking place in the parking garage. My second clue was the man behind me who got very angry when I managed to grab a spot before he did. In Los Angeles, you could get shot for lesser things. You would think my stupidity would have given way to common sense at this point, but no—I had to achieve new heights of stupidity on this particular evening. I still imagined that, somehow, this would be fun.

Getting into the mall was no small task. Literally thousands of shopping-bag-laden shoppers were coming and going at breakneck pace. By this time, the kids were hungry, one had to use the restroom, and we were forced to press on. I'll never forget the sight when we stepped inside the mall. It was like stepping into a million-man march for chaos and anarchy! Before us were more people in a single mall than I had ever seen in my life. People of every age, size, shape, color, and background jammed the corridors of that mall in a mass pandemonium of shopping hysteria. I looked at my wife, Dana, she looked at me, and then we looked at the kids. We were both thinking the same thing at exactly the same moment. We knew we had to find a potty fast—and some fast food—and yet we knew that forging this sea of humanity with our family intact would be a minor miracle.

Like a massive undertow on a stormy beach, we felt that any one of our kids could get "swept away"—never to be seen or heard from again. The thought paralyzed us. Suddenly, as if cued by the same inner radar, we all grabbed each other tightly. Dana grabbed my arm and one boy, I grabbed the other boy and the stroller with Haylee, and we fearfully began our trek into the sea of strangers.

Christmas shopping was never so miserable and fearful! Every three seconds, I checked both hands and the stroller just to make sure we weren't missing anyone! We gripped tightly and walked briskly—knowing that one mistake could separate us for the rest of our natural lives. I was envisioning late-night police searches…my boys were envisioning life in an orphanage…this was not fun. It was only a matter of moments before we *all* had to go potty.

I honestly can't explain the panic that we all experienced in that mall, but we all felt it at exactly the same moment, and it remained until we were safely in the car and cruising up the freeway towards home. We were only too happy to give our parking place to some other crazy lunatic shopper! Merry Christmas, Glendale Galleria…and good riddance!

Surviving the Current of Culture

There you are—parent and teenager—entering a very busy, fast-paced time of your family life. Up until now, things have been relatively light and manageable during the elementary years. Children are more obviously dependent upon parental affection, care, and involvement during these years. (Notice the word "obviously"—they are no less dependent upon these things as they become teens, although their dependence *is* less obvious.) The pace of traffic has been manageable but you've recently taken an exit, and you're entering a whole new world.

Suddenly, school schedules increase; sports practices are more frequent; music lessons, youth activities, church events, ministry service, extra curricular activities, time with friends, homework, and endless other good things begin to fill the calendar of your life. At the same time, for Mom and Dad, financial burdens increase; orthodontist bills begin; career demands become greater; family needs become more expensive; time as a married couple becomes more difficult to find; and worst of all, you actually start to feel the early effects of your age! (I know, it's almost like I just said a curse word—I never said that all of this book would be pleasant!) In addition to this, our culture keeps upping the standard of living that we try meet to "keep up with the in-crowd—our peers"—tempting us to keep looking for that extra dollar, at any cost.

The truth is, life changes for both parents and teens during this critical time. If you're not careful, the fast-paced current of life could quickly and easily sweep you downstream in a raging torrent of activity and commitments. Before you realize it, you could be separated from those you love, estranged from those you were once close to, and distanced from those you most desperately need. I don't mean physically. You may still live in the same house and eat out of the same refrigerator, but you can become strangers nonetheless. The fact that you share the same space and draw from the same resources doesn't mean you are functioning as the family that God intended.

Yours is not the only family that has to navigate and survive this shopping-mall experience, and unfortunately, most families simply let it happen. Most families let the "current" of commitments pull them farther and farther apart—and all for good reasons. After all, what could possibly be wrong with sports, music lessons, homework, ministry service, and all the other good things that come our way? And how are we going to pay for all of these things if Dad doesn't work more—and Mom too? So for most, this separation, this fragmentation, becomes a normal way of life. But it couldn't be more *abnormal*, and it couldn't be more dangerous.

Let me insert this clarification. I do not believe that church or ministry involvement is harmful to a family. In fact, I believe exactly the opposite. Our families cannot know God's best if we are not actively and faithfully involved in loving, worshipping and serving Him together in a local church body. We'll mention more on this later. Yet, even good opportunities, when too many in number or too carelessly pursued, can pull us away from the best opportunities.

The families that survive this phenomenon are the ones that look deep into each other's eyes and choose to enter this frenzy holding tightly to each other, no matter what tries to pull them apart. It's a two-way commitment. Dad and Mom must absolutely determine, against all odds, to hold out a firm hand of stability, and son and daughter must determine to reach out and grasp that hand against the pressure of mainstream society. Each must hold to the other, swimming upstream together, until safe passage is obtained!

Just as that shopping-mall experience threatened to tear my family physically apart, even so, the teen years will threaten, in countless ways, to pull parents and teens apart. A barrage of good things will soon be squeezing every last minute of family time away from your schedule and every last drop of nurturing energy from your life, unless you determine to take preemptive action against what we will call "family fragmentation."

*"And he shall turn the heart of the fathers
to the children, and the heart of the children
to their fathers, lest I come and smite
the earth with a curse."*
—MALACHI 4:6

Six

Portrait of a Fragmented Family

Family fragmentation: the accelerating tendency of families in the 21st century to spend increasingly less time together and more time involved in other pursuits and interests. For many, family life is nothing more than a pit stop—a place to refuel and rest—before heading on to more important things. Parents are pulled in a myriad of directions involving career pursuits, hobbies, and advanced education while teens are pulled to their rooms, their friends, their sports teams, their schoolwork, their video games, and their music. Again, there may not always be something wrong with these things when kept in check with higher priorities; yet they become idols at worst, and major distractions at best when they pull our lives out of balance with the will of God.

While many of these things are necessary and even vital to our lives, society has taken these pursuits to a new extreme. We are content to allow weeks and months to pass without spending any quality and quantity time together as a family. Many families have chosen to "roll over and play dead" to the process of fragmentation. We rationalize that we don't want to withhold any good thing from our kids, and so, in our efforts to provide every good thing, we end up withholding the best thing—nurturing time together. It becomes easy to say "yes" to every good opportunity without truly evaluating the spiritual cost.

The more members you have in your family, the more extreme this fragmentation can become as everyone develops separate life interests. To some degree, this process is natural and unavoidable. I'm not talking about a utopian society where kids never grow up. I just believe that we have taken this to an unhealthy extreme, and I believe we're seeing the dramatic, negative effects upon the next generation—a generation with no moral compass or conscience.

The portrait of many Christian families goes something like this. Dad often works 12 hours a day, plus drive time. Mom often works too, in order to help provide a certain standard of living. Kids go to school, come home to an empty house, and take care of themselves until the evening hours. Everybody does their own thing for dinner, and by that time, Dad and Mom are so exhausted, all they want to do is collapse in front of the TV for a couple of hours. The kids usually end up hanging out in their rooms—door closed, headphones on and video game in hand—until bedtime. Somewhere between the bathroom and the refrigerator, kids and parents cross paths, exchanging a quick goodnight. The sum total of today's exchange—less than ten seconds. Then we wonder why things go wrong and our kids mess their lives up. We thought the church and Christian school were taking care of things…

How easily we have devalued our core relationships and sacrificed them on the altar of lesser, more self-centered pursuits.

I don't know how closely this resembles your family, hopefully not at all. Why not take a quick inventory? In the last two months, on average, how much time a week do you get to spend with each of your kids? Is this time filled with brief exchanges that never venture beneath the surface, or are they true times of nurture and heart-level connection? Even as you read this question, you may find yourself with good excuses why you don't spend more time together. How easily we have devalued our core relationships and sacrificed them on the altar of lesser, more self-centered pursuits.

Teenager, do you spend most of your time at home locked in your room with your headphones, your video games, or your computer—blocking out the rest of the world? Do you take every chance you can to get away from your family? Do you talk more on the phone to your friends than you do to your own parents? Do you live and fantasize away much of your life in a virtual world created by today's video game producers? If so, you're swallowing the bait and you'll regret it someday.

Parent, have you forgotten that parenting cannot be done on "auto-pilot" once your kids become teenagers? Are you finding yourself over-committed to every good thing in life, but radically under-committed to nurturing time with your children? A pastor friend recently said to me, "Every day that passes before you make a change, is a day that will never return!" You have only a few brief years with your kids. Everything else in life can wait until after they leave the house, but nothing will slow their growth. You will never be able to recapture the moments you've lost to lesser causes.

What I'm describing is one of the most destructive family patterns that exists in our culture today. Nothing could be more spiritually destructive to our kids, and quite often it's not a choice between good and bad—it's a choice between good and best. Are you saying "yes" to all the "good things" in life only to find that you are saying "no" to something far more important?

Malachi 4:4–6 says, "Remember ye the law of Moses my servant, which I commanded unto him in Horeb for all Israel, with the statutes and judgments. Behold, I will send you Elijah the prophet before the coming of the great and dreadful day of the LORD: And he shall turn the heart of the fathers to the children, and the heart of the children to their fathers, lest I come and smite the earth with a curse."

God makes it clear that in the last days, as people get farther and farther from Him, the product is that their hearts—parents' and children's—will turn away from each other. This pattern ultimately results in a "curse." God must feel pretty strongly about this issue!

Second Timothy 3:1–2 refers to this problem from the heart of the child when it says, "This know also, that in the last days perilous times shall come. For men shall be lovers of their own selves, covetous, boasters, proud, blasphemers, disobedient to parents, unthankful…" The spirit of disobedience and thanklessness that exists in this generation is evidence of an entire culture of fragmented families.

Let's take a close look at what this fragmentation creates, and how we can turn the tide…

> "…*Every kingdom divided against itself is*
> *brought to desolation; and every city or*
> *house divided against itself shall not stand:*"
> —MATTHEW 12:25

Seven

Designed for
Time Together

No kid ever feels more alive—more secure—than when they are with their parents. Do you remember getting separated from your mom in the grocery store when you were little? Do you remember the fear that gripped your soul when you realized the person you were following—the one you thought was your mom—wasn't?! Suddenly, life as you knew it came to a grinding halt as panic paralyzed your tiny heart! Life suddenly had one focus—find Mom.

There's nothing more terrifying for a kid than to be separated from the security of Dad and Mom. And, in the same sense, there is nothing more secure, more emotionally and spiritually healthy than nurturing time with Dad and Mom. Though my dad traveled some when I was growing up, he always made it a priority to have an occasional football game, pillow fight, or Monopoly round. He always made "playing together" a family priority. I could fill a book with the incredible things we did together as a family—rafting, skiing, vacationing, camping, hiking, swimming, family devotions, and just generally having fun together. Looking back, this family playtime is what kept us connected, soft, and pliable in the hands of the Holy Spirit.

Kids were made for this. Families were designed for this. We all came into life with a desperate need to be nurtured, cared for, and to deeply, emotionally connect with our parents. To be sure, there is a time in the young adult years when leaving Dad and Mom and cleaving to a spouse becomes a normal part of transitioning into adulthood, but that's later. Until a young person leaves for college, he needs his parents' involvement and nurturing, progressively more with each passing day.

Somehow, we as parents reason that the time our children needed us the most was when they were little—when they were so dependent upon us. We limit our vision to the physical world. The fact that your teenagers can feed and dress themselves is no reason to conclude that they no longer need you.

Teenagers need their parents more during the teen years than at any other time in their lives! They may not need help brushing their teeth (though there may be some argument against that), but they desperately need spiritual guidance and mentoring. Their needs transition over the years— less physical (though affection is still a huge part of their spiritual and emotional well-being) and more spiritual. Less seen, more unseen—beneath the surface. The silent, unseen needs of their hearts become a sort of silent scream— growing greater the closer they get to adulthood.

> *We all came into life with a desperate need to be nurtured, cared for, and to deeply, emotionally connect with our parents.*

Is it coincidence that the devil creates more family distractions, more fragmenting opportunities, more life pressures when our kids become teenagers? I think not. The fact that there is more opposition should clue us in to the greater spiritual need.

As a youth pastor, I can tell you that the kids who struggle the most in life are those who have lost this connection with their parents— sometimes by their own choice, sometimes by the choices of others. Every teenager craves and needs this time, though few will recognize it, and even fewer will admit it. When a family becomes fragmented in this way, there is no end to the spiritual damage that can be done in a young life. It's as though this disconnection literally opens the spiritual floodgate of opposition. The enemy gains free, unhindered access to inflict any and all kinds of spiritual blight and destruction!

We Need Time Together

Face it, family—you were designed to nurture each other! Ephesians 6:4 reminds us, "And, ye fathers, provoke not your children to wrath: but bring them up in the nurture and admonition of the Lord." How are fathers provoking their kids to wrath today? Sure, some are abusing them. Some use harsh words. Yet, most simply don't "bring them up in the nurture…." Most angry kids are provoked to anger simply through the silent absenteeism of those they call Mom and Dad.

Honestly, when you consider Ephesians 6:4, there is no way around spending large amounts of time together. There is no "Readers Digest Condensed Version" of parenting. There is no shortcut or timesaving solution. God never gives parents permission to hand off this responsibility to a pastor, teacher, or youth pastor. God commands that we (parents and teens) spend large quantities of time together during the bringing-up years.

A friend recently told me that his father gave him every Friday afternoon after school during his teen years. His dad wasn't the wealthiest man. Surely he could have chosen to earn some extra money for family needs. Surely he had other hobbies and interests; yet he chose his son. Every Friday, this man and son would spend several hours together doing whatever the son wanted to do. That man said, "It was the greatest gift anybody ever gave me! It's the primary reason why I love the Lord today." Wow!

Now, you may be thinking, how in the world could I do that? I'm not saying you have to. Yet, you cannot ignore God's command either. How you "flesh out" that command into your life every week is up to you, but be sure you do it. Be sure that nurturing time becomes a reality, not just a concept. And be sure that you combine quality time with quantity time—they go together.

Teenager, in the same passage, you too are given a command. Ephesians 6:2 says, "Honour thy father and mother...." We'll get to the obey part later, but for now, think about that word "honor." That literally means "to highly value." If you've been shrugging off your parents' involvement in your life, shunning them to your friends, and avoiding them, you're not only deeply hurting them, you are getting reeled into the devil's fishing boat! It's a trap! Don't fall for it. Resist the course of culture. Determine that you will honor—highly value—your parents. Highly value what they say and highly value who they are. Recognize that you need them! Then, get out of your room, say "no" to some friends, and get to know the two most valuable people in your life—they are the greatest gift that God has given you next to His own Son!

> *Be sure that nurturing time becomes a reality, not just a concept.*

Teenager, realize that your heart craves and your spiritual life desperately needs time with your parents. Most kids suffer from a lack of time with parents, and they spend the rest of their time trying to find "pain killers" in friends, illicit relationships, harmful substances, and other experiences. No friend, no music, no interest, no substance will heal the spiritual hole in your heart. Time with your parents is foundational to your spiritual stability now and in your future. You were designed to need it! So go get it!

Big Challenges in Fighting Fragmentation

Parent, balancing the demands of your life and the needs of your teen is among the greatest of responsibilities that God has given you. God challenges you in Deuteronomy 6:4–9, "Hear, O Israel: The LORD our God is one LORD: And thou shalt love the LORD thy God with all thine heart, and with all thy soul, and with all thy might. And these words, which I command thee this day, shall be in thine heart: And thou shalt teach them diligently unto thy children, and shalt talk of them when thou sittest in thine house, and when thou walkest by the way, and when thou liest down, and when thou risest up. And thou shalt bind them for a sign upon thine hand, and they shall be as frontlets between thine eyes. And thou shalt write them upon the posts of thy house, and on thy gates."

God's first challenge to you, as a parent, is to love Him with your whole heart, soul, and strength. This means total, unreserved, unquestioning commitment to Jesus Christ. God must have first place above everything else in your life. Before you can be the parent He wants you to be, He must have all of you and you must live daily in full abandon and surrender to His good pleasure. Your whole life must flow from a passionate love for your Saviour and from your personal relationship with Him. This is huge!

God says, exemplify this life before you try to teach this life. Let me ask it this way—why should your teenager obey you if you are not obeying God? Why should your teenager love God if you love anything else more than God? Why should your teenager spend time with you if you aren't spending time with your Father? Your family will ultimately reflect, in many ways, the true heart commitment that you have to the Lord and the personal relationship that you have with Him. The buck stops there.

God's second challenge to you is to keep His Word in your heart. Before He says to teach, He says for you to "learn." Perhaps the reason that we become silent parents as our kids become teenagers is that we just don't have the answers. Perhaps we don't know what to tell them, so we opt not to tell them anything.

God's first challenge to you, as a parent, is to love Him with your whole heart, soul, and strength.

Your kids need a lot more than what they can get from church on Sunday. They need a parent who can speak with biblical skill and knowledge. Far more than they need a youth pastor, they need a parent who values, knows, and keeps the Word of God. By the word "keep," I'm not referring to being perfect. Until eternity we will always fall short of God's perfection. I'm referring to honoring and protecting God's Word—showing the supreme value of it in your life and home. Determine to protect God's Word and His place and priority in your family! Determine to know and do (through His power) all that God has said from His precious Word!

You may not feel like one who could speak very wisely. That's irrelevant—neither did Moses. It was God who did the speaking, and Moses simply became the willing mouthpiece. As you value, hear, know, and live the Word of God, you are becoming a vessel—a mouthpiece—for God. He will give you the words, the applications, and the teaching moments so long as you allow Him to fill you with His truth.

Pretty big challenges! Are you up to the task? Parent, are you up to loving God that much? To knowing His Word that well? Teenager, are you up to having a parent who will guide you into a true committed relationship with the God who made you?

God's final challenge is to "teach them" (the truths and laws of God) diligently to your children. He then goes on to list the specifics—you are to teach when you're sitting, when you're standing, when you're lying down, and when you're rising up. So it's simple. God wants you to exemplify and teach His love and His Word to your children every time you're standing, sitting, lying, or rising. Guess that means you can catch a break every time you float.

"We will not hide them from their children,
shewing to the generation to come the praises
of the Lord, and his strength, and
his wonderful works that he hath done."
—Psalm 78:4

Eight

What a Difference Time Together Makes

Over the past few years, I've noticed a recurring theme in counseling parents—especially when talking with fathers. Nearly every time I've talked to parents about a struggling teen, somewhere early in the conversation, the dad mentions having a strained relationship or not being as close to this child as his other children.

As the conversation continues, the parents proceed to describe how the teen is struggling. The dad is usually shocked that I go right back to his early statement as the biggest part of the problem. Somewhere in the early stages of this problem, the father and the child were divided, sometimes for years. As time passed, the distance grew. Somewhere along the way, Dad felt completely cut off.

The same conversation has happened with teen young men. "I'm not close to my dad." "I never get to see my dad." "Me and my dad used to be good friends, but we haven't been for a long time."

Dad, can I insert a loving prod here? Don't be content "not being close" to one of your children. God was so discontent about "not being close to you" that He gave His very life in the person of His Son, the

Lord Jesus, to restore you to His side. Don't accept distance in your relationship with a child as normal in some way. It's not normal. It's not right. It's not what God created you for. What price are you willing to pay to close the gap?

Early in youth ministry, when confronting these statements from teens, I used to try to talk about and deal with the surface, behavioral problems. Yet, in never dealing with the real issue, no lasting solution was achieved.

The real issue was family fragmentation. So the real answer was time and nurturing. In every case in recent years, I have urged the father to spend large quantities of time with this particular teen—whatever the cost, whatever the challenge, or whatever the battle. If this meant shifting priorities, making personal sacrifices, selling the house, changing jobs, cutting off an arm, or poking out both eyes with an ice-pick—whatever it took—time together was the key.

Don't be content "not being close" to one of your children.

Examples of Fragmentation Fighting

One dad took his son away for four days to an athletic event. Another dad took his daughter on a business trip. One dad spent three hours each week alone with his son. Another dad began praying every night with his son before bed. One dad began taking his daughter out for dates weekly. One by one, over the years, I've seen dads re-enter the lives of their sons and daughters. I've seen them pray for different work schedules, turn down pay raises, and make personal sacrifices; and in time, I've seen the hearts of those kids begin to soften. That time together with a godly parent became the catalyst of every other spiritual decision that would follow.

One young man in particular was struggling with many spiritual issues. Rather than try to attack those issues one by one, I simply begged his father to spend time with him. This father, being a godly man, worked hard at this solution. Gradually, the heart softened, the spirit became receptive, and that young man began to respond to preaching and spiritual truth for the first time in a long time! The change was undeniable.

After eight months of restored relationship with his dad, I commented to him that he seemed to be doing so much better. "This all sort of started when you and your dad went away on that trip didn't it?" I asked. His nodding reply: "Everything in life goes so much better when you are close to your dad." The smile on his countenance told me that indeed, everything *was* going so much better.

Another young man, in a similar story, was actually close to suicide. His friends, his music, and his rebellion were getting the best of him. He was literally being reeled in—quickly. This time, Dad entered the spiritual battle with prayer, time, and focused energy invested into his son. Within three months, this young man became a different person. That once hardened heart and cold spirit became soft and pliable. The scornful face melted into spiritual contentment. The entire demeanor of this young man gradually, but surely, transformed.

Not long after, this teen began making amazing spiritual decisions—getting rid of wrong music, leaving old friends, restoring his walk with God. Eventually, he gave his life to God and began preparing for full-time ministry!

One young lady was incredibly "boy crazy." Her true craving was for her dad's acceptance and love, and her need

Time together with a godly parent became the catalyst of every other spiritual decision.

began to be met as her dad re-entered her life with regular dates, talks, walks, and interest. Amazingly, her boy-craziness all but disappeared, and her whole countenance transformed from an attention-craving girl to a deeply satisfied, Christian, young lady.

What brought about the changes in these young people? Great preaching? Partially. Faithful church attendance? Surely that was part of the equation. A Christian school chapel? Though these things are all valuable, I'm talking about something much deeper and more foundational. What was it that suddenly made hearts responsive to influences that had always been there? What radical thing made a cold heart soft—a scornful spirit receptive—a frustrated countenance peaceful? What foundational change led to all the other spiritual transformation?

Simply—time with Dad.

I may be seemingly over-emphasizing the role of Dad in the life of a teenager. Let me explain. From the beginning of a child's life, his mother is a very present force. This applies to both boys and girls. In the early years, in most cases, the mother is naturally the primary care giver. Mom does the dressing, the feeding, the nursing and especially the diaper changing! It's usually Mom that mends a skinned knee in elementary school, while Dad might say, "Suck it up son, you'll be fine!" There's nothing wrong with this pattern. It's somewhat natural in God's design of the Christian home.

> *Simply—*
> *time with Dad.*

During the early teen years, a son begins to naturally distance from his mother and begins to need more of his father's influence. For boys, this distancing from Mom and drawing to Dad is a natural craving for Dad's love. During these years, a boy desperately needs the manly love and masculine character of his father. The distancing from Mom is seen when a son begins to feel less and less comfortable with Mom's public displays of affection, like hugging and kissing. The drawing to Dad is seen as boys like to do things that dads enjoy—fishing, hunting, shooting stuff, blowing up stuff, climbing, sports, and camping!

Not Your Average Hunting Trip

A few weeks ago, I decided to take my boys hunting. If you knew me, that would give you a good laugh. I've never done any real hunting, and don't really live close to any real hunting areas. So, we just made do. We grabbed a couple of BB guns and hit the trail for some birds, chipmunks, lizards—whatever we could find. You would have thought I bought my boys a one-month hunting safari pass! What ensued was comical!

Since we live in the desert, there just aren't many trees—where birds generally hang out! It took us about thirty minutes just to find a tree that wasn't in a populated area. When we finally found one, Larry, my youngest, got so excited to shoot a bird, he bounded out of the car like a pack of wild hyenas! Every bird within a half mile flew away immediately.

So, after another thirty minutes, we found another tree, and this time we snuck up on 'em. This time, we found a small grove of trees on the edge of some farm land, and we sort of "camped" there for about an hour. Every time Lance or Larry took a shot at some unsuspecting bird, they missed, and the bird flew to a neighboring tree. So, we would carefully move to another tree. Shot after shot flew by these birds and nothing ever fell to the ground.

Eventually the birds just stayed where they were and laughed at us. I'm sure they were mocking us, and honestly, this got under my skin a little. After all these shots, we hadn't hit one bird!

"Give me that gun," I told Lance. His gun was one of those more powerful pump guns, and I had my eye on one big, ugly raven that hadn't moved for about fifteen minutes. The Antelope Valley, where we live, has the biggest, ugliest ravens you have ever seen in your life, and this one was mine! He was going down!

With a rugged strut and Clint Eastwood glare, I loaded that chamber, pumped that gun about twenty times, took aim, and let that crow have it. I was sure I hit him, but he wasn't sure. He fluttered, almost lost his balance, but regained control and just glared down at me, as if to say, "Is that the best you've got!?"

Three more times I repeated my efforts, pumping the gun even more, and three more times that bird squawked back at me in mockery. On my last effort, I pumped the gun so many times that it broke, and about that time my prey gingerly flew off, laughing at me as if to say, "Better luck next time, ladies!"

A few moments later, we loaded the car up and returned home—and honestly, I was somewhat dejected. I was sure we would kill something. I had no idea it could be that difficult. On the way home, we were rehearsing our failure, "That's okay," I said, "we'll get something next time, guys." I was trying to breathe hope into the failed mission.

In that moment, Larry piped up with great pleasure and optimism, "Hey, Dad…we didn't kill any, but I really think we wounded a few!"

In that moment, hope revived in the car and I knew that killing a crow or not, we had definitely shared some masculine adventure and manly love with one another. We had definitely made some memories, and my boys were more fulfilled in their heart and soul for the journey we had experienced together.

It's hard for a mom to understand why boys need to shoot things. It's hard for women in general to understand why men like to blow things up. It's just in us, and in every boy is a need for a kind of love that only a dad can give.

A girl needs her father, too. All of these principles apply to a daughter—taking the form of dates, walks, and more tender exchanges. And, in the absence of a father's love, girls become boy-crazy, and ultimately immoral—looking for a father's nurture in the ill-intentioned arms of whatever boy will have her.

As a side note, none of this discussion minimizes the role of a mother in the family need structure. Mom, you are incredibly needed and vital in the life of your son and daughter! In fact, your relationship with your teen son in many ways will foreshadow his relationship with his future wife. Your relationship with your teen daughter is pivotal to her becoming the young woman that God intends for her to be. It's impossible to say one parent is more important than the other. Family life by its very design is very much a team effort.

Your family will ultimately reflect, in many ways, the true heart commitment that you have to the Lord.

We're dealing with a culture that distances fathers and their children. This is a common, albeit unhealthy, phenomenon. Mom, don't feel rejected by the fact that a teenager naturally needs and longs for a father's love. Embrace this and recognize your role as a supporter and facilitator of this need. It will often take your gentle prodding (not nagging) for your husband to sense and respond to these needs. Dad, recognize that you can easily be distracted by the "cares of this life" and give your wife a listening ear when she is encouraging you to spend more time with the kids! Her ability to sense and support this need is a gift for your family. Embrace it and be grateful for it.

Perhaps you are reading from the position of a single-parent family. Though my words are geared towards a traditional family with Dad and Mom both living under the same roof, the needs in your teenager's heart are more real than you can possibly comprehend. Volumes could be written on the issues a teenager faces when growing up in a broken home, and I can really only "skim the surface" in this chapter. I believe the most common way teens from broken homes express this craving for Dad is by wanting to spend more time with him or even to go live with him during their teen years. I've seen teens with the worst of fathers—fathers who forsook them and fled for drugs, money, and wild living—still long to live with and spend time with this kind of father! It doesn't add up to human reasoning, but it certainly exposes the deep need of the heart.

This deep craving generally shows up between seventh and ninth grades. Your son or daughter

> *Family life by its very design is very much a team effort.*

may have seemed to adjust to a break up years ago, but you can always expect this issue to hit hard—I'm talking "train-wreck"—during their early teen years. Don't be surprised by it.

Many parents I've talked to are shocked that a long-ago divorce resurfaces during the teen years. Questions arise. Accusations are thrown carelessly, seemingly from nowhere. In the case where there is a step-parent—even a long-time, loving step-parent—usually hurtful words are tossed out suddenly and unexpectedly. "Well, who cares, you're not even my real dad!" "I just wish I could live with my real dad!" Ouch. These arrows hurt! They pierce deeply. Don't take them personally. (Sure, right…easier said than done!) Just see the crying, desperate needs of the heart and try to help your teen see them too! They don't really mean these words. They just don't have a way to verbalize the pain and confusion of the heart, so this is what generally comes out.

In the absence of a godly father, only the wonderful grace of God can fully meet the deep needs of a teen's heart. Though the efforts of good men at church may help to fill some space, a wounded heart needs much more. I don't write this to cause despair, but to cast your gaze to Christ. No human being—no earthly man in a pastoral support role can completely fill the deep void left by an absent father. Only God's boundless grace and perfect love can fill this void. God may choose to nurture that need with some key leader—a step-father, a youth pastor, a pastor, but most of all, He chooses to heal that wound with Himself. I'm not saying that godly, male role models aren't important for a young man who is being reared by a single mom. Mom, surround your son with as many godly men as you possibly can! Yet, don't expect these men to be able to completely fill the place of Dad—only God can do that. The earthly father son relationship, as awesome as it can be, is merely a shadow of what your child's relationship with his true Heavenly Father should be as you nurture that relationship through the Word of God and other godly influences.

In the absence of a godly father, only the wonderful grace of God can fully meet the deep needs of a teen's heart.

It will take something far beyond human effort to fill the needs of this heart, and trying to fill the void with a human substitute can often cause you to divert your attention away from the true provider—the Lord Jesus Christ. It will take nothing less than His awesome power to fill this space. Single parent—take hope in Christ. Trust Him to do what only He can.

Good Friends

In 1984, my dad took a new job. He was the manager of a new music store in the Atlanta, Georgia area. The goal in taking the new job was that he might have more time at home. The opposite happened. Six months into my ninth grade year (the most spiritually critical time of my life, and for most teenagers) he was working sixteen-hour days just to get this store operational. His only day off was Sunday, which was committed to morning church, a long afternoon nap (from exhaustion), and then Sunday evening services. As I look back on this scenario, I'm amazed now at how the devil tried to fragment my family at the most important time of my spiritual development.

Fortunately, my dad and mom were more sensitive to the needs of our family than to a paycheck or a career. Thankfully they didn't relegate the job of raising us to the church, the youth group, or the Christian school (though we were actively a part of all of the above). When it came down to it, the only way for my dad to get his old sales job back—one with more freedom to operate by his own schedule—was to accept a different sales territory. I'll never forget the night my parents sat us all down to explain that we would be moving. Ultimately, that move took us to California and gave way to untold divine appointments in my life and future. Yet, in the short term, it was an incredibly difficult thing for me to accept.

I remember going to my room and crying—hating the thought of leaving friends, sports, and life as I knew it. My dad came back and sat on my bed for a few minutes, probably not sure what to say. I don't really remember his words. I do remember his presence. I remember him putting a hand on my back. I regret not opening up to him, but at least he was there. I knew I was making him feel terrible. That wasn't my desire. I was just intensely confused and reeling inside with disappointment. In that moment, being the decision maker, he was the only one I could project my displeasure on.

Looking back, I needed what my parents did in that decision! I needed my dad and mom to put everything on the line to keep our family from becoming fragmented. And they did. They seemed willing to move heaven and earth to maintain our family time—our connection. Far more than I needed my sports, my friends, or my "life"—I needed Dad and Mom, and they went to great lengths to protect "us"!

Why didn't I run to rebellion, sex, drugs, alcohol, or other forms of "pain-killers" when I was a teen? I simply didn't need to. I had Dad and Mom, and we were really good friends.

"My son, give me thine heart, and let thine
eyes observe my ways."
—Proverbs 23:26

Nine

Putting a Fragmented Family Back Together Again

Perhaps you're reading this and it's hitting you hard. Perhaps your family is right where I've been describing. There's no time to lose in getting back on track. Every day that passes is another day lost. Whatever ground you've lost, whatever time is gone—put the past behind and let's talk about getting back on track.

Realize that the battle, at least in the beginning, will be uphill. Your teenager will probably resist your efforts, question your sincerity, and even fight to maintain the fragmentation. Let's face it; in a fragmented family a teen usually has a lot more freedom and self-autonomy. Losing this, at first, will possibly result in a bitter battle. Be ready for it, persist through it, and maintain a loving spirit and spiritual focus in spite of it. Remember that the resistance is a surface issue; you're fighting to meet a heart level need that may have been buried and forgotten about.

1. Seek God's direction through prayer and Bible study in making critical changes in your family. Every family is different, and there is no static recipe. God will lead you individually to make the changes He wants you to make. He may lead you to make some tough choices. He will never lead you to lower His priority in your life. In other words, God will not lead you to stop attending church so you can spend more time together. That would be like a doctor telling you to cut your head off so that your acne problem will go away. The proposed solution creates more destruction than the original problem! Together, with God's leading, you must decide what stays on the schedule, what goes, and when you will begin restoring your relationships.

2. Make tough choices about good things. Maybe there will be some sports practices that will just be missed. (I know…"cardinal sin" if your first priority is sports or if your nickname is "coach.") Maybe there will be a night when homework just doesn't get done. (Now that's a catastrophe of global proportions, especially if you are a school teacher!) Perhaps this isn't the year to learn the trumpet. (Can we say "Advil"?) Maybe the best thing for everyone would be to miss a day of school, sleep in, and go shopping. (And all the teen girls said: "Amen"!) Maybe this isn't the night to "go out with the gang"! Maybe the bowling league, night classes, or side job will have to wait until the kids are grown. Maybe you can say "no" to some good opportunity with a clear conscience. I don't know what choices you will make, but be willing to make them. Be courageous enough to choose the *best* over the *good*.

Honestly, as a youth pastor, I even appreciate a family who occasionally chooses that the teens miss a youth activity so they can have a family night! The key is, make sure you are actually getting the higher priority. Exchanging a youth activity for a TV night would be a bad choice.

In seasons of need, these choices are tough, but necessary.

3. Make a week-by-week assessment of your family time. Every seven days, sit down with a calendar and make prioritizing choices that help you stay in balance. This is huge! Dad, I believe this is your responsibility, since it's your heart that the devil will try to take AWOL. Perhaps this is something you can do together—Mom and Dad—on Sunday afternoon or evening.

Find a quiet time to look at the next seven days in your life. Look at the days spread out on a calendar or a sheet of paper. For me, it even helps to have the sixteen to eighteen waking hours of every day clearly laid out before me. Every "spoken-for" time slot is filled in—every appointment, every class, every work hour, every sports practice, every time commitment. Write it out. Look at it plainly before your face. You may be shocked to find that there simply isn't any time. No wonder you're struggling.

While looking at that schedule, ask yourself when you will spend time with each kid. When will you spend time as a family? When will you spend time with your spouse? Place those times physically on the schedule. Write them down, bank on them, and commit to them. Then, force yourself to stay in balance. Keep your commitments. Understand that these commitments are every bit as valid as a doctor's appointment or a college class, and they are a lot more important!

I may be stupid, but for me this is what it takes to stay in balance. My commitment to my family must drive me to these critical times of planning and decision-making when tough choices are made. I cannot afford, as a husband and father, to default into my life—week after week—and neither can you. If you have a habit of defaulting into your week with no planning, no preparation, no forethought—you're probably losing the battle. Who would fight a war this way? Isn't this why fish are hooked so easily—because they just swim around and bite stuff that looks good?

My commitment to family must drive me to critical times of planning and decision-making...

Finally, on this point, accept temporary seasons of imbalance, but not blindly and not for prolonged periods of time. In other words, there may be seasons of your life when you are required to be out of balance - like the arrival of a new baby, a two-week business trip, or a prolonged family need. These seasons should have a definite beginning and ending, and balance should return quickly! Have a heart to stay consistent and to stay connected. With a review every seven days, you'll never get more than seven days out of balance!

4. Be willing to schedule extended time with a struggling member of your clan. If you are dealing with a teenager who is really struggling with spiritual issues, take some time off work, save some money, and get away together. Do something fun. Don't feel like you have to go away just to deal with problems, just go away and play together. Being together, having fun, making memories *is* dealing with the problem—in a deeper way than you can imagine. Beyond this, pray that God will soften the spirit and open a window to the soul, when you as a parent can courageously yet compassionately confront and resolve the real issues of the heart.

5. Don't expect an overnight miracle. Please understand, this is not a crisis-mode, temporary adjustment. Don't think you can change your family schedule for two weeks, fix the problems, and then go right back to your fragmented lifestyle. And don't be fooled into thinking you can solve a five-year problem on a two-day retreat. Surely this will start the healing, but only the Holy Spirit of God over time can bring the long-term healing. There are no quick solutions or lasting results in fast-food style relationships. The kind of change we're talking about only comes from a prolonged pattern of consistency and faithfulness.

In pre-reading this manuscript, one pastor friend shared these thoughts that really struck a nerve with me:

"Many dads are king of the 'one night stand'—and I'm not talking about an affair. They way overdo a single activity in an attempt to make up for months of nothingness, and then go another year without anything. They often go so overboard financially and with time, that they don't see how they can do it again soon. The kids don't need a different theme park every five days, they need three hours every Friday afternoon for a year. They need family Pictionary, throwing the baseball in the front yard, working on the car together, family hide and seek, and wrestling on the floor. We have forgotten how to make fun. We only know how to buy it. There's time for an occasional pay event—batting cages, go-carts, sporting events, etc. but they are not necessary."

6. Look for teaching moments. Nurturing isn't forced. What new mother has to force herself to lovingly cradle her newborn? What toddler has to be forced to run to his mother when he skins his knee? Even so, teaching moments that are forced usually feel awkward and are received resentfully. More than your lecture, your teen needs your heart. As you spend time together, in the ebb and flow of family life, teaching times will become self-evident. These are the times when a unique situation surfaces and the Holy Spirit prompts you to seize the moment to bring about spiritual insight. The more you look for them, the more they will show up. For this reason, the more you know the Word of God, the more ready you will be to give a biblical application at the right moment.

7. Connect with the heart. There are many activities you could do that put you together as a family without connecting you. The September 13, 2004 edition of *Newsweek* magazine stated that today's "families spend 'quality time' at the mall instead of in the backyard." In other words, sometimes our focus is more on having more stuff than it is on connecting with each other.

Work to find and create family settings that are conducive to connection! Many parents have told me that their teens open up emotionally just before bedtime. There is something about the end of the day, the quietness of the night, and the fact that the kids like to stay awake a little longer. One father told me he would sometimes sit on the beds of his teens for an hour or more at bedtime, talking about whatever they wanted to talk about. He credited these moments as some of the most important of their family life.

Whenever and wherever your teenager opens up, you want to find that moment and connect. Teenagers often feel that their parents don't even know them. You cannot afford to let a week go by when you don't feel an intimate connection to the heart of your son or daughter. The enemy is too crafty, and your connection is the first line of defense against his gaining ground in your teenager's heart!

Teenager, honestly, I've had many teens tell me that talking with their parents is just plain awkward, especially when it's a new concept! Don't let that stop you from opening up. It's normal to feel weird about this sometimes, but once you get beyond that, some great moments with your Mom and Dad are just ahead!

8. Pray with them and for them. There are few things that speak to the heart like prayer. I recently encouraged a father to kneel by the bedside of his struggling son every night before bed to pray. "Pray out loud, pray specifically, and pray pleadingly—asking God to help you be the right father and asking God to soften the heart of your son. Whether or not your son agrees to pray, just pray, with him sitting there listening to you."

The son resisted and refused to join his dad in prayer, but Dad prayed anyway. I'm sure he felt foolish praying while his son sat there stone faced. After prayer, he told his son he loved him and left the room. Ten minutes later, that young man burst out of his room in tears and threw his arms around his father's neck in apology. The prayer of his father was more than his hard heart could bear.

9. Show frequent, appropriate affection. Parents with grown children have often told me that physical touches of affection are critical in child rearing. One sign of a tender heart and spiritual bond is when a teenager responds favorably to the appropriate affection of a godly parent. If your son or daughter refuses a hug, pulls away from a loving arm, or rejects a tender touch—something is terribly wrong. This outward closure is a warning sign of a much deeper and more dangerous issue. Many parents shrug this off and eventually get "numb" to this behavior. "You know how teenagers are," we reason. Yet, as the spiritual heart-connection is restored between parent and child, there will always be a naturally favorable response towards these expressions of love.

"I'm not the affectionate type," you might be thinking. Hmmm... wonder where that thought came from? The truth is, your teenager *needs* you to be affectionate. Whether or not you ever received this type of affection, you are more than capable, by God's grace, to express it. Teens of every age still need a hug, a kiss, a loving arm around the shoulders, etc. A spiritual connection takes place with these affectionate exchanges. My own kids love a good back tickle during prayer time or a good night hug before bed. If this is missing in your relationship, bring it back, but be patient—it may take some time before it feels "normal" or before it's received readily.

This affection is especially critical during times of discipline. Your loving embrace will soften whatever punishment you are handing out, and more importantly, it will communicate that you are not rejecting your child, but that you are simply dealing with a problem. Your love becomes the foundation of the discipline in this case, and your affection speaks volumes as to the true motives of your heart. If you can't hug your son or daughter after a session of discipline, then this is probably a sign that you acted out of anger or with a wrong spirit or motive.

In much the same way, if your son or daughter refuses to hug you after a season of discipline, it's probably a sign of a wounded or closed spirit. Don't be content to let this remain—it is a dangerous fragmenting trap! Work through it together, and when all is said and done, restore your ability to express affection one towards another.

Recently I had a discipline session with my boys. Without embarrassing them, suffice to say, there was some lecturing, some spanking, and some praying together. Yet, when the episode was done, Lance's heart was still closed. His countenance was fallen, his spirit was closed, and his physical posture towards me was resistant. When I tried to hug him, he was stiff and unresponsive. Little red lights went off in my head—warning signals were sounding. But I was tired, ready for bed, and didn't want to go through this ordeal.

> *If your son or daughter refuses a hug, or rejects a tender touch—something is terribly wrong.*

Yet, I didn't have a choice. I knew I could not leave his room with his heart closed to me. So, I stayed. I sat back down, looked into his eyes, and said, "Son, what's wrong here… am I being unfair?" At first, he didn't open up, so I persisted. Fortunately, this was not an all-night ordeal. Soon enough he came out with the facts. Indeed, he had felt I was unfair. He felt I didn't know all the facts in the situation. So, with an open heart I listened. In some sense, he was right. There was more to the story, and I believed he was being honest. Though the "rest of the story" didn't affect my approach to the discipline or the basic outcome, it did affect Lance's heart. It was critical to his heart that I understand the truth. It was critical that he be heard and that I apologize for jumping on him too quickly without giving him my ear.

After just a few moments, Lance's entire demeanor and countenance shifted and his warm response to my affection returned. He did hug me, and we both slept better for it.

10. Don't stop serving God. I can already anticipate that the devil is telling you to "get out of the choir so you can spend more time together," or "if you didn't go soulwinning, you could have an extra family night," or "it's that ushering you do at church," or "stop teaching Sunday school; that's the way to get more quality time." Unless you have too many ministry hats, you cannot stop serving God and hope to gain ground with your family. Isn't it interesting that we're not willing to give up a TV night, but we are quickly willing to give up a visitation night for family time? Ouch.

Before you start taking the ax to the eternal investments of your life, take a good long look at the self-centered things you do with your time. Be willing to lose some selfish things and remember that your kids need to see your love and commitment to Christ. It also wouldn't hurt for your son to know he means more to you than the jalopy you're building in the garage.

Most of my life my dad taught Sunday school, attended revival meetings, ran a bus route, and involved himself in actively serving God and studying His Word. This service was not a hindrance to our family; it was a pillar of strength! Don't fall for the lie that ministry will hurt your family, unless you are already extremely over-committed (in which case, learn to say "no"). In the case of being over-committed to ministry, realize, it's not the ministry's fault. Ministry is not the enemy, though your true enemy would love for you to think it is.

Surely your family is your first ministry, but it probably shouldn't be your only ministry.

11. Serve God together. Why do we miss this incredible solution? One young lady recently shared with me that her most treasured time with her parents was when they went soulwinning together. They would talk, visit new Christians, and even grab lunch together. In a two or three-hour period her parents were connecting with her heart, serving God with her, and investing their lives into others! What a fantastic combination. These parents, with their daughter, were able to lead people to Christ, disciple new Christians, connect as a family, and make valuable memories together all at the same time! Teach your kids to love serving God by serving God with them.

Again, don't let the devil tell you that "too much of God" is going to be harmful. There couldn't be a more man-centered false concept. God is not a cultural experience. Church is not a social club. You and your family might possibly overdose on Boy Scouts, soccer, or cheerleading, but you cannot have too much of God! God is the solution to the deepest needs of our lives. Church services, Bible studies, revival meetings, and ministry opportunities—when shared—are huge contributors to the spiritual connection of your family. How subtle Satan is to tell us that these good things actually hurt our families, while we simultaneously leave so many other areas untouched and undisputed—like the video cabinet, the remote control, or the internet connection. Let church and ministry commitments bring you together, and don't swallow the lie that you can have "too much." God's Word says, "so much the more, as ye see the day approaching." (Hebrews 10:25).

Parents who give up ministry or church attendance to "spend more time together" usually just end up getting another TV night—as if ministry is a time waster and TV isn't. Parents who keep God first will always find that there are plenty of other time wasters, and God's priorities are vital for a healthy, spiritual family.

At the deepest part of your family connection, your children are evaluating your sincere love for God. Is it just for show? Is it a hobby? Is it socially motivated? Or is it true and real!? They are deciding right now whether this God is really that lovable and whether you truly are pursuing Him with your whole heart. If you are looking for every excuse to avoid Him, His house, and His family, you are communicating the wrong message. Yet, as your passion for God becomes outwardly apparent and bubbles over into true worship, sincere service, and life commitment, there are proven results that your child will most likely want to love Him and serve Him too!

12. Recognize that only you hold the power of choice for your family. We humans are incredibly quick to blame our bad choices on others! If we're not spending time with our spouse and children, it's always somebody else's fault. The boss, the pastor, the company, the church—somebody else is to blame.

Can I bring this down to the very bottom line? When you stand before the judgment seat of Christ to give an account for your life, you will not be able to point the finger of blame at anyone or anything else when it comes to the personal choices of your life and family! You hold the power of choice. God has made you responsible and able to respond to the circumstances of your life. He expects you to. His commands are clear; His promises are true; but He requires you to step onto the playing field and act upon the truth.

Don't wait for your circumstances to change so that the right choice becomes "easy." That time will never come. It's always difficult to make the right choice in decisions between "good" and "best." Only you have the power of that choice for your own family. Use it and don't fall prey to the blame game!

The list for fighting fragmentation could go on, but it boils down to one thing. Give yourself to your teenager. There really is no formula. There is no quick fix. There is no microwaveable solution. If you're looking for a quick fix so you can move on with your life—this is the very problem. The Lord God and your family should be your life. Everything else is negotiable when it comes to these two priorities. Until you are willing to make this priority shift, nothing will change.

Teenager, break down the barriers in your heart! Let your parent into your life. Accept the changes that your family needs to make, and embrace them with an expectant heart. Realize that you desperately need your parents' nurturing—more than you need friends, fun, food, or even oxygen! Your teen years will soon be gone (though they feel like forever), and you will soon be establishing a family of your own. When it comes to de-fragmenting and reuniting your family, don't resist it; embrace it! Contribute to it, for your own good.

"Train up a child in the way he should go:
and when he is old, he will not depart from it."
—PROVERBS 22:6

Ten

How God's Fiery Love Overcame Fragmentation

Consider our Heavenly Father. He not only provides our needs, gives us salvation, and cares for us in crisis—He's just there. He promised to never leave us or forsake us. He pursues us with an unrelenting love. He promised to guide us with His eye.

There has never been a moment of your life that you didn't have all of His attention. You have never uttered a prayer or needed His presence when He wasn't there. You have never needed to fear that He would leave you or reject you. He is all yours, all the time. And when you were "fragmented" far away from Him, He journeyed across the universe, spanned all of time and space, put on a body, and died a brutal death—taking upon Himself your sin to "defragment" and restore your relationship to Him.

He came through time and space to save you and to make you forever His child! He did this for all men, and offers this wonderful gift to all who in faith believe, trust and receive His offer of salvation and forgiveness. And He wants us to fully love and accept each other by His love with the same faith, in spite of our shortcomings and less than loveable qualities.

Parent, you may not be omnipresent. You may not be all-powerful. But then again, your kids don't expect you to be. Yet, deep within their innermost being, in ways they cannot consciously express or understand, they deeply need and want you to be with them frequently, generously, and faithfully. They long for you to span the canyon of their callousness, to fight the forces of darkness, to lay your own life and dreams on the line, if necessary, to restore them to your love!

I have never seen a spiritual problem in the life of a teenager that couldn't be solved through nurturing time with godly parents. No wonder the devil fights so ruthlessly to fragment us. He is striking at the foundation, and if the foundation crumbles, everything else will follow.

Survive—Together

So, we're done with hook number one. The number one way that teenagers destroy their lives—they disconnect from their family. How do their parents help them? They too disconnect and allow the process to worsen with time. It's time to reverse the process. It's time to break out of the cultural norm and to start swimming against the current! It's time to do what God would do!

There you are, a shopping mall of thousands of ruthless shoppers in front of you. The slightest lack of concentration could rip you apart and sweep you away in the rush of culture. The risk is great. The threat is real. The enemy is cold-blooded and merciless. Link arms, grab hands, lock eyes and determine that nothing—absolutely nothing—will pull you apart. No force can come between you. No power can sever your connection. Together, make a covenant that come what may, you're going to get through this together.

Guess what?

You will.

"…a child left to himself
bringeth his mother to shame."
—PROVERBS 29:15

Part Three

Hook #2
Draw Out
and Devour

Overcoming Rebellion

The enemy's lie to a teenager...

"Authority is for kids! I'm 18 now, I'm a legal adult! I can finally do what I want and nobody can say anything about it…"

"Authority is holding me down, keeping me from the fun, the friends, and the frills of real freedom! That's what I want…freedom. I can't wait to get away from my home!"

"I'm sick of people telling me what to do all of my life. I'm tired of having things crammed down my throat. Finally, I'm an adult and I can make my own choices without somebody breathing down my neck! I've waited a long time for this kind of freedom from authority…"

The enemy's lie to a parent...

"All teenagers are rebellious—it's normal—and I just have to learn to put up with it. After all, I was rebellious too when I was a teenager. In fact, my teen is better than I was—who am I to try to be an authority? I was far worse than this, I have no right to discipline my teen."

"I'm tired of fighting. I don't have the will or the energy to get into this. I'm just going to give in and let him have his way. It's not worth fighting over."

"Maybe this rule is too harsh or extreme? I mean, really, isn't the pastor and the church a little 'overboard' in this area? Is there really anything that wrong with…? After all, too much Bible…too much God might actually push my daughter away from me!"

Eleven

Authority 101:
Basic Concepts for Mr. Brain

This second hook of destruction—rebellion against authority—follows closely on the heels of the first, and usually goes hand in hand with it. It too strikes at the roots, the very foundation of spiritual stability. Biblical authority, for both a teen and a parent, is a protective fortress intended by God to shield from spiritual attack. Thus, the attempt of the enemy is to literally draw you out from behind the protective hedge of biblical authority so he can get a clear shot at you!

Authority is a word that most teenagers hate to hear about—and increasingly adults do too, but I'm going to ask you to simply work with me through this chapter. Don't close the book. Don't think I'm simply building a case so your parents can control you. Every page of this book has your absolute best interest at heart—period!

"Question Authority"—that's the popular bumper sticker, the mantra of this generation. Unfortunately, what the statement really means is "suspect authority" and "resist authority." The subtle lie embedded in that little phrase is that authority is bad and that it must be broken free from. Actually, godly authority wouldn't mind being questioned! In fact, godly authorities in your life would love for you to question them, and then listen with an open heart to well-reasoned answers from God's Word.

So go ahead. Take your best shot! Think of the toughest questions you can and open up! Bring those questions to your parents, your pastor, your youth pastor. Go ahead—really make 'em sweat. But play fair. Listen to the answers; consider the proof they offer—really research the outcomes. You might be surprised at what you find.

Biblical authority, for both a teen and a parent, is a protective fortress…

I have three children. Early in their lives I discovered that the primary focus of parenting between the ages of birth and five years is simply "to keep the child from killing himself." You cannot imagine the incredible ways a child can create near-death experiences! It's like they are bent on dying an early death as soon as they become mobile.

All three of my children stood on chairs above hard surfaces—before they knew how to keep their balance. All three of them crawled directly to the fireplace the first time they saw a fire. All three of them attempted to run directly into the street as soon as they could walk. The list goes on. Crawling up stairs, hanging from ledges, eating rubber balls or quarters, drinking cleaning fluids, touching electrical sockets, and hitting their heads on rock-solid surfaces—these things just barely scratch the surface! These kids came out of the womb bent on their own destruction, and they couldn't even understand plain English warnings of danger.

Larry could be actively sticking his finger into an electrical plug when I yelled, "Hey, kid…don't do that! What are you, stupid?" These words meant nothing to him.

There was only one language that could protect this child from his own insanity—preemptive force! Little terrorist! Yes, I (his authoritative, abusive, overbearing, controlling father) would physically run to him, grab his hand, and physically remove him from the danger. What a control freak I must be! What a mean father—to restrict my own son from experiencing the firsthand joys—the exhilarating feeling of 120 volts of electrical current coursing up and down through his entire body!

And then there was Haylee! That girl had no fear of fire. "Hey, don't go over there! Don't stick your hand in there, you'll get burned." These commands had no effect! On she went, straight to the fireplace every time it was lit. The little pyromaniac! What's the matter with these kids?

Again, only sheer forceful restraint would work. So, once again her obsessive-compulsive parents would freak out every time she crawled within eight feet of the fireplace doors. We would jump up, pounce on her, grab her up, and physically remove her from the danger. Cruel of us, wasn't it? I mean really, to rob our daughter of the vibrant heat, the smell of burnt flesh, the excruciating pain of melting skin and blistered tissue! How coldhearted we were in those days! Surely her tears, her screaming, her kicking, her defiance caused us to give in. Not a chance! No emotional tactics can break through my authoritarian armor.

Then there is the backyard thing! We have a nice backyard, complete with swing set, playground, castle, Barbie house, and grass play area. But, again the authoritarian spirit and control mentality shows through because there is a six foot, locked fence all the way around it! "Aha," you're thinking, "a prison yard. You treat your kids like inmates!" Exactly. We control when they go out there, how long they stay, and we fence 'em in tight. No escapees from my backyard. I'm even considering placing guard towers, security cameras, and gun turrets at the strategic corners!

If they ever escaped they might discover the joys of getting eaten alive by a pit bull, grabbed up by a kidnapper, or better yet run down by a UPS truck. I can't possibly risk them experiencing all of these wonderful life blessings—it would cost me all control and completely undermine my authority in their lives! After all, that's the only reason to have kids, right? So you can control them—make them miserable—invent new ways every day to torture them with rules and restraint!

Surely that's why your parents had you, right? Think back. There they were, just "them"—nothing to do, nowhere to go, nobody to pick on. They had nobody messing any diapers, no one to wake them up every night, no one to eat all their food, and nobody to spend all their money on. So, instead of toilet papering the neighbor's house or holding up a gas station, they had a better idea.

"Let's have a kid," one of them suggested. "Then we could have a real, live, little person to torture and make miserable. We could invent terrible rules, unreasonable demands, and unrealistic expectations. It would be so much fun."

"Kids are expensive," the other one replied. "Yeah, but it would be worth it. Sure, we'll spend a hundred thousand dollars or so in the next 18 years, we'll never have another private moment, we'll endure constant stress and responsibility—but it will be worth it, just so we can make someone else miserable!"

And so, they had you.

And ever since, they have been having so much fun dominating your life with horrible restraints that cause you nothing but problems and inconvenience. If only they would have left you alone, you could have killed yourself with the electrical outlet years ago! What's the matter with these people. Authority…Bah-Humbug!

Okay, enough stupidity. Hopefully my point is clear. Without the loving authority you have in life, Mr. Brain, you would have killed yourself a long time ago. So before you rule authority out and let rebellion breed a higher level of stupidity in your heart, you'd better take a second look at that hook!

"For this is the love of God, that we
keep his commandments: and
his commandments are not grievous."
—1 JOHN 5:3

Twelve

Authority:
God's Original Plan

Psalm 147:11–13 says, "The LORD taketh pleasure in them that fear him, in those that hope in his mercy. Praise the LORD, O Jerusalem; praise thy God, O Zion. For he hath strengthened the bars of thy gates; he hath blessed thy children within thee."

There are two ways to take the first part of verse thirteen. Jerusalem sounds like a pretty tightly locked up place! "He hath strengthened the bars of thy gates." What's that all about? Prison camp? Sounds pretty rough. Obviously, this is a skewed perspective of the "bars and gates" mentioned in this verse.

In ancient times, if the people of a city wanted to be safe, protected, and "blessed," they would fortify the city. They would build thick walls, strong barred gates, and heavy defenses against potential enemies. The walls and gates served not to imprison people, but to protect people by keeping the enemy out!

This is also why I have a fence around my backyard—for the protection of my children, not their imprisonment! And friend, this is why God has placed authority in your life—for your protection.

Coming back to this verse, any sane person living in Jerusalem at the time would have been happy to hear the report that God was strengthening the bars of the gates! Any Israelite with half a brain would be thankful for the walls around the city. I doubt there were many dinner-time conversations along the lines of, "I sure hate those walls…They really block the view…I feel like a prisoner in this city!"

Similarly, I've never one time wandered into my backyard to see my kids crying, stomping their feet, and bemoaning the existence of the fence! I've never seen Lance, Larry, or Haylee resist the fence, hate the fence, fight the fence, or try to break through the fence. Usually they are so captivated by the fun they are having inside the fence, that they never even notice the fence!

I *have*, hundreds of times, sat across a desk or table from a "fence-fighting" teenager though! I can't for the life of me understand why they resist the fence. I can't figure out why they want to play in the street, risk the pit bull attacks, hazard a UPS truck, and chance biting into a razor-sharp hook!

Rebellious teens only see the fence! They completely miss the protection, the safety, and the advantages that the fence gives them. They never see the love, the compassion, and the care that the fence-builders of their lives have for them. They ignore the blessings of the great things within the fence—the fun, the freedom, the safety. They are too busy trying to break free, that they never realize they are breaking free from safety and will soon enter the freedom of the hungry-lion cage!

Rebellious teens are not prisoners to rules, they are prisoners to their own blindness and ignorance. Those who fight godly authority fight against their own safety. Eventually they break free from authority, only to find themselves exposed, vulnerable, and easily reeled into a bloody fish cooler.

God's Original Plan for Authority

1. God's design of authority is universal to the human race. Everyone is under authority! You will never live a day of your life, ever, when you are not required to answer to some authority. You will never outgrow it, never get beyond it, and never escape it. Everyone lives under authority, and the sooner you accept authority as a part of life, the sooner you will grow in spiritual maturity.

If you're just absolutely sick of authority—you just can't take your parents anymore—move out, get a job, pay your own rent, drive your own car, and answer to the boss, the landlord, and the traffic patrolman. If you can't take that, consider joining the military.

2. Earthly authority is not and never will be perfect. We could all bemoan the failures of earthly authorities. These failures are everywhere! Our national justice system is imperfect; our law enforcement agencies sometimes fail; and no school teacher is always right. At home, Mom and Dad will sometimes be wrong, act out of anger, or react with less than Spirit-filled responses. If you're looking for failure as a reason to distrust and defy God's plan for authority, you will never have to look very far! Humanity is fallen; our world is a corrupt place; and no earthly authority will ever be perfect or accurate 100% of the time!

Certainly there are times when lines are crossed and those in authority, by reason of a choice, naturally forfeit their right to authority or influence. In the case of a father who leaves his family, his authority in the lives of his children is somewhat forfeited. In the case of a government official that breaks the law, his authority is forfeited and his position must be filled by another. These illustrations could go on.

You will never live a day of your life, ever, when you are not required to answer to some authority.

Make no mistake, I'm not advocating deliberate abuses of authority. Exactly the opposite! I believe that when God gives someone authority, He holds them to the strictest accountability, and I believe (as one who holds some authority in my own home and some in the lives of others) that authority brings a huge stewardship of influence! Everyone in authority must answer to those they serve and ultimately to God for how they used that authority. If you have a position of authority, you know how unworthy you feel to have it, and how pressured you feel to exercise that authority in the grace of God! It's a huge weight of stewardship that no wise authority figure takes lightly.

I'm simply stating the fact that human authority falls short. This doesn't negate authority in our lives. In other words, just because there are a few bad policemen in the world doesn't mean we can disrespect and disobey all of them! The fact is, we need every one of them. Just because there are some abusers of power in religious and governing institutions doesn't mean we should resist every pastor, church, or public officer! The fact is, our spiritual health and our national freedom depend on these authorities, and these positions need to be filled with trustworthy people—people who understand the stewardship and labor diligently to serve, protect, and honor those they serve.

Everyone in authority must answer to those they serve and ultimately to God for how they used that authority.

Bringing it a little closer to home, the fact that your parents are human does not give you a right to resist their God-given place in your life. They will not always be right; they will not always respond with perfect grace and godliness; and they will not always make the right calls. Nevertheless, they are still your parents, and they are still God's greatest gift to you!

3. Earthly authority is given for our protection, not our persecution. Ezekiel 22:28–30 says, "And her prophets have daubed them with untempered morter, seeing vanity, and divining lies unto them, saying, Thus saith the Lord GOD, when the LORD hath not spoken. The people of the land have used oppression, and exercised robbery, and have vexed the poor and needy: yea, they have oppressed the stranger wrongfully. And I sought for a man among them, that should make up the hedge, and stand in the gap before me for the land, that I should not destroy it: but I found none."

The picture in this passage is one of oppression, fear, distress, and devastation. One group of people is being afflicted by another group. God is displeased, and He is searching, seeking, looking for a man who will "stand in the gap"—a man who will "make up the hedge." This hedge that the Lord refers to was the one thing that could have restored safety and protection for the oppressed people. The gap in the hedge—the hole in the wall—was allowing tyranny to reign and freedom to die!

In your mind, let that hedge be the authorities in your life—the spiritual wall of protection. Your parents, your pastor, your teachers, your youth pastor—they are diligently laboring to stand in your gap—to make up your hedge. They are willing to fight off the spiritual enemy, to force back the oppressor on your behalf. They are willing to shoulder the burden of your spiritual safety! They don't have to, but they are being obedient to their own authority by doing what God has assigned them to do. They could move to the mountains and raise fish in a hatchery if they wanted to, but no, they opted to fight on your behalf. What a gift! Those standing in your gap have expressed the greatest kind of love known to humanity—they are giving their lives for yours!

Yet, because you can't see the enemy, you opt to distrust them. All you see is the hedge! It's blocking your view. It's ticking you off! Who do these people think they are? They are hedging you in, cramping your style, keeping you down! They are restricting your freedom and controlling your life! So, you, in all of your grand stupidity and ignorance start kicking, screaming, punching, biting, and spitting at "the wall." You decide you're going to break free—escape—resist at all costs.

Just over that hedge is a desert wasteland of spiritual desolation. Just beyond that wall is a fierce lion—a vicious meat-eating enemy—hoping you break out! Did you get that? He's cheering you on, "Yeah, break free! Look at you locked in all those rules and authority…come on out here where the air is clean and the view is wide." He hopes you *do* break through that hedge.

Depending on the strength of your ignorant persistence and the resolve of those standing in your gap—you just might break free. And when you do, it will be "open-season" on you. You'll suddenly be all alone in a bloody land of slaughtered rebels and fat lions! You'll be the devil's ground beef in no time.

Young man, young lady, that hedge is there as God's greatest gift of spiritual protection in your life. You cannot see the battle or the enemy, but those in authority in your life can. You can trust them and stay safe, or resist them and break free. You will then see for yourself in painful reality that the enemy is real and you are vulnerable.

4. Authority is a protective gift from God. Those who shoulder true biblical authority shoulder spiritual battle on the behalf of others. It's no picnic or pleasant thing. The easiest way to live life is to avoid becoming anyone's authority. Those in authority in your life carry a spiritual pressure for your well-being that you cannot understand and fight a battle for your protection that you cannot see.

Can you comprehend the indescribable gift that it is to have someone in your life who will fight the forces of darkness on your behalf? Have you ever realized that when your parents go toe-to-toe with you, when your pastor powerfully declares spiritual truth from the pulpit, when your spiritual authorities engage into battle on your behalf, that this is an act of passionate, fiery love? They risk your hate, your resentment, your rejection, but they love you too much to let you get hurt! They would rather be rejected or hated than to see you go down without a fight.

That's the kind of amazing love your heart craves. Why would you resist it? Why would you try to break free from it? Why would you run from it? Why would you mistreat it?

Stop fighting the fence and start being grateful for the safety—the fiery love that God has placed in your life! Start thanking your spiritual authorities for standing in your gap and for making up your hedge. Most importantly, start taking advantage of the incredible protection that you have as you prepare for your own adult journey! That wall of authority around your life will give you a fantastic advantage as you become an adult—unless you break out and don't live long enough to get there…

"He that diggeth a pit shall fall into it;
and whoso breaketh an hedge,
a serpent shall bite him."
—ECCLESIASTES 10:8

Thirteen

Responding to Biblical Authority

I was fourteen years old and I loved video games. I mean I really loved them! I couldn't walk past one in a grocery store or a mall without playing. If I couldn't find a quarter, I would bum one from my mom. If she wouldn't give me one, I would very nearly come to tears! Go ahead, laugh. I know; I was stupid. I still am in many ways. These things just had a hold on me. Are you ready to laugh again? My favorite game of all time was Ms. Pac Man! Go ahead—get it out of your system. The book will be here when you're done with your belly laugh.

Yes, I must admit the humiliating fact that if I saw Ms. Pac Man and couldn't play it, at fourteen years old, it was quite literally the end of my life's joy and purpose. Strange.

Well, my parents saw this unhealthy addiction to blinking, digital life forms and they tried to curb it. Usually they would just flat out say "no." On rare occasions, when the planets were aligned just right, they would let one or two games slip. Those were the two days that I was happy during my ninth grade year. The rest of the year was basically a wash—no happiness whatsoever.

On one occasion, we were at an event in a large downtown area in Atlanta, Georgia with some friends. There was an arcade just around the corner, and during the week-long event the planets aligned and I was permitted on a couple of occasions to go and play Ms. Pac Man with some friends. Yet, for some unforeseen reason, about midway through the week, my dad flip-flopped on me and said, "No more video games."

Now, parent, whether you realize it or not, teenagers have the ability to hear what you actually say but then completely re-interpret it into what you really mean! Every teenager knows that parents have a difficult time expressing thoughts, stringing words together into intelligible sentences, keeping saliva from running down their chins—things like this. So, early in our teen years we devise an interpretation system.

Somewhere deep in our inner recesses we have a translation mechanism that kicks into gear when you speak. At first, it hears the words. Then it asks a simple question, "Why is my mom or dad saying this and what do they really mean?" Upon providing its own answer, our interpretation mechanism then begins to re-interpret your directives, using past experiences and inner desires as a guide. By the time your words are actually put into action, they usually mean something entirely different to the heart of your teen than what they meant when they were actually spoken.

This interpretation mechanism is truly a wonderful thing. With it, we never have to do what you actually say, and we can always explain how we reasoned what you really meant!

It is for this reason that your teenager can look at you and honestly say, "I didn't know that's what you meant"—and be truly sincere.

Well in this case, my inner translation mechanism kicked into high gear. "No more video games." "Why is my dad saying this and what does he really mean?" The inner voices whirred into motion. "Video games cost money—quarters to be exact. My dad is a frugal person and he is concerned about spending too many quarters and driving our family into poverty. In addition to this, he is concerned that I will spend too many quarters when I'm married, and that I will drive my own family into poverty. Money—that's the root concern." I was sure that my "why" question had been answered accurately. "For how long? Hmm...this is a tough one. He let me play video games yesterday... does he mean forever? No, that can't be right. So...for how long can I not spend quarters? Well…so long as it isn't my quarter or his quarter, why should he care. So long as I don't spend our quarters, he won't mind, since his real concern is saving money. Surely he isn't burdened for all the quarters in the world!"

Like your oven when the timer goes off, a little buzzer went off in my head as if to flash, "Interpretation Complete!" And then this message followed: "'No more video games' when translated from parent-ese to teen-lingo actually being interpreted means 'don't spend quarters.'" I was so pleased that I could still play video games so long as I didn't spend quarters. This was easy. Being as addicted as I was,

> *Teenagers have the ability to hear what you actually say but then completely re-interpret it into what you really mean!*

I was very good at begging quarters from strangers, carrying a sign that says "will work for quarters" etc. Finding a quarter that didn't belong to me or my dad was an easy fix.

So, first chance I got I was off to the arcade with a friend. I told my dad, "we'll be right back."

Now, teenager, you need to know that parents have an inner translation mechanism too; only theirs actually works—it actually tells the truth! In that moment my dad's inner mechanism began to translate, "We'll be right back." Actually, when using a teen translator to process this phrase you get something like, "We're going to do something perfectly innocent that will take a mere fraction of a second. We will return with angelic behavior faster than you can worry about where we've been."

Amazingly, when using a parent translator to interpret this phrase you get a completely different meaning. To a parent the interpretation of "we'll be right back" goes something like this, "We're probably up to no good but we don't want you to know it. Don't follow us. Don't question us. What you don't know won't hurt you. Stay here; wait for us to return at our leisure (no matter how long we are gone) and don't ask questions when we get back." At this point, a little buzzer must have gone off in my dad's head saying, "Interpretation complete! Follow teen immediately! Warning, Warning…Danger…Danger!"

So, a few seconds on my heels, was my dad—coming to make sure I wasn't spending any of his (or my) quarters. But rest assured dear reader, I wasn't. I was spending someone else's! I was completely obeying my inner translation of my father's directives. Aren't you proud of me?

When we got to the arcade, though I knew my interpretation was false, I swallowed it anyway. See, for teens, it's not about knowing the truth, it's about having an alibi! Deep in my heart, I knew well what my dad meant, yet my conscious mind didn't want to accept it, so my translator provided a neatly packaged explanation if needed. But surely, it wouldn't be needed, because we told Dad that we would be right back.

Parents have an inner translation mechanism too; only theirs actually works—it actually tells the truth!

It only took a few seconds for my friend to start playing Ms. Pac Man, and then to offer me a turn. Carefully looking around, not wanting my dad to think I was spending his quarter, I gratefully accepted the opportunity, like a drug addict escaped from rehab. It was a wonderful two minutes of sheer video game bliss!

Well, my turn only lasted a moment and the screen flashed "GAME OVER" soon enough. Then the moment of truth hit. Suddenly all of my reality came crashing back down upon me as I turned to see my dad standing directly behind me. He was about ten yards off, arms folded, standing squarely, and staring a hole right through me. How long he had been standing there, I do not know. Too long. Way too long, obviously.

He just stood, stared—glared is more like it—and waited. I scrambled, like a kid caught with his hand in the cookie jar. I tried to explain, tried to paint a light-hearted approach to the whole thing. "Dad, hey, Dad, I didn't spend any quarters on this! My friend let me borrow a quarter, Dad," expecting that he would be proud that I was so obedient to his directive *not to spend quarters.*

I was getting nowhere. He just stood, stared, and waited. Finally he just said, "Come with me." At this point I looked at my friend as if to say, "It's been nice knowing you," and I followed my dad to what I was sure was an early grave. My dad then dealt with my rebellion, and let's just say I'm lucky to be alive today and recounting this story as a humorous memory. That was the day I learned how broken my translator was! It was also the day that I realized, even when I think authority is being absolutely ridiculous about the smallest of things, I'm still under it! My game truly was OVER!

You cannot escape authority—ever. No matter where you run, where you hide, or what you do—you are forever predestinated to live under God's structure of authority in some form or fashion. You don't even get to escape it when you die! It's just here— which means you have two basic choices.

You can choose to respond to it correctly—to experience the protection and care that God intends to provide for you through it. Or...

You can respond incorrectly and suffer a life and perhaps an eternity of destruction. First, let's look at what not to do...

The Wrong Response to Godly Authority

Most teens and often many parents resist this wonderful gift—authority. The Bible calls this rebellion, and God places no small consequence on this in His Word. One of the most dangerous, confused, frustrating, and vulnerable positions you can be in is "in rebellion to God-given authority."

If you are in a position of rebellion against authority in your life right now, you are among the most miserable people walking the planet. There is no peace for you—no true happiness. You are confused, frustrated, angry, and probably depressed. And you're convinced that it's everyone's fault but your own. You are convinced that happiness will come as soon as you break free from authority. Your life is consumed with breaking free. Soon you will. Soon you will be more imprisoned than you ever imagined.

First Samuel 15:22–23 reminds us of God's position on rebellion versus obedience. It says, "And Samuel said, Hath the LORD as great delight in burnt offerings and sacrifices, as in obeying the voice of the LORD? Behold, to obey is better than sacrifice, and to hearken than the fat of rams. For rebellion is as the sin of witchcraft, and stubbornness is as iniquity and idolatry…"

"Rebellion is as the sin of witchcraft." Wow, that's pretty strong language. Can God really mean that? Absolutely.

In this story, Saul was disobeying God so that he could do something good for God. Have you ever been in that position? Have you ever done something wrong so you could do something good? Have you rationalized your rebellion as being acceptable because you don't have bad intentions!? Your intentions are not the issue here—your actions are.

God tells Saul, obedience is top priority! Obedience comes first over all other spiritual exercises and good intentions. God says, "Obedience is what I want more than any other thing you could sacrifice for me or to me. Submit to my authority. Do what I say. Don't do it your own way."

Saul rebelled. Saul was greatly rebuked for disobeying God to do something good for God. Saul's rebellion was listed in God's book on the same page as idolatry and devil worship. Whoa!

Rebellion is like the very act of turning from God and worshipping Satan. Rebellion ranks up there with curses, satanic rituals, and human sacrifice. (In this case you're the sacrifice and Satan is the idol you are worshipping.) In God's Book, deliberately fighting against authorities that He has placed in your life is among the worst things you could do.

In the Old Testament, devil worship was quite often tied to drug use and mind-altering substances. Satanic rituals, idolatry, and witchcraft employed the use of these substances to induce altered states of consciousness and spiritual vulnerability. You might say that these substances did (and still do) open up the mind and soul to spiritual powers of evil.

When God says "rebellion is as the sin of witchcraft," He is including these practices. He is saying that rebellion has the same effect on the heart that the use of these conscious-altering substances have. In the same way that drugs and alcohol take away your conscious ability to discern reality, so rebellion distorts and destroys spiritual reality. In the same way that substance abuse makes you physically crazy, even so rebellion makes you spiritually crazy—self-destructive.

I once read about a man on drugs who climbed a telephone pole and tried to fly. Another man drove his car down a road and straight over a cliff. Another killed his family because he thought they were trying to kill him. People who are on drugs or alcohol cannot see clearly. Reality is distorted. This makes them see things that aren't so and make choices that aren't healthy. Substance abuse puts a person on a very real path of self-destruction. It places a person in an artificial reality—a world of distortion—where destructive decisions are made.

If you are rebelling against a godly authority in your life—you are there—in a distorted world of "drunkenness" that will cause you to hurt yourself and others. You are on spiritual drugs! Your spiritual reality is messed up; your senses are dulled; and you will destroy yourself. It's a law of God's spiritual universe. You cannot resist and defy spiritual authority in your life and win. No one ever has; no one ever will! It cannot be done.

> *If you are in a position of rebellion against authority in your life right now, you are among the most miserable people walking the planet.*

Rebellion makes you high on self—drunk on stupidity. Rebellion makes you say and do things that anyone in their right mind wouldn't. Rebellion confuses, distorts, and frustrates your spiritual life in ways that you cannot comprehend. If you are rebelling, you know what I'm saying is true—and you're even thinking you can rebel against my words. See the lie! Wake up! Don't continue down this path to your own demise. Sober up! Get out from under the effects of this dangerous, spiritual substance abuse.

The Right Response to Godly Authority

So, if the hook of rebellion—the lie of resistance—is the second most dangerous way teens are destroying their lives, what is the right response? In light of the truth of godly authority, how should we respond to this gift from God?

First, the right response goes back to honor. In Exodus 20:12 God says, "Honour thy father and thy mother: that thy days may be long upon the land which the Lord thy God giveth thee." We talked about this in the last chapter, so we won't deliberate. Let me just say, that you can obey without honoring, but you cannot honor without obeying. Surface obedience—conformity—is not the answer. You can rebel in the heart while externally doing what you are told.

One little boy was told to sit down in Sunday school. After several times, the teacher finally threatened that if he did not sit down, she would take him to his mother and father. At this point the little boy sat down and defiantly said, "I'm sitting down on the outside, but I'm standing up on the inside!"

You can do that. You can obey outwardly but still rebel inwardly. This is why honor comes first. If you truly honor your authority—respect them, highly value them, value what they say—you will obey from the heart with a right spirit. Honor will create within you a right spirit that will generate true obedience.

Second, a right response involves surrender and submission to God first and to human authority second. Ephesians 5:21 teaches us this way, "Submitting yourselves one to another in the fear of God." To submit means literally to "lay down your arms and stop fighting." Are you tired of the fighting? Fighting authority is one of the most miserable, depleting, spiritually exhausting ways to live. There is nothing more empty and frustrating!

When I was teenager, there was a season when I chose a girlfriend that my parents were less than approving of. This young lady wasn't necessarily a bad person; it was just that my parents had a God-given uneasiness about her, and they made that clear to me. Rather than submitting, I chose to resist. Though this was a relatively brief season in my life, it stands out as the most miserable!

I wanted to date this girl and my parents didn't approve. This drove a wedge between us for several weeks. It was always there. It gave way to heated exchanges, frustrating dialogs, harsh arguments, and cutting throwbacks. I stiffened my neck, hardened my spirit, and resisted their guidance. I wanted my will above theirs! All the time, the wedge was there, keeping us apart. I often thought, "If they would just give me my way, things would be much better between us!" And that wedge…was just…there…

They could have forced their will, and in some instances parents should. In this instance, however, they chose to continue making their will clear, letting me suffer in the mire, guilt, and frustration of my own. The lesson I learned was stronger than if they had forced obedience. I was miserable and the whole world knew it! It was my parents' fault—every last bit of it. But I knew better.

A few weeks of this was all I could take. No beauty, no girlfriend, no love note was worth this! Life was horrible and I wanted my good life back. It's amazing how we wallow in the pig slop of our rebellion longer than we really need to.

Finally, I broke up with this girl, giving in to my parents' desires. Like a long lost friend, peace came flooding back into my soul. Like a heavy fog lifting in the morning sun, clarity was restored and I could see reality. It didn't take me long to find out that this girl didn't like me all that much any way. I was pretty much "bait" she was using to make her old boyfriend jealous (the one I didn't know about). My parents knew far more about dating than I did, and their authority in my life could have spared me some emotional trauma if I had but submitted to their guidance.

One of the hardest things you will ever do is submit, or stop fighting your parents. It's a matter of pride—not wanting to "give in to them" and let them win. It's a struggle of the will—seemingly losing something you desire so strongly. Yet, it's really just a trap! It's a hook. The sooner you learn to give your will over to God and to your parents, the sooner God will begin to bring your life back into clear focus. I can't entirely explain it—it's just a law of God. It works.

> *Honor will create within you a right spirit that will generate true obedience.*

Third, it ultimately boils down to obedience. My issue with my dad and Ms. Pac Man was not an interpretation problem. It was an obedience problem. When his will directly clashed with my will, I disobeyed his and followed mine. This was the exact wrong response to authority! No matter my reasoning, no matter whether I had an explanation, I was choosing to respond wrongly to authority. I chose to disobey. My game was over soon enough, and so will yours be, unless you understand more fully what obedience is all about.

You've heard the verse all your life—Ephesians 6:1, "Children, obey your parents in the Lord: for this is right." You could quote it backwards and forwards. You've sung songs about it. You've memorized it in every Sunday school class you ever attended. So by now, when you need it the most, you're completely de-sensitized to it. So, let's look at some things you probably never knew or never really realized about obedience. See you in the next chapter…

"…Obey, I beseech thee, the voice of the LORD,
which I speak unto thee: so it shall be
well unto thee, and thy soul shall live."
—JEREMIAH 38:20

Fourteen

God's Premium on Obedience

Obedience isn't just a word in a kid's song or a verse for children. In fact, in God's Word, adults are often commanded to obey, too! Interesting fact, isn't it? Sort of makes you want to write a new song and create a new Scripture memory program for Christian adults, after all these years of having obedience crammed down your throat, doesn't it? Not a bad point, Mom and Dad. Obedience would fall under the category of things we are supposed to first model by example, and then teach.

Deuteronomy 13:4 says to God's people, "Ye shall walk after the LORD your God, and fear him, and keep his commandments, and obey his voice, and ye shall serve him, and cleave unto him." Time and time again in His Word, God commands His people to obey His voice.

Obeying your parents is just a learning curve for real life! Learning to obey Mom and Dad is "boot camp"—spiritual training for learning to obey God. You see, obedience is central to the Christian life. From Adam and Eve until now—until you—God has been eagerly blessing those who obey Him and warning those who disobey Him. He commands obedience, rewards obedience, and responds to obedience.

Adam and Eve disobeyed when they ate the forbidden fruit, and we're all paying the price for that disobedience. Abraham obeyed God by leaving his hometown for an undisclosed location and future. Abraham obeyed God again when he was told to kill his only son Isaac. Jonah disobeyed God. It took a few days of being "gastro-intestinal distress" inside a whale to change his mind. He ultimately obeyed against his will. Saul disobeyed by sacrificing against God's command. Peter obeyed by getting out of the boat. Paul obeyed by fulfilling God's call to take the Gospel to the known world.

Learning to obey Mom and Dad is "boot camp"—spiritual training for learning to obey God.

The Bible and history are filled with the stories of billions of people. In every case, each person made a simple choice: obedience or disobedience. Isn't it amazing, that with all of these historical proofs of the products of obedience and disobedience, we still convince ourselves that we can beat the system! Don't be so foolish. This obedience thing is about you and God—no one else. It's just about the two of you. When you resist authority, you are resisting God. In your life you will either obey Him and reap the benefits, or disobey Him and reap the problems. It's that simple.

Obedience is central to your walk with God. In every decision, every choice, you are either obeying or disobeying God's direction in your life. If you struggle with obeying Mom and Dad, you will most likely struggle the rest of your life with obeying God. In the end, you will miss out on unbelievable blessings.

God is very clear that those in spiritual authority over you should be honored, obeyed, remembered, and submitted to. Hebrews 13:7 says, "Remember them which have the rule over you, who have spoken unto you the word of God: whose faith follow, considering the end of their conversation." Hebrews 13:17 says, "Obey them that have the rule over you, and submit yourselves: for they watch for your souls, as they that must give account, that they may do it with joy, and not with grief: for that is unprofitable for you."

Romans 13:1–3 speaks so powerfully on this subject. Read and think about what God says here. "Let every soul be subject unto the higher powers. For there is no power but of God: the powers that be are ordained of God. Whosoever therefore resisteth the power, resisteth the ordinance of God: and they that resist shall receive to themselves damnation. For rulers are not a terror to good works, but to the evil. Wilt thou then not be afraid of the power? do that which is good, and thou shalt have praise of the same:"

God says so many powerful things about authority here. He ordains authority, wants us to be subject to authority, and warns against resisting His plan. He caps it off by saying that those in authority in your life are ministers (servants) to you for good.

I love what the people of Israel told Joshua when he was preparing to lead them across the Jordan. Look at Joshua 1:16–18, "And they answered Joshua, saying, All that thou commandest us we will do, and whithersoever thou sendest us, we will go. According as we hearkened unto Moses in all things, so will we hearken unto thee: only the LORD thy God be with thee, as he was with Moses. Whosoever he be that doth rebel against thy commandment, and will not hearken unto thy words in all that thou commandest him, he shall be put to death: only be strong and of a good courage."

Those in authority in your life are ministers (servants) to you for good.

To paraphrase, "So long as you are courageous enough to follow God and obey Him, then we will follow you and obey you!" What a fantastic commitment! Joshua committed to stay under God's authority, the people committed to stay under Joshua's authority—each obeying the higher authority for the good of all! That's what true authority is really all about!

God Chose Your Choices for Disobedience

When God created time and space, He created laws. Some of those laws He chose to make mandatory. Other laws He gave you a free will to choose to obey or disobey. In other words, God chose, long before you came along, in what areas you could disobey. He predetermined which laws you could rebel against and which ones you couldn't. And guess what? You've stayed right in His plan all along.

For instance, you've probably never rebelled against breathing oxygen! The fact that you're reading this book means, no matter how you've rebelled in other areas, you have managed to take a breath of fresh oxygen every few seconds without fail over the past however many years. You wimp! If you're a real rebel, why don't you take on something significant—like breathing! I mean, if you're really tough, rebel against something impressive—start breathing water for a few weeks! Prove to the world that you really can stand alone!

Some rebels are so wimpy; they've never thought of rebelling against eating food. They resist in other areas, but when it comes to eating, they always manage to down a healthy plate of real food! Why not fight this? Why not rebel and start eating wood chips or grass clippings! Why submit to God's design? If you want to defy His plan, go for something bigger than just "fighting your parents." That's so wimpy! Anyone can do that!

If you're going to fight God, really fight him! Breathe water, eat concrete, resist gravity, grow another head, move to another planet, live underwater, eat through your ears, sleep on the ceiling, grow a few more eyes, arms, or legs…whatever! Just do something that really proves your individuality, your true power, your total lack of submission to God's authority and design! Do something original for once. Anyone can fight his or her parents. Anyone can resist God. Anyone can get a bad attitude. How childish of you. How petty. Move up in the world of rebellion!

I hope you get my point. You don't choose how to rebel. God chose that for you. You only get to rebel in the areas that God allows. And, it stands to reason, that you only get to rebel as long as He allows. He could stop you at any moment! You'll be far better off if you give in to Him of your own free will. That's what He calls "faith!" That's what pleases Him most.

Maybe it never occurred to you quite this way, but God is the one who determined that resistance against your parents could be tolerated, while resistance against oxygen would be lethal. God is the one who determined that disobedience to Him would sometimes be put up with, while disobedience to eating would be fatal. Call it mercy. Call it patience. Call it love. No matter how you slice it, God is putting up with your position—giving you time to rethink your direction and change course. Isn't He great!

Obedience—the Place of God's Blessing

I think Deuteronomy 11:26–28 puts it best, "Behold, I set before you this day a blessing and a curse; A blessing, if ye obey the commandments of the LORD your God, which I command you this day: And a curse, if ye will not obey the commandments of the LORD your God...." In these verses, God gives you options—obey or disobey—be blessed or be cursed. It's that simple. God has chosen whom He will bless. Yes, He plays favorites! Those who obey are His favorites. Yet, He isn't a "respecter" of persons—anyone can obey Him and have His favor! This is another one of God's laws—His blessing follows obedience. If you want God's blessing on your life, you must be in the place of obedience.

Do you know why your parents are commanded to obey God? Because He wants to bless them! Do you know why your parents should make you obey them? So that God will bless you! Up 'til now you thought it was about control! You think people are just trying to control your behavior—to hold you hostage. Not at all. The reason your parents discipline you, your teachers lecture you, your pastor rebukes you is that you might be in the place of God's blessing on your life. Period!

The reason I'm writing you now to say "Obey your parents" is all about God's blessing for you! When you obey, you place yourself in the direct path of God's best blessings. Obedience places you in God's sights—registers you on God's radar! He said very plainly that He blesses those who obey Him and that "it may be well with thee and thy days may be long upon the Earth..." for those who obey their parents.

Got blessings? No? Try obedience...

The World's Greatest Unknown Secret of Obedience

Rebels are stupid. I hate to be so blunt, but they are. Rebels never get what they want, and are always more and more uptight about it—like more and more rebellion is going to magically get them there! Listen carefully, Einstein…most teenagers completely miss this point altogether.

Just as obedience is God's way of blessing, it's also a parent's way of blessing. Wait a minute, I can tell you didn't get that. Let me say it more clearly—kids who obey their parents always get better stuff!

Now, I'm not saying obey only for selfish ends, but I am saying that obedience is the world's best-kept secret! Obedience is no prison—it's exactly the opposite when you're dealing with biblical authority—it's a world of freedom, trust, blessing, and privilege! Kids who obey their parents always have the trust, respect, admiration, and blessing of those with the true power in the world—the money-makers!

Think of it this way, your friends may make fun of you for honoring or obeying your parents—but then again, your friends aren't planning to help you BUY A CAR! Yet, I've never met a parent who didn't want to help provide an obedient, honoring sixteen-year-old son or daughter with a car! And, I've never met a sixteen-year-old who didn't want one. I've never met a parent who didn't want to provide their teenager with any good thing that God provided for!

The provision of these things always hinges on two things—God making a way financially, and the teenager making a way spiritually. God has to provide the resources, but the teenager has to provide the track record, and there's no greater track record than one filled with obedience and honor!

Don't believe me? Just look around your youth group or friends. Those who are the most obedient and honoring to their parents always have better blessings, greater freedom, and bigger privileges! They have a treasure that you cannot buy—trust! (I realize, you may have a friend whose parents give no control or boundaries, who appears to have more freedom and trust than you do, but that's just not the case. Teens whose parents give no restraints have no tough love in their lives. I've met many who only wish their parents loved them enough to discipline them.)

Most teenagers never see this, though it's right before their eyes. Your parents would love to give you more freedom, more trust, more privileges! Your parents are craving to provide you with some really cool opportunities. They are simply waiting for you to get over yourself long enough to show them some maturity! Obedience and honor are the keys! So quit wasting time with rebellion. Figure it out already.

Parent, grab your crash helmet, you're up next...

"Now therefore, if ye will obey my voice indeed,
and keep my covenant, then ye shall be a
peculiar treasure unto me above all people:
for all the earth is mine:"
—Exodus 19:5

Fifteen

Obedience:
Like Father, Like Son

This book is about how parents and teens are collaborating on self-destruction, and if rebellion is the second biggest "hook" or destroyer, then I would have to submit that rebellion is the second biggest parental contributor to this problem! In other words, "Monkey see, monkey do." I'm trying to be funny, not disrespectful. Have you ever heard the phrase, "Like father, like son?" I believe it applies here. Consider this...

Why should your son obey you, if you aren't obeying God? How can you expect an obedient child when you aren't being one? The image of a father telling his son to "never smoke" as he personally lights up another Camel comes to mind here. God's expectations of you are no less than yours for your own teenager. It's complete hypocrisy to demand or expect or even hint at obedience from your child if you are deliberately, willfully disobeying God in your own life.

Let me get specific for a moment. How about tithing? Are you obeying God? How about church attendance? Are you obeying God? How about your music, your TV watching, or your service; are you obeying God? If obedience is central to the Christian life, how is your obedience to your Father? We cannot teach what we do not know. We cannot exemplify what we are not doing. We should not expect what we are not willing to give. Ouch…I know that's a painful thought, but needful nonetheless.

Maybe you should stop right here and review your own heart with God. Maybe we've hit a nerve center and the light bulb has just come on. Disobedient parents have no reason to expect obedient children—plain and simple. Are you, perhaps, struggling with a disobedient child in your home because God is struggling with one in His? If so, I beg you for the sake of your teen, to make this right. Some readers at this point will choose to become passive parents—to stop expecting obedience. Wrong choice.

How often I have seen parents unwilling to obey, simply take a passive position in their teen's life. Why are they passive? Because they would rather not make any personal changes with God. They accept their own disobedience; therefore, they accept their teen's. Putting up with their teen's disobedience becomes the price they must pay to continue their own.

I'm not trying to be harsh, just direct. And I'm certainly not suggesting that the only reason teens rebel is because their parents do. And I'm not excusing any disobedience to parents *for any reason*. I'm just saying that the issue of rebellion is something we all deal with, not just teenagers, and that dealing with our own rebellion as parents should be the starting point for helping our teens deal with theirs. How can we ever help them through their rebellion towards us, if we don't deal with our own towards God? After all, the point is to help them through rebellion, not just to squelch it. You cannot imagine the wonderful inroad you will have into the heart of your teenager, when you have openly and consistently displayed an obedient heart toward your Heavenly Father. Your own spiritual obedience will speak louder, longer, and far more effectively than your commands or verbal confrontations.

> *We cannot teach what we do not know. We cannot exemplify what we are not doing.*

In Isaiah 1:16–20, God has just completed a clear indictment against the spiritual formalities that the nation of Israel was following.

He decries their sacrifices, their oblations, and their "religious activity." He literally denounces the things they were supposedly doing "for Him." Then, He turns His attention to the solution. Here is what He says, "Wash you, make you clean; put away the evil of your doings from before mine eyes; cease to do evil; Learn to do well; seek judgment, relieve the oppressed, judge the fatherless, plead for the widow. Come now, and let us reason together, saith the LORD: though your sins be as scarlet, they shall be as white as snow; though they be red like crimson, they shall be as wool. If ye be willing and obedient, ye shall eat the good of the land: But if ye refuse and rebel, ye shall be devoured with the sword: for the mouth of the LORD hath spoken it."

Your own spiritual obedience will speak louder, longer, and far more effectively than your commands...

After telling these people to stop their game of religion, He calls them back to Himself in humble repentance. He offers to wash them, to make them clean, to clear the slate. Then He puts before them two simple options. "If ye be willing and obedient, ye shall eat of the good of the land: But if ye refuse and rebel, ye shall be devoured with the sword...." God says to these adults—His people—"you have two choices. You can be willing and obedient or you can refuse and rebel." Simple, direct, impossible to escape. The place of God's best blessings for both teens and their parents is simply willing obedience to Him.

In addition to this, as a parent, even dealing with discipline in your teenager's life becomes an issue of obedience to your Heavenly authority. When you guide your teenager and enforce rules that God has led you to put in place, you are literally obeying God. No longer is it merely a matter of control between parent and child. No longer is it simply about behavior and surface performance! It's no longer a surface struggle of the wills.

When you choose to be the authority God has appointed you to be, for your teenager, you are obeying God! Therefore, when you stand in the gap as a biblical authority, you are modeling, to your teen, obedience to your own Heavenly Father! What a great combination. You cannot fathom how this position changes the depth and magnitude of your parental position and influence on the heart of your teen! A teenager is much more likely to honor and obey (from the heart) both father and Heavenly Father when the foundation of all discipline in the home is submission to God first.

In other words, when your teenager knows that you are standing on biblical grounds, submitting to your own authority, obeying your own Heavenly Father—it becomes clear that your discipline is driven by pure motives rather than self-centered ends such as behavior control, embarrassment, irritation, or anger.

Teenagers easily sense and are deeply hurt by impure motives in discipline—these impure motives actually counteract whatever good was intended through the discipline in the first place! Yet, no matter how much a teen resists discipline, he will always respect authority that is truly under Authority and guided by higher principles. Parent, before you can expect or demand obedience, you must first exemplify it in your Christian life—walking with God and obeying Him on a daily basis. And Second, you must obey Him by being the authority He has commanded you to be for your family.

A Lesson from Larry

I'm continually amazed at the lessons the Lord teaches me during family vacations. One of the most humorous lessons came when our son Larry was a mere three years old. Larry has always been a deep thinker at heart, and generally a pretty funny kid on top of it. He has always had a different way of seeing the world around him.

For instance, for the first five years of his life, he couldn't comprehend the concept of a "day." He couldn't grasp the idea of "tomorrow" or "three days from now." When he needed to measure time, he measured it by "how many times he had to go to bed before an event happened." He even went so far as to coin his own term for this measurement of time—a "bed-night"!

So, Larry was constantly asking questions like, "How many bed-nights until Christmas, Dad?" "How many bed-nights until vacation?" "How many bed-nights until my birthday?" We were constantly hearing about bed-nights. People started staring at us in public places. It was rather embarrassing. But no matter how we tried to explain, he just couldn't get it. In Larry's world, there was no passing of "days"—just "bed-nights"!

On another occasion my wife was cooking something in a pot on the stove. Larry walked in and said, "Hey Mom, what are you cooking in that fire-bucket?" On another occasion, he was afraid of a bee but didn't know what to call it, so he coined the term "stinging-fly"!

On another afternoon, we were walking by a freshly seeded grass lot on our church campus. A truck-load of manure had been evenly spread across the budding lawn which provided for a rather unpleasant nasal experience! The entire southern portion of our campus smelled like a cattle ranch! After taking a few whiffs, Larry shook his head incredulously, and said, "Man, we've got to get a better smell for that grass!" (As if choosing a smell for the grass was like selecting your air-freshener at the car wash!)

All that to say, Larry sees the world with a slightly different slant than most people—hilariously so!

Rewind to family vacation 1996. We're staying at a hotel with my parents. Larry is just figuring out "family relationships"—he's just getting the idea that Dad has parents too! In fact, it was apparently a wonderful discovery for him! Sometime about midday, while walking to our hotel room, Larry inquisitively asked me this question, "Hey, Dad, is Grammy your mom?"

Thrilled that he was finally getting it, I said, "Yes, son, Grammy is my mom."

"Okay." And with that he was silent, pensive, calculating. I could tell the little wheels in his three-year-old mind were turning, but that's all he said. The subject didn't come up until four hours later, when we were all together at dinner.

Little did I know, Larry's mind had been working all afternoon on this subject of family relationships—he must have been quite pleased to discover that his own dad had a dad... and a mom! As we entered the restaurant and took our seats, he deliberately chose a seat close to Grammy. He had some negotiating he needed to take care of. Halfway through dinner, he found his long awaited strategic moment—a moment when I turned away in conversation with my wife.

Seizing his window of opportunity, he leaned over to Grammy, motioned for her to bend an ear, and whispered stealthily, pausing for emphasis, "Grammy…your kid…has been giving me spankin's…and you need to make him stop!"

My mother burst into immediate laughter—completely blowing Larry's well-planned cover! A few moments later, after hearing the story, we were all belly laughing at the table, and Larry was quite unexpectedly the "star of the show"!

The simple fact of the matter is, just like Larry, your child understands that you have a Father—you have a Heavenly Parent! You have a Dad that you must obey. And, while your teenager may not be able to appeal to grandma as Larry did, he certainly understands that you too must live in obedience to your Heavenly Father. Somehow, even in the mind of a little child, the concept of parents answering to a higher authority is understandable. Why is it that we, as parents, seem to lose sight of this?

Simply put, the best way to deal with disobedience is from a position of complete obedience. Refuse to give your teen even one reason—even one justification—for rebellion.

Fortunately, giving "spankin's" wasn't the devastating news to Grammy that Larry thought it would be! Little did he know Grammy's own dark and sordid history of giving "spankin's" in her day! My brothers and I still bear the deep emotional scars to prove it. I still flinch a little when I get around those wooden cooking spoons that my wife uses in the kitchen!

Parent, quite sincerely, here is my question:

If you were sitting at the dinner table with your child and God… what could your child whisper about you?

"…for I the LORD thy God am a jealous God,
visiting the iniquity of the fathers upon the children
unto the third and fourth generation of them that hate me;"
—EXODUS 20:5

Sixteen

Passivity Breeds Rebellion

Remember my Ms. Pac Man story? This may be hard for teenagers to believe, but my dad would have preferred not to deal with my disobedience. I know, teenager, you think your parents actually enjoy slam-dunking you. This just isn't the case.

The easiest thing to do, for my dad, would have been to just tune my problems out. My issue was an unhealthy addiction to video games—idolatry. It was about the control that video games had on my heart. His directive to me was in an effort to loosen that control so that it wouldn't become a greater stronghold for the enemy. Yet, he didn't have to engage for me. He could have disconnected himself from my predicament and just let me have my way. This would have been the easiest path—the path of least resistance—that path that most parents in our culture today would have chosen.

Our culture is plagued with passive parents—parents who take a non-role in their kid's lives—the path of least resistance. Passive parenting is the current standard approach to teen-parenting. When you're dealing with a fighting teenager, the easiest thing to do is nothing—to not fight. Many parents become passive because they are simply tired and don't have the energy to deal with the battle; others are passive because they simply don't know what to do. Still others choose passivity because they'd rather not change their own relationship with God.

Whatever your reason, passivity is the worst route you could take in this spiritual battle. The September 13, 2004 edition of *Newsweek* magazine contained an article entitled "The Power of No." The second paragraph of the article hit the nail on the head with this statement, "It's an unexpected legacy of the affluent '90's: parents who can't say no." The article went on to say that modern-day parents have "confused permissiveness with love. Experts agree: too much love won't spoil a child, but too few limits will."

Passivity is the choice (whether deliberate or not) to disengage from the spiritual battle for the life of your teen—the choice not to fight. This choice is one of the most damaging you could make because it says, at the core, "I don't care about you. I'm too tired, too ignorant, too comfortable to get involved in your spiritual battle. I don't love you passionately enough to fight for you." This is the ultimate form of neglect, and it's the temptation of every parent.

Our culture is plagued with passive parents—parents who take a non-role in their kid's lives—the path of least resistance.

A key to spiritual victory in the life of a teenager is parents who choose to stand strong, engage actively, and stay in the battle—no matter what. The devil will do everything he can to wear you down and disengage you from an active spiritual battle for your teen. He will exhaust you, intimidate you, misdirect you, all in an effort to make you passive.

Nothing is more intense than spiritual battle. When you are going head to head, late at night, with one of your teens, you are engaged in spiritual battle. Paul makes this clear in 2 Corinthians 10:3-4, "For though we walk in the flesh, we do not war after the flesh: (For the weapons of our warfare are not carnal, but mighty through God to the pulling down of strong holds;)." Your confrontations with your teen are, at the core, spiritual. You must see this and understand that there is a far bigger battle, and far greater stakes than just the surface conflict itself.

This battle may feel like an exercise in futility and the temptation, which most parents are giving in to, is to "give in." You need the sleep, you don't have the energy, you are beyond exhaustion—and so you quit. You actively choose not to stand in the gap. You vacate your place in the protective hedge. And your teen knows it. There is not a bigger parenting mistake.

Fighting a spiritual battle is no easy thing! It's exhausting, depleting, and risky. It takes true spiritual courage, trust in the Word of God, and full spiritual engagement—and it must take absolute priority over every other life commitment. Dad and Mom, there will be times when you feel as though your back is against the ropes, your strength is completely gone, and you can't go another round! Don't just walk out of the room and go to bed.

There will be times when your emotions are at their limit, your wisdom seems exhausted, and there are no other options. Don't quit the battle. In those times—keep swinging (spiritually, that is), keep fighting, keep praying, keep exerting your full spiritual energy. Keep asking the Holy Spirit to give you His words, His promptings in penetrating into the heart of your teen. If it means you have an all-night discussion once a week for

> *Fighting a spiritual battle is no easy thing! It's exhausting, depleting, and risky.*

the six years your son or daughter is a teenager, if it means your plans for the moment must radically change, if it means your teen misses a day of school or you are three hours late for work—it doesn't matter! Fight the battle. Be the authority that God appointed you to be—not for selfish reasons or control. Be the hedge! Stand in the gap for your teenager. Face the forces of darkness head-on in the power of God's Holy Spirit. Face down the devil for the life of your teen. James 4:7 says it this way, "Submit yourselves therefore to God. Resist the devil, and he will flee from you." Note that submission to God is a prerequisite for resisting the devil.

Don't Engage Without the Holy Spirit!

The only thing worse than passivity is carnal engagement in battle. In other words, fighting the fight in your flesh. Many parents do this. They enter the fight in their own flesh, their own human reason and strength. They fall to the temptation of temper—throwing angry, hurtful words like fiery darts—heaping rejection and impatience upon the heart of their teenager. Most often the teen is just as guilty—firing back hot responses and angry outbursts. In a sense parents lower themselves into the immature boxing ring of teenage conflict. They lose control, respond in carnality, and never gain spiritual victory.

When you "put on the gloves" and lower yourself into a flaring exchange of verbal explosions, the devil wins. He succeeds in dividing your home. Imagine him—there in the background—laughing his heart out at how he is destroying your relationship with each other. He is the silent, invisible victor. Regardless of who wins the argument, you both lose the relationship.

Your battle with your teenager is not physical—it's not a war of words in which one of the two of you must win. It's not merely a war of wills that can be won with a loud voice and a flaring temper. Your battle is spiritual. Your battle is you and your teen together, against the forces of the wicked one. It must be entered with prayer, in the power of Christ, with the sword of His Word, and with the filling of His Holy Spirit.

Parent, when you fully submit yourself to God in total surrender and obedience, and then you actively resist the devil on behalf of your teen—the forces of Hell itself cannot come against you. In Christ, you are a spiritual "force to be reckoned with"! It's the fantastic design of God—His plan for protecting every young life. The devil cannot win against an obedient, Spirit-filled, engaged parent who chooses to "stand in the gap"!

When you engage in your spiritual battle in the power of Christ, there will be no shouting match, physical force, or venomous exchange (though these things might be thrown at you, they will not come from you). In other words, you will not fight to save your life. You will lay yours down to save the life of your child. There will be prayer—passionate pleading with God for victory and courage. There will be Scripture—verses that the Holy Spirit brings to your heart to use against the enemy.

There will be a sacrifice—of energy, of sleep, and more critically, of a deep part of your heart. You will feel as though you are dying a miserable death. This is the kind of intense love that ultimately leads to spiritual victory. May God grant you courage to fight—not in your own strength, but in His.

A Biblical Story of a Passive Parent

First Samuel 3:12–13 is one of the saddest parenting passages in the Bible. In this story, Eli is the priest of God who has two sons—Hophni and Phineas. Eli's sons were "sons of Belial"—wicked young men who chose not to follow God. In spite of the terrible wickedness of his sons, Eli chose a passive path. Here is what God says in response to Eli's passivity:

"In that day I will perform against Eli all things which I have spoken concerning his house: when I begin, I will also make an end. For I have told him that I will judge his house for ever for the iniquity which he knoweth; because his sons made themselves vile, and he restrained them not." God pronounced judgment on the house of Eli, not because of the sons' rebellion, but because of the father's failure to restrain his sons. Eli chose not to fight for his sons. He chose to break down the hedge, to leave the gap. In response, God chose to judge his house. What a powerful indictment against passive parenting in the 21st century.

Ezekiel 13:3–5 gives another insight as to how God truly feels about those who vacate their place in the hedge of protection. He says, "Thus saith the Lord GOD; Woe unto the foolish prophets, that follow their own spirit, and have seen nothing! O Israel, thy prophets are like the foxes in the deserts. Ye have not gone up into the gaps, neither made up the hedge for the house of Israel to stand in the battle in the day of the LORD." In this case, the Lord rebukes the prophets (the pastors) who refuse to stand in the gap and to make up the hedge.

Make no mistake about it, parent, pastor—you are called to stand in the gap—to make up the hedge! You are called to engage in battle on behalf of those under your care. No matter how intense the rebellion or how harsh the resistance—passivity (leaving the hedge) is not an option.

"*And I sought for a man among them,*
that should make up the hedge, and stand in the gap
before me for the land, that I should not destroy it:
but I found none."
—Ezekiel 22:30

Seventeen

Rules Without Relationships Breed Rebellion

Our pastor has often stated from the pulpit that "rules without relationships breed rebellion." This statement reveals another extreme in society and in many Christian homes today—the reverse of passivity. Oftentimes I see aggressive, zealous parents seize on structure—they pounce on putting a rigid set of guidelines into place in their home, in the hopes that this structure will become the guiding force, the salvation for their family.

In this scenario, rules become far more than a means to an end—they become the end in and of themselves! These homes are something like Marine boot camps and the kids are something like inmates. Often it happens in committed Christian homes where parents are busy and fail to offset the rules with relationship. Often it happens in homes where spirituality is artificial and surface behavior is the primary concern—"we want our happy Christian family appearance to hold up with our church friends."

Rules are necessary. Rules are a product of love. Guidelines are necessary in any strong relationship. Parents who truly care will establish and enforce rules. Yet, the guidelines are only a means to an end, and yes, rules without relationships do indeed breed rebellion.

Perhaps you're dealing with a rebellious teenager because your rules do not rest on the foundation of a close, loving, de-fragmented relationship. Perhaps the cure for your home is laughter, fun, memories—a family canoe trip, or a day trip to the beach. Every rule in your home must rest upon the soft bed of a loving relationship. With that foundation in place, your teen will accept, eventually submit to, and one day even own your biblical guidelines.

> *Every rule in your home must rest upon the soft bed of a loving relationship.*

Please don't fall for the lie that your rules will harm your teenager. That's just not true. Rules show your teenager's heart that you really care. They may resist your rules on the outside, but they know they need them on the inside. The two worst things you could do as a parent—have no rules and have no relationships. You must have both, in balance.

While I'm not dealing with the specifics of what rules you should have, hopefully through the course of this book, you will find biblical principles to help you in forming your own guidelines for your own home. The key is, they must be biblical; they must be reasonable; they must be explained clearly; and they must be enforced consistently within loving relationships.

Realize that part of the testing your teenager puts you through is about verifying your beliefs! A teenager will push you in an effort to verify your sincerity and resolve—your true love and your true commitment to Christ. A teenager needs to know you love enough to fight the fight, to persist in battle. If you give in, it makes two huge statements about you. You don't believe what you claim to believe. You don't care enough to exhibit tough love.

Consider the tough love of our Heavenly Father. He gives us His Word, which is replete with guidelines for living—rules, if you will. Shamefully, in modern day Christendom and in most pulpits, we do our best to minimize those rules—the laws of God—as though they are grievous! We cower to a world that accuses our God of being legalistic. How sad that we are so afraid to express and teach the tough love of

God. His rules and commands are for our blessing! How do we know this? Because His same Holy Word also teaches us of His boundless, measureless, limitless love! The same God who said, "Thou shalt not commit adultery," (Exodus 20:14) also says that no power in time or eternity can ever "separate us from the love of God" (Romans 8:38–39)! Yes, God's love and God's law are one and the same—and perfectly balanced towards us. They work together to provide us with the love, the blessings, the protection that we need to survive this physical existence at war with a world we cannot see.

> *The same God who loves you warmly will also fight for you passionately! His fiery love drove Him to the cross.*

Sadly, many Christians want only the soft-love and never the law. They want only the "warm and fuzzies" and never the "thou shalt nots." Friend, in a world where there is an enemy bent on devouring you, you cannot separate the two. The same God who loves you warmly will also fight for you passionately! His fiery love drove Him to the cross. His passionate, protecting love warns us of sin. His jealous love pursues and chastens us when we wander. And His avenging love will one day redeem us into eternity and banish evil to Hell forever! Yes, God's love is both tough and gentle.

Ouch!

Within the first three years of each of my children's lives we had a "stitches" incident. In all three cases it was their heads that were "cracked," and in all three cases—since my wife faints at the sight of needles, gashes, and blood—I was the one elected to take them to the emergency room. By the third time, at least I knew what to expect, but the first time I was clueless! Do you know what they do with a small child so they can stitch his head? I didn't. It's no pleasant thing, that's for sure.

First, they lay the child down flat on a sheet. They fold the sheet over both arms (from underneath) and then back under the body so that both arms are forcibly strapped down. They tightly wrap the legs the same way—all while the child is wide awake—now screaming bloody murder. You feel as though the entire world is coming to an end. There are few things less bearable to a parent than hearing his child in this much torment! But that's not all. We're just beginning. Then they take a papoose or cocoon type of wrap and Velcro wrap the entire body of the child. Now, lying on a table, you have a completely restrained two-year-old—screaming in absolute terror and panic. It's almost enough to make a parent say, "Thanks but no thanks, we'll just leave the gash the way it is…."

From there, the doctor proceeds to numb, stitch, and staple—all while the child is screaming uncontrollably. As a father, I would have rather had my head removed than to see my children have to endure this. In all three cases, what I chose to do was to physically place myself (not all my weight, but my presence) on top of the bodies of my children, with my face directly in front of theirs. In that position, they felt more of the pressure of my body and less of the pressure of the restraints. Also, they saw my face more than anything else. Several times I was so close that the doctor asked me to move back slightly so he could see what he was doing.

Every time, I tried to actively engage my sons and daughter in loving, joyful conversation. I have to confess, my throbbing headache (from the screaming) was a part of my concern, but only a small part. My primary concern was settling their nerves, calming their fears, drawing their attention away from the pain or problem and to their loving father. I wanted them to know my presence, hear my voice, be calmed by my caress on their cheek.

Guess what? It worked. Every time, within just a few moments of being physically and emotionally that close—the torment subsided, the bonds seemed to disappear, and the process became bearable (for all of us). It was an amazing lesson.

No matter the bonds that held my child, no matter the needles and staples that punctured them—just my presence, my face, my voice, my touch saw them through! The stitches were a necessary process to healing. It was my responsibility to provide the medical attention that led to a Velcro wrap and stitches, but it was also my responsibility to provide the comfort, the love, and the strength to endure the process.

In the same way, sometimes rules and restrictions are like that Velcro wrap—uncomfortable and binding, but necessary. Your loving relationship and your presence in their lives offsets the pressure of the rules and the guidelines. As a parent you must provide the rules necessary to guide your family, but you must also provide your presence, your love, and your strength. You must strive for the balance between the rules and the relationship! May the weight of your presence and the closeness of your heart cause the pressure and discomfort of the rules to sort of blend into the background of your family life.

"The LORD *hath appeared of old unto me, saying,*
Yea, I have loved thee with an everlasting love:
therefore with lovingkindness have I drawn thee…"
—JEREMIAH 31:3

Eighteen

Inconsistency Breeds Rebellion

Consistency is huge for a teenager. A mom and dad who are constantly flip-flopping, unsure of what they believe, insecure with each other, unable to ever fully commit to Christ can wreak havoc on a growing heart and mind! Parents who love the pastor today and hate him tomorrow; parents who are faithful to church today and unfaithful tomorrow; parents who enforce a rule today and let it slide tomorrow—all of these send mixed messages. Inconsistency creates a short circuit in the spiritual development of a young person.

In more than a few cases that I'm aware of, Dad and Mom, while appearing to be faithful committed Christians at church, have become incredibly critical and harsh towards the church and the pastor when away from church. This kind of negativity and critical spirit can become addictive to the point that in every setting outside of church, these parents pick, bite, jab, and devour every possible perception of inconsistency in their church or pastor. It's amazing that we fall for this behavior pattern as supposedly mature adults. Given that pastors are human and churches are made up of humans—there is never a lack of things to become critical of! And there never will be—"Till we all come in the unity of the faith, and of the knowledge of the Son of God, unto a perfect man, unto the measure of the stature of the fulness of Christ:" (Ephesians 4:13).

In spite of this, these parents descend into the mire of this harsh criticism, literally biting and devouring good people who love them deeply. The addiction becomes habitual, so that every Sunday after church and in every possible setting these criticisms fly along with sarcasm and slight. All the while, little ears and little hearts are off in the corner quietly listening and contemplating these criticisms—confused by this inconsistency and duplicity of life. Heart perceptions are being solidified in young lives, and conclusions are being drawn. "Church is stupid, pastors are hurtful, my parents are unhappy—why should I ever want to be this kind of Christian, in this kind of church, with this kind of pastor?"

The product of this kind of inconsistency and hypocrisy, which often takes ten years or more to see, is rather unpleasant. In nearly every case, these kids end up leading godless lives of immorality, deception, and device. It's sad, but it's quite predictable and even avoidable.

As a side note, consider this: God blesses you in spite of your flaws and inconsistencies as a Christian. He loves you and blesses you when you've had your quiet time and when you've missed it—when you've prayed and when you haven't. His love is unconditional and isn't performance-based. In the same way, He blesses every good pastor and every Bible-believing church in spite of our flaws and humanity. May God give you the grace and maturity to extend the same to your pastor and church family—if only for the sake of your consistent example in the life of your children. Your teenager doesn't need a heart filled with criticisms toward the man and the place that prepares and presents the Word of God in his life! Don't you see the subtle trick? Satan will use your criticisms to destroy the very formational years of faith in your child.

"Well," you might say, "what if the criticisms are true?"

> *Inconsistency creates a short circuit in the spiritual development of a young person.*

A few thoughts: first, again, I present the problem of our humanity. Someone could pull your teen into a corner and criticize you, truthfully, just as easily. How would that help your relationship?

Second, it's up to you to evaluate the legitimacy and weight of such criticisms in light of the Scriptures. Are these minor preference issues that are being blown out of proportion by imagination? If you are in a good, Bible-believing church, this is probably the case. You would be wise not to allow Satan to throw gasoline on those tiny critical sparks. He wants to.

Third, if the criticisms are truly legitimate violations of scriptural principles (in which case you should personally talk openly and honestly with your pastor about them, face to face and heart to heart) then you may conclude that God would lead you to a more Bible-centered church where the bar of integrity in leadership is raised higher. Or better yet, perhaps God would use you as "iron sharpening iron" to bring about change with a godly spirit of humility and kindness. Perhaps He could use your Christ-like approach and honesty to actually mature and

Willful rebellion, quiet sarcasm, subtle criticisms, vain imaginations—he doesn't really care what it takes. He just wants you out of the hedge, and your children with you!

grow those in leadership in your church. Yes, this can actually happen when Christians exhibit the honest and loving spirit of Christ towards each other.

In any of the above cases, prolonged criticism and inconsistency before your child is simply not an option. To state it simply, criticism of this kind breeds horrific rebellion. Resolve the issues, whether by repentance, compassionate confrontation, or quietly finding another church and pastor—whichever is the more scriptural approach in your situation. Whatever the case, don't stay in a willful position of criticism and sarcasm—lest you reveal your own immaturity and addiction to the negativity. There are far better things to do with your time and with the formational years of your child's faith!

Are you seeing, parent, how we as adults can fall for this same hook, rebellion? If the Word of God, the church, and the loving, shepherding leadership of your pastor represent the hedge in your life, it only makes sense that the devil wants to break down that hedge. Willful rebellion, quiet sarcasm, subtle criticisms, vain imaginations—he doesn't really care what it takes. He just wants you out of the hedge, and your children with you! Don't bite that hook!

James says it this way in James 1:6–8, "But let him ask in faith, nothing wavering. For he that wavereth is like a wave of the sea driven with the wind and tossed. For let not that man think that he shall receive any thing of the Lord. A double minded man is unstable in all his ways." The surest way to build an unstable home is double-mindedness. The cure is a pure heart before God. James 4:8 says, "Draw nigh to God, and he will draw nigh to you. Cleanse your hands, ye sinners; and purify your hearts, ye double minded."

In many ways, we all struggle with consistency, and until we reach Heaven, we will never perfect it. I believe the key is purity of heart. There are issues of consistency in our daily lives that are less than willful. Paul said in Romans 7 that the power of sin in him was influencing some of the inconsistency in his life. Yet there are other areas where inconsistency is a deliberate act of the will, out of a double heart—an impure heart. This kind of blatant inconsistency or willful double-mindedness is not only a lack of submission to God, it is one of the quickest ways to spiritually confuse and frustrate a young person.

The effect of this inconsistency will not only be rebellion, but total aversion. Inconsistency of this kind will breed in your young person a total aversion to God, the Christian faith, the church, and the pastor.

So parent, please resist rebellion, but do it at a level that's far deeper than most parents ever really venture. First, check your own life with God. Are you submissive to Him? Second, engage. Place yourself in the hedge, and choose to fight the spiritual battle for your teen. Third, select biblical rules that will guide your home and establish them on the strong foundation of loving relationships. Then, be consistent. Don't doubt or second-guess your spiritual course. Don't willfully be double-minded or arrogantly critical and sarcastic of the spiritual things you pretend to value. With these principles in place, you will find, in time, that the rebellion in your teenager will give way to better days!

*"And Elijah came unto all the people, and said,
How long halt ye between two opinions? if the
Lord be God, follow him: but if Baal, then follow him. And the
people answered him not a word."*

—1 Kings 18:21

Nineteen

Divided Authority Breeds Rebellion

When the vice-president of my college called my name, I knew it couldn't be good news. It was my first semester in foreign territory, and this was the man who handled all the campus discipline. When he wanted to see you it generally wasn't to take you for tea! I was walking down the corridor by his office; he didn't know me, and I didn't want to know him. Yet, just as I passed, he stepped out of his office and asked his secretary to "find Cary Schmidt as soon as possible."

Now, I have to be honest with you. At this moment, the Holy Spirit said, "He doesn't know you, just keep walking…that's right, walk on…." I'm kidding. Those were my thoughts but they didn't come from the Holy Spirit, that's for sure. I probably should have kept walking. But, in all of my grand stupidity, I stopped, turned around and said, "Did you say Cary Schmidt?"

"Yes, is that you?" Again at this point, the voices in my head impressed me to deny ever even knowing a Cary Schmidt, but my mouth spoke before I could stop it.

"Yes, sir…" though I wasn't sure I wanted to be me at that moment. Even though my conscience was clear, I had a feeling I had broken some terrible rule without even knowing it. My heart began to beat in my throat, my breath became shallow, and I was sure my end was near.

After having to wait for an excruciating twenty minutes or so, I was finally invited into the vice-president's office—a place I had hoped to never see, and this was only my first semester! Not a good start. As I sat down, he placed a shoebox on the desk in front of me—one that I recognized because my mother had sent it to me as a care package.

"When is the last time you saw this box, Mr. Schmidt?"

My mind raced with confused panic. Are shoeboxes against the rule? Oh, my, I had no idea! The last time I had seen that box was during white glove inspection when I had thrown it in the trash and I told him so.

"What was in it when you threw it away?"

Again my mind raced, "Uh, a paper towel, a Styrofoam plate, a Styrofoam cup…some other trash…I don't get it, sir, what's the problem here?"

Well, long story short, somebody from another floor of our dormitory was dipping snuff (against the rules at Bible college) and chose to throw his snuff canister away in my shoebox on my dorm floor so he wouldn't be caught. Later that evening, someone was plundering through the trash and found the snuff in my shoebox and turned me in for it. Talk about unfair. Talk about not understanding the "rest of the story." I had never in my life even touched a can of snuff, much less used it!

Obviously, in that appointment with the vice-president I assured him that this was "not my snuff," regardless of the fact that this was my box, with my name on it. He wasn't sure what to believe, understandably so. Let's face it, this man was earning his living listening to students lie to him. Towards the end of the conversation he asked, "Would you be willing to take a polygraph test to verify that this isn't your snuff?"

I didn't know whether to laugh or cry. Here I was an eighteen-year-old kid, two thousand miles from home in a Bible college to prepare for the ministry and within my first few weeks I'm being asked to take a polygraph test. At first I thought he might be joking, but the seriousness of his face told me otherwise. At that moment, in all of my innocence I said, "Sure, I guess so...."

You're not going to believe the rest of this story, but it's the honest truth. Within a few days of that appointment, I was actually sent to a local polygraph office with my roommate. As I arrived, I was taken to a small, fully carpeted room with one-way mirrored windows on every wall. In the center of the room was something that looked like the electric chair, and there next to it, what I guessed to be the polygraph machine.

As the examiner entered the room, I was asked to remove my shirt, whereupon little electrodes were then attached to my upper body. Once I was strapped in and hooked up, the machine was turned on and I was officially being tested by a real, honest-to-goodness lie detector machine. I mean this was no laughing matter. These are the things that killers, murderers, terrorists, and rapists are attached to—generally not Bible college students.

To make matters worse, after the hook-up was complete, the examiner left the machine running and left me alone in that room for about thirty minutes—just to contemplate the horrific crimes I had done and the terrible fate that was about to be handed. Those one-way windows really bothered me too. I felt I was constantly being watched. I mean this was one of the creepiest experiences I have ever had in my life!

I honestly sat there incredulous! This was like a freakish nightmare directly from the mind of a Looney-Toons artist! I kept wondering, "Is this really happening to me? Am I really here right now? Oh...if only Mom and Dad could see me now...they'd surely be proud!"

The interview proceeded with a barrage of questions. Was it my snuff? Did I taste the snuff? Did I know about the snuff? Did I know whose snuff it was? Was there more snuff? How long had the snuff been in the room? Did I ever use snuff? Seemingly dozens of questions, and all the while I'm thinking, "What if that machine says I'm lying, when I'm really telling the truth!?" My whole future ministry and the fate of my calling seemed to rest in the abstract flitting back and forth of the needle-like fingers of this machine!

Well, needless to say, I passed the test, and so did my roommate. In spite of my serial-murderous past, I managed to slip by the snuff test.

Authority Standing Together

The thing that stands out about this incident is the incredible balance my parents had in this exchange with authority. If there was ever a time in my life when false accusation put me through an unfair ordeal with the help of God-ordained authorities, this was it! If there was ever a time that my parents could have become righteously indignant and angry with other authorities, this was it. I could have exercised my own right to be righteously indignant. After all, I truly hadn't done anything that could justify a polygraph test.

Looking back on that incident, do you know what it was? It was the enemy's attempt to get me out of Bible college. He would have had me become bitter, angry, and resentful at being treated unfairly or unreasonably. He would have loved for me to quit right then and there, and all it would have taken was upset parents. My parents had every right to send me a one-way plane ticket home and we could have justified the decision… "Well, if that's the treatment I'm going to get, I'll find another Bible college!"

Never in my entire Bible college experience was I more vulnerable to quitting and walking away than I was in that moment. Yet, something kept me in balance. Something kept me from getting caught up with fury. Something "stayed together" in my heart that kept me standing on the solid ground of God's will for my life. In the perfect will of God, I was at the right Bible college and I knew it. So, somehow this incident was foreordained of God as a testing or proving experience, and there was one key factor that kept me focused on that truth.

My parents never sided against authority. They always supported and backed those appointed by God to stand in my gap. I remember calling home and telling them of the pending polygraph test. Do you know what they did? They actually laughed. Why…of all the nerve! Here I was being labeled among America's most wanted, and they found it humorous! How dare they!

Honestly, they shrugged it off. No big deal. Do it. Take the stupid test. Life goes on. In a moment when they had every reason to rise up in disgust, cry out against the establishment, and side with me, their loving, innocent son, they laughed it off. They helped me keep perspective. When they could have enraged me against good influences, they calmed me and helped me stay in balance. They explained that in a large Bible college, maybe this is necessary. They encouraged me to go with it and not to get ticked off.

Read very carefully here. A moment ago I mentioned "something stayed together" in my heart that kept me in God's will. Do you know what it was? My hedge.

Divided Authority Defeats Itself

Matthew 12:25, "...Every kingdom divided against itself is brought to desolation; and every city or house divided against itself shall not stand."

As a youth pastor, one of the most uncomfortable things I have to do, as an authority figure, is confront a teenager about a problem. It comes with the territory—I think it's in the job description somewhere, but it's never fun. It ranks right up there with a root canal or having an ingrown toe nail removed. It's not the sort of thing that you wake up in the morning and "can't wait to get to"! For me, I put it off as long as I can—or at least that's what I'm tempted to do.

For the next moments, I want to bear my heart to you on a subject that few people ever stop and think about. As you read, please understand, I was once a teenager (as were you), I am now a parent, and I am now a youth pastor and teacher. In some form or fashion, I've been in every position that I'm about to address. I'm going to try to approach this issue from a big picture perspective of everyone involved. I beg your hearing on this, for the sake of your teenager.

Do you remember the illustration of the hedge of protection around your child's life? Do you remember God's call to stand in the gap and to make up the hedge? Can you imagine a hedge divided against itself? What kind of safety would the inhabitants of a city have if the protective wall around the city tore itself down or punctured holes in itself? Obviously, none. And this is a subtle tactic of the devil that is becoming more and more prominent.

Let me be direct here. A wall of authority that is divided against itself cannot protect the inhabitants, and in fact, leaves gaping holes where the enemy can proceed undetected to destroy a young life. I do not know of a teenager who grew up with authority divided against itself who turned out to love and live for God. Conflicting authorities—divided protectors—create a mixed message and confusion in the heart. To avoid this confusion and to avoid sending a conflicting spiritual message, godly authorities in a teenager's life must stand together!

The enemy will do everything within his power to divide parents against the other authorities in your teen's life. He will even use your teenager's complaints to do it.

A wall of authority that is divided against itself cannot protect the inhabitants…

At some point, and perhaps many points on your parenting journey, your teen will come home from school with a demerit or a detention slip, vehemently denying that it was deserved. Or perhaps your son or daughter was sent out of class for talking, but insists that this was unfair. On some occasion they will take offense at something said or at some misunderstanding with authority. They may be simply protecting themselves and trying to throw up a smoke screen in your face. Or, they may be correct—they may have been legitimately treated unfairly. In this moment, the rightness or wrongness of the action taken by the authority is a secondary issue. I'm not saying it's unimportant. I'm just saying it's not most important in this moment.

The first and foremost issue is that you maintain a supportive heart, recognizing that this other authority stands in a very important gap for your teenager. If you immediately side with your teen and jump on the authority-bashing bandwagon—picture this—as you stand in the hedge for your teen, you have turned towards another place in that hedge and started launching missiles at it. You have just removed and perhaps destroyed all respect that your teen has for this part of his hedge, and now that space stands vacant. You have effectively endangered your teen by turning against yourself! Scary thought.

You see, parent, you are authority. And when you attack authority, right or wrong is inconsequential. You are attacking a position of authority from a position of authority. This is like an army turning against itself in battle. The enemy wins with little effort. As you destroy the position of another in the heart of your teen, you destroy your own position as well. For your position is grounded upon the same foundation—God's principle of authority—as the position you attack. When you destroy the foundation under one authority, you destroy the foundation under all authority.

In an emotional moment of conflict, the enemy will try to immediately incense you against other authorities for treating your child so unfairly. You must stand guard and determine to support until the entire story is completely understood.

As a side note, this goes both ways. Teenagers often try to incense their youth pastor or teacher against their parents in much the same way. This is the enemy's tactic to divide authority and to break down the hedge. If he can't get you to leave the hedge, he will at least try to make a crack, to bring a division between authorities.

Be on the Same Team with Other Authorities

The first and most important thing to do, in the presence of your teenager, is to support authority. It's vital that you not jump to any extreme conclusion based on the emotional plea of your teen. This is true for all authorities. Teachers and pastors must support parents, and parents must support teachers and pastors. It is vital! In any particular disciplinary case, there are always two sides of the story, your teenager's and the other authority figure's. In

> *When you destroy the foundation under one authority, you destroy the foundation under all authority.*

many cases both have their own paradigm and both have valid points. In time, you can sort out the details, but it is vital that authority remain a united hedge in the life of your teen.

To do this, you must be a team with those in authority in your child's life. You must know them, understand them, share common values with them, and trust them. This is huge. You cannot support someone who you do not agree with, and therefore you must choose these teachers, pastors, etc. with great care and discernment. In a great sense, you, parent, are responsible for who makes up the rest of the hedge for your teen. You make these selections! You choose the church, the school, the youth group, and the outside involvements. These choices fall on your shoulders.

As a side note, please know, I recognize that authorities are imperfect! In my time as a youth pastor, I have jumped to unfair conclusions, handed out discipline, and even made wrong assumptions plenty of times. This was never, ever intentional, but as a human it's unavoidable! Though I can honestly say my motives in disciplining teens are always pure, my judgment is sometimes flawed. Sometimes there is more to the story that I didn't know. Sometimes there were others involved that I wasn't aware of. Sometimes I implicated the wrong person. I am not saying you should turn a blind eye to the potential wrongs of those in authority. Exactly the opposite.

As a parent and a youth pastor, I realize the mutual accountability that I must have. I am accountable to every parent for every discipline situation that arises. I must be approachable—willing to talk, to reason, to hear the rest of the story, and even to apologize and ask forgiveness when I'm wrong (more often than I care to admit). Yet, to be effective as a youth pastor, I must also have support from parents as I lovingly yet firmly confront issues in the heart of their teen.

One of the most damaging things any adult can do is tear down any part of the hedge in the life of a young person. Pastors and teachers must stand with parents, and vice-versa. It's a law of the universe!

Ecclesiastes 4:9-12 says, "Two are better than one; because they have a good reward for their labour. For if they fall, the one will lift up his fellow: but woe to him that is alone when he falleth; for he hath not another to help him up. Again, if two lie together, then they have heat: but how can one be warm alone? And if one prevail against him, two shall withstand him; and a threefold cord is not quickly broken."

When I Blew It—One of Many Times!

Several days ago, I sent some teens out of class for being disruptive. After class I was able to talk to two of them, but the third was already gone. I hate to do things like that. It's the least enjoyable part of my life. Yet, it is sometimes necessary.

In the follow up of the event, I personally phoned the parents, just to make sure we stood together. I wasn't sure whether I would find angry parents upset with me, or supportive parents backing me. In every case, the phone calls, which could have been discouraging, were very encouraging! In every case, those parents stood with me and appreciated the loving but strong confrontation in which I engaged. We all recognized we were on the same team fighting the same enemy on behalf of the teens!

In one of the cases, I found through follow-up conversation with the teen, that I had indeed been somewhat unfair. At the first hint of a closed spirit, which the parent made me aware of, I rushed to this teen, dropping everything in my day to make things right. We drove to a local fast food place and grabbed a bite to eat as he told me the rest of the story. Had I known then what he was telling me, I wouldn't have sent him out of class and I felt terrible for the misunderstanding.

In short, we had a great time together. I apologized and he did too (for the times he deserved to be sent out but wasn't) and we ended the time together closer for the conflict. Most importantly, this young man's heart for God was still intact! Even though I was wrong and had unfairly embarrassed him, his heart for God was still soft. Why? Because his hedge stood together! His parents believed I wanted what was best for him and they gave me the benefit of the doubt! Thank you, parents! And I believed the same about them.

Together we reached into this young man's heart and tried to engage in resistance against the enemy. Even where authority was wrong and parents could have been justifiably ticked off, the united hedge gave stability and protection during a vulnerable time.

The Bible is clear that this kind of division is dangerous. In I Corinthians 1:10 God gives us this admonition, "Now I beseech you, brethren, by the name of our Lord Jesus Christ, that ye all speak the same thing, and that there be no divisions among you; but that ye be perfectly joined together in the same mind and in the same judgment." Again, in 1 Corinthians 3:3, "For ye are yet carnal: for whereas there is among you envying, and strife, and divisions, are ye not carnal, and walk as men?"

Parents, recognize that divided authority breeds rebellion. It destroys the hedge. Right, wrong, or indifferent—authorities must give each other the mutual benefit of the doubt in front of the teen and work things out in private (with right attitudes) when necessary. Don't break down the hedge. Don't stand divided against those who would come alongside of you and fight the spiritual battle for your family, with you! Lock arms, join forces, communicate often, and cooperate diligently. After all, as parents, we can use all the spiritual help, all the reinforcements that the military can possibly send in!

"And Jesus knew their thoughts, and said
unto them, Every kingdom divided against
itself is brought to desolation;
and every city or house divided against
itself shall not stand:"
—MATTHEW 12:25

Twenty

A Sushi Bar of
Our Own Making

Recently, I spoke with a man who has been in family ministry for several decades. I couldn't resist in the course of our conversation asking for a bit of counsel. In answer to a parenting question, he said this, "Cary, everywhere I go, I ask parents what is their number one goal for their children. They usually answer, 'I just want them to be happy.'" He proceeded to say, "That's the stupidest answer anyone could ever give. Happiness is no parenting goal. A child can giggle his way straight to Hell. Now joy, on the other hand, is a much higher goal, because true joy comes from knowing Christ and doing His will."

Most parents' greatest fear is their own children's unhappiness. We cannot bear to see them disappointed, let down, or unhappy. We cannot deal with their sorrow. And all too often, we allow our fear of their unhappiness to keep us from truly helping them discover lifelong joy. Friend, when it comes to rules, rebellion, and relationships—make joy your goal and don't fear a necessary moment of unhappiness that will lead to lifelong joy. The last time I checked, the dentist office wasn't a very happy experience—but having healthy teeth surely is a blessing!

A while back, Pixar released the film "Finding Nemo." While I certainly can't endorse or condone the philosophies or messages of every family-oriented movie, I have to admit, we look forward to an occasional family feature at our house! When "Nemo" came out on DVD, we planned a big family night around the release. It was much anticipated, probably by Dad as much as anyone else.

As the story line unfolded we laughed, we anticipated, we cried—the whole emotional spectrum was covered in a matter of 90 minutes or so. As the story goes, little Nemo defies his father's orders, gets captured by divers, and ends up in a fish tank in an Australian orthodontic office. From this point, the movie turns to Nemo's dad, who lays everything on the line and embarks on a legendary journey of mythical proportions to rescue his son. He braves deep waters, befriends hungry sharks, defies death more than a few times, and takes unparalleled risks for the love of Nemo. As you might imagine, the journey ends as the two are wonderfully reunited and every sea-going creature lives happily ever after.

On this kind of family night it's almost as much fun for me to watch my kids watching the film as it is to watch the film itself! In tense moments, they are stressed. In sad moments, they are hopeful. In happy moments, they are laughing. Their body language and physical responses are hilarious!

As the film came to its grand conclusion, everyone breathed a collective sigh of relief that Nemo was once again safe in the care and nurture of his loving father. Whew…(Although I'm sure he will disobey again so there can be "Nemo II.")

It was in this moment, closing credits still rolling across the screen, that reality hit me! It was like all of my collective consciousness finally put it all together. Nemo was a little rebel! Nemo was a disobedient little brat, a self-centered ingrate. This whole emotional journey that I had just been on could have been avoided if that little mischievous sea urchin had submitted to his God-given authority! I just spent 90 minutes watching all chaos break loose in the Pacific Ocean; a series of near-death experiences nearly destroy a life; and the gut-wrenching journey of a father's search and rescue attempts—all the fallout of this little monster's devilish disobedience. I felt betrayed. I was outraged!

What a waste of time. What a mockery of my intelligence. I know, I was getting a little carried away.

But then, I saw it…teaching moment!

I looked over at three-year-old Haylee, who was still trying to comprehend the experience. We were, and still are, trying to help Haylee understand the importance of obedience to Mom and Dad. "Obey" is a word that we are working on all day at our house. So, I put on my fatherly teaching voice and seized the moment.

"Haylee, do you know why Nemo got lost from his daddy and almost never saw him again? Do you know why Nemo's daddy almost got killed by all those mean fish? Do you know why this movie lasted so long and why Nemo had so many problems?"

Her face was blank. No clue! I'm sure she was wondering where I was going. So did my boys.

"Because he disobeyed! His dad told him not to swim beyond the reef and he disobeyed his dad. If Nemo had obeyed, he would never have been lost; his father would have never been in all that trouble; and this movie would have only lasted about 10 minutes!"

Her quick response, "Yeah…he needs a spankin'…"

We all got a good laugh out of that one.

I can hear you now. "Hey, Nemo rebelled, and lived to tell about it. He won! He fought authority and lived the adventure. That's what I'm going to do."

Wrong. You're forgetting a few things. Your life is not an entertainment venue. Rebellion never leads to a happy ending. You are not a Pixar character.

And one final thought…in reality, Nemo could have just as easily ended up as dessert in a Japanese sushi bar…

New movie title? "Tasting Nemo."

> "He made a pit, and digged it, and is fallen
> into the ditch which he made."
> —PSALM 7:15

Part Four

Hook #3
Pollute and Plunder

Overcoming Heart Corruption

The enemy's lie to a teenager...

"It's just entertainment…"

"Everyone else is watching, listening, doing…it can't be that bad! I don't see how it can be so harmful!"

"My pastor and parents just don't understand the entertainment and music of my generation! It's not all that bad, they are just extreme and out of date in these issues…"

The enemy's lie to a parent...

"It's just entertainment…"

"I have no influence over what kind of music or entertainment my kids enjoy! Besides, I've always had my own favorite style of music too! And, everybody knows…God likes all styles of music!"

"TV is funny, movies are fun, and music is entertaining—that's all it is…nothing more. There's no spiritual conspiracy here…just a few good laughs, some romantic adventures, and a nice rhythm to carry me through the day!"

"I don't like that kind of music, but as long as they keep the headphones on and keep it turned down, I guess it can't hurt too much! At least they aren't out 'carousing'!"

Twenty-One

A Little Infection Infects the Whole Body

Vacation around our house is a much-anticipated event. About two days after we get home from one, we start anticipating the next one! It's not that we don't love our lives and love what we do. We just love being together, making the memories, and sharing the long days. We never get enough of each other.

This past year, we were able to spend a few days outside of the Pensacola area on a very unpopulated beach, alone as a family. It was solitude at its finest, and when your life is busy, solitude is a WONDERFUL thing! The weather was perfect. The water was emerald blue and green. The sand was sugary white, and the kids were primed and ready for some adventure. This trip was their first extended stay anywhere near a beach and it was incredible fun just to relive my childhood through their eyes as they discovered seashell hunting, bodysurfing, sand-castle building, snorkeling, sand-crab catching, and jellyfish evading—all for the first time! It was a treasure.

Every morning we awakened and embarked on the sunscreen mission—slicking down every exposed body part of every family member. It's quite a job! Boy, I really hate when I miss that one spot on my foot! It never fails! I always end up with a "quarter-size" sunburn somewhere on the top of my foot!

Every evening we took long walks on the beach, collecting seashells, holding hands, watching the sunset, and gathering memories. It was a vacation I will never forget!

Sometime during the second day of our stay, something began to happen inside me—physically. I didn't catch on as soon as my wife did, but by the end of the day, my head hurt; my chest was congested; my sinuses were swollen; and my entire body ached. In short, I was miserable! Why is it that the woman of the house always knows who is getting sick, before they actually get sick? My wife can tell every time!

When women get sick, the world goes on—especially the fun. But when men get sick—all fun ceases!

Now, when women get sick—the world goes on, especially the fun. But when men get sick—all fun ceases! In fact, fun no longer exists! This rule is true with our family as well. Throughout the course of that day I gradually went from being a pretty nice guy to being one of the grumpiest human beings you've ever met. I was short-tempered, punchy, irritable—well to put it plainly— downright carnal. By the day's end, nobody was having any fun. I made sure of it. All I wanted to do was go to bed, and my wife was only too happy to send me there!

In all honesty, I have an incredible wife. I married way over my head. She is unbelievably patient with me. If I had gotten what I deserved, she would have killed me a long time ago. This was one of those times when I really deserved to be put out of my misery (and everybody else's).

The kids were disappointed that I went to bed early, but I think they were hopeful that tomorrow would be different. No such luck. I woke up only worse. Though I felt clammy and though I was still crabby, we persisted into the day, determined to have fun whether we liked it or not! My wife offered medicine; I declined. What's with men and declining medicine!? Are we mentally handicapped in this area? Are we afraid of being weak and having to wimp out and actually swallow a pill? I guess I was. What kind of a wimp did she think I was? Then, she did the unthinkable—way worse than medicine! She actually suggested that I go to the doctor. Now, it's one thing to suggest this on a regular day (though that's bad enough!) but this was a vacation day! Who in their right mind would go to the doctor for vacation! No! I didn't care how bad I felt, the doctor's office was no place to spend a vacation day! So, I refused. Twelve more hours of grumpiness, just ahead.

By the end of the third day, I was ready to die and the rest of my family was ready to help me! I was miserable, and looking back, I'm ashamed that I let physical illness so affect my disposition towards my family. It was one of those days when absolutely everything was irritating! Ever had one of *those* days?

Day four came only too quickly, and as we awoke my wife calmly but firmly asserted that today "we were going to the doctor." She smiled one of those smiles that seemed to say, "I'm nice right now, but this smile can quickly belong to the strongest, meanest person you have ever seen, so don't even think about saying anything but 'yes dear'!" I've seen that smile a few times in my life. Yes, I've had a few of these near-death experiences. I knew I had two options—either give in and say, "Ok, we'll go…" OR have my entire family full-body tackle me, gag and hogtie me, and forcibly take me to the doctor. They were ready to do so! Whatever it took, we were going to the doctor.

So, in all of my grumpy gratitude I conceded defeat. A few phone calls and a thirty-minute drive later, I was sitting in an emergency room in Fort Walton Beach, Florida, little name bracelet and all. And my family supported me by going shopping while I waited! As I sat alone in the waiting room, I was trying to remember my wife's words—what I was supposed to say to the doctor… "I have a sinus infection that is affecting my entire body and life, and I need (what was that medicine she kept telling me to ask for?)…Zith—something…Zithromax!" Yes, that was it.

Well, you know the routine. After a long wait and another long wait, the doctor finally came in. Sure enough, he diagnosed a severe sinus infection and began to prescribe an antibiotic.

Now at this point, I should tell you there's something terribly wrong with my telling the doctor what my wife told me to tell him. Somehow all of my masculinity—my manhood—my individuality was at stake in that exact moment! It was an emotional and intellectual crisis of gargantuan proportions! Do I say something and risk looking childish, foolish, hen-pecked to this doctor? Or, do I keep silent, maintain my masculinity, but risk being killed by my wife when I return to the car? I nearly kept silent, but in the last moment I gave in. I couldn't bear the thought of what I should say when she asked me, "Did you tell him...?"

Sort of sheepishly, like I was speaking a foreign language to a national for the first time, I interrupted his prescription, "Uh...sir... my...uh...my wife wanted me to tell you...uh...well...she thought you should prescribe zithro-something." Somehow not saying the whole word preserved what little manhood and self-dignity I had left at this point. Playing the macho zithro-something card somehow made it easier to bear.

The doctor laughed, more at me than with me, I think. "I knew it," I thought, "I should have just kept my stupid mouth shut!"

After his laugh he responded, "Oh, she did, did she?" as if he was thinking "Perhaps I should have talked with her from the beginning!" But rather than insult me, he just laughed again and said, "Well, you tell her thank you so much for the assistance; that is exactly what I will do."

I have since been told that "Zithromax" or a "Z-pack" is like the atomic bomb of antibiotics! Z-pack. That would have been much more manly. "Doc, give me a Z-pack! I'll take the atomic bomb!" Yeah, I could've handled that! You can't even say "Z-pack" without sounding manly! Now, anytime I go to the doctor, that's what I say. "Doc, can you give me a Z-pack for this?" Usually they say something like, "No, that would be like using an atomic bomb to kill a mosquito." Now, what could be more manly than trying to atomically blow up a mosquito!? Yeah, I like this Z-pack thing!

Well, I walked out a few moments later, name-bracelet still on—but somehow my masculinity had been retained, because there in my little medicine bag was my "Z-pack"—my atomic bomb! Little did I know at the time, that this Z-pack is unlike any other antibiotic because it works very fast and with only a few pills. No days and days of taking pills...just a few pills, taken in succession in less than 24 hours—KABOOM! You're all better, and every germ or molecule in your entire body that was even thinking about making you sick is wiped out instantaneously. Cool!

Well, needless to say, I took the medication. And to the delight of my entire family, it worked fabulously! Literally, within five hours I was a different person. I was my laughing, light-hearted, fun loving—albeit stubborn—self again. The atomic bomb worked, and our fun vacation returned.

Recognizing the Internal Problem

This illustration has two applications. The second we'll come to in a later chapter, but the first begins right here.

I'm stupid. No, really, I am. Let's consider for a moment that I felt crummy for nearly three days. All the while my family telling me to take corrective action, yet I refused. I chose rather to suffer affliction in my own misery than to seek medical treatment to restore my health.

The sickness inside of me literally and completely transformed my personality—my attitude and spirit—from joyful, jovial, and enjoyable to irritable, cranky, frustrated, and miserable. And stupid me didn't see it at all! I really thought it was just everybody else—the world around me—being irritating! I never would have concluded for even a second that it was in me—that the problem was within me. No, no. It was the kids—they were too loud, too talkative, too rowdy. It was my wife—she was too happy, too questioning, too annoyingly concerned! And, when everyone in the family was being quiet and still—they were breathing annoyingly too loud!

I ask you, what was the source of my problem—external or internal? I couldn't blame my family or my surroundings. This was supposed to be vacation—fun, light-hearted, relaxing! My problems were internal, and yet not me. It was the sickness in me, altering me, bringing about a behavioral and emotional change.

I'm not making excuses for my wrong attitudes, but rather explaining that a foreign substance—an infection—had invaded my otherwise healthy body, inflicted internal harm, and that harm was affecting my external behavior and relationships more drastically than I was willing to admit! The internal cause was fueling external problems, and no external treatment could bring about a change. Taking a shower, changing my clothes, or getting a different family couldn't cure my sickness! This was an internal corruption that required an internal treatment to root it out, kill it, and destroy its influence on my life.

The Bible refers to this internal "sin infection" in Romans 7:17–23, "Now then it is no more I that do it, but sin that dwelleth in me. For I know that in me (that is, in my flesh,) dwelleth no good thing: for to will is present with me; but how to perform that which is good I find not. For the good that I would I do not: but the evil which I would not, that I do. Now if I do that I would not, it is no more I that do it, but sin that dwelleth in me. I find then a law, that, when I would do good, evil is present with me. For I delight in the law of God after the inward man: But I see another law in my members, warring against the law of my mind, and bringing me into captivity to the law of sin which is in my members."

Applying my illustration, we might say that I delighted after the inward man in a happy vacation, but the power of the infection in me was bringing me into captivity to another behavior. The first step to killing the infection and regaining the joy was *recognizing* that it was not *me*, but the infection *in me*—which my wife so aptly did!

In the coming chapters, we will expose a process of corruption that is very much the same, on a spiritual level. Your enemy will attempt to corrupt you on the inside so he can change you on the outside! He will plant an internal spiritual infection that will wreak havoc on your life and family. You honestly won't know what hit you or where it's coming from, but it will devastate your life.

I warn you, the following pages are not for the blind-hearted. Take a moment before you continue and ask God to "enlighten the eyes of your understanding" right now…

"Unto the pure all things are pure: but unto them
that are defiled and unbelieving is nothing pure; but
even their mind and conscience is defiled."
—TITUS 1:15

"A little leaven leaveneth the whole lump."
—GALATIANS 5:9

Twenty-Two

Spirits—Speaking and Being Heard

This third hook that teens and their parents are swallowing is huge! Hook #1—family fragmentation, hook #2—rebellion against authority, and hook #3—corruption of the heart—all work together to form a tightly woven trap to destroy our homes. This hook of internal corruption defiles the heart, addicts the inner man, and then literally rewrites the attitudes of the heart and resulting actions.

This internal corruption comes at us in a multitude of ways and in millions of varieties, but the net effect is the same—it redefines who I am on the inside, which in turn redefines how I look and how I behave on the outside. This lie is incredibly subtle because it is spiritual in nature, seemingly harmless upon "ingestion" and silent at its work. It transforms effortlessly, redefines who I am with seemingly no external warning. It takes time too! This isn't an overnight thing. No, it often takes months and years for the full effect to be in place. With this corruption, the devil is exceedingly patient! He is content to work slowly, gradually, and methodically.

On my vacation, an internal infection caused my entire personality and behavior to change. In the process, I was miserable, and so was the rest of my family. In the same way, your enemy would love to sneak an infection into your spiritual heart. He has tricky ways of doing this without you realizing it. As the infection settles in, it changes how you think, how you feel, and what you desire. This literally happens without you realizing it. He has ways to numb you in the process. His tools and devices deaden the spiritual senses and then reprogram the heart with new attitudes. The enemy's corruption lodges deep in the heart where it can root and grow without detection. For a period of time, on the surface, Satan's tricks seem harmless and even enjoyable; yet over time they corrupt and reprogram the heart.

Before identifying what this hook is, I want you to understand what it does and how. We'll unveil it specifically later in the chapter, so stay with me. This hook of corruption is so powerful that I truly believe it is "public enemy #1" for teenagers—especially Christian teenagers. It seems harmless on the surface; yet it is as destructive spiritually as any other force I know of. This hook has a redefining influence to the spiritual heart—very similar to how drugs or alcohol redefine reality in the human brain! What drugs and alcohol do to the mind and body physically, this corruption does to the heart, spiritually. This is what makes it so much more dangerous than physical substances. At least when a person is drunk or under the control of some mind-altering substance, you can see the physical signs and take proper action. This corruption hides beneath the surface and leaves you wondering what's wrong with this person. The effects are seen, but usually not easily tied to the hidden cause.

> *This corruption hides beneath the surface and leaves you wondering what's wrong with this person?*

When a person comes under these seemingly harmless spiritual influences, there are no immediate physical signs. That's why we reason them as harmless. Yet they are absolutely destructive in an invisible way! The corruption happens within—the vision is skewed; the heart is drunken; and it all happens under the surface. All the while, on the surface the warning signs are rarely taken seriously enough. It's as though a deadly cancer is eating away inside, while we diagnose a common cold or cough on the outside.

Exposing the Spirits of this World

To understand where we are headed, you must first come back to the reality of the spiritual life—the inner man—and the spiritual battle for that part of your life! Everything that we will uncover in this section will have to do with the alteration and annihilation of a healthy inner man. In other words, you must believe that the spiritual world is more real than the world you see.

The Bible says it this way in 2 Corinthians 4:18, "While we look not at the things which are seen, but at the things which are not seen: for the things which are seen are temporal; but the things which are not seen are eternal." Again in Hebrews, God says, "Through faith we understand that the worlds were framed by the word of God, so that things which are seen were not made of things which do appear" (Hebrews 11:3).

Second, you must realize that your spiritual enemy uses devices of the physical world to carry his messages into your spiritual being. He uses physical gateways and physical tools to penetrate a spiritual message into your spiritual heart.

Look at 1 John 4:1–6, "Beloved, believe not every spirit, but try the spirits whether they are of God: because many false prophets are gone out into the world. Hereby know ye the Spirit of God: Every spirit that confesseth that Jesus Christ is come in the flesh is of God: And every spirit that confesseth not that Jesus Christ is come in the flesh is not of God: and this is that spirit of antichrist, whereof ye have heard that it should come; and even now already is it in the world. Ye are of God, little children, and have overcome them: because greater is he that is in you, than he that is in the world. They are of the world: therefore speak they of the world, and the world heareth them. We are of God: he that knoweth God heareth us; he that is not of God heareth not us. Hereby know we the spirit of truth, and the spirit of error."

I want to call your attention to several truths here. First, there are two kinds of spirits that speak in our world today—the Spirit of God and those spirits not of God. Again, this verifies the spiritual battle, the lies and deceptions that we are going to be hounded with so long as we live on this planet.

Second, John repeatedly reminds us that we are "of God." He is emphatically stating that there are some spirits that we should have nothing to do with, because we are of another Spirit! In fact, God has gone to great lengths to help us overcome these spirits! Remember we're not talking about "Casper, the Friendly Ghost" here. We're talking about bait, hooks, battle, deception, lies, and spiritual butchery! These ungodly spirits intend to lead you astray, lie to you, and destroy you. Third, he assures us that God is greater than these spirits. In actuality, they are not something to fear, just something to be aware of and to avoid.

The most important application I want to draw from this passage is in verses five and six where it says, "They are of the world: therefore speak they of the world, and the world heareth them. We are of God: he that knoweth God heareth us; he that is not of God heareth not us. Hereby know we the spirit of truth, and the spirit of error." Think about this. These spirits of the world actually speak and the world hears them! These spiritual entities, enemies of the cross, actually have voices that can be heard in the physical realm—voices that are pleasant enough to be listened to. Obviously, the destructive power of these voices is masked by something much more attractive—bait that the world wants. Yet, they speak—clearly and physically. And the world hears them! Think about that. The world listens to, absorbs, physically understands and accepts these voices.

> There are two kinds of spirits that speak in our world today—the Spirit of God and those spirits not of God.

In the next verse, John says that we who are of God have given our ears to a different source—the Word of God, the truth of God, and those who speak His truth. Amazing! John so clearly tells us that in the world, we will be surrounded by the voices of ungodly spirits speaking and being heard by the world. Then he reminds us that we are "of God" and should give our ears to a different voice!

Finally, you must recognize the significance of this heart level corruption of which we speak. God says in Proverbs 4:23, "Keep thy heart with all diligence; for out of it are the issues of life." Again in

Proverbs 23:19, He says, "Hear thou, my son, and be wise, and guide thine heart in the way."

Your heart is the source, the wellspring of your life. If the devil can corrupt your heart, it's only a matter of time before he will destroy your entire life! It's only a matter of time before he will reinvent you without you even knowing it! In fact, he would rather destroy you slowly from within than quickly from

> *We are "of God" and should give our ears to a different voice!*

without. He is after spiritual destruction! He wants to build a stronghold in your heart and then he will fight you through that stronghold as long as he can, undetected by you.

It's amazing! This is his master tactic at "sneaking up on us" from within. You don't see him, hear him, feel him, or sense him. You just think you're taking in some harmless voices—but at the core, you're opening your spirit to the destroyer.

We're often completely blind to the process. In fact, even after years of youth ministry, I often find myself blind to this hook as I'm trying to help families! Sometimes, after hours of counseling and exploring life issues, it seems that the Lord finally lifts the veil and gives the enlightenment that Paul spoke of. Finally, the true issue comes to the surface so clearly and plainly, and nearly every time, this hook is somewhere near the root! In recent years, this very hook is often where I go first in counseling—and it's always right there, hidden from view, but tightly lodged in the inner man.

Your heart is literally your mind, your will, and your emotions; in other words, your "thinker," your "chooser," and your "feeler." It's who you really are in your innermost being! Through these voices, the enemy can literally influence, alter, and control your mind (thoughts), your will (desires), and your emotions (feelings). Consider this for a moment. I know many teenagers (some of whom we will hear from later) who have literally been driven to thoughts of destruction, desires towards suicide, and emotions of despair through the very voices that we will look at! All of this resides in the heart—a place where parents and pastors cannot see their existence. That's a pretty powerful hook!

As we delve into these principles, recognize that parents and teens are both susceptible to these voices on a daily basis and the corruption process works equally well on both! In fact, the corruption is most effective when it's happening in both at the same time—which aids in fragmenting the family even more. Let's take a close look at this process of corruption.

> *"Be not deceived: evil communications*
> *corrupt good manners."*
> —1 CORINTHIANS 15:33

Twenty-Three

Understanding the Process of Corruption

I had a beautiful tree in my back yard. Large trees are rare commodities in the high desert. When we were looking for a house, that was my one requirement—a tree. I don't care if we have running water, bedrooms, or toilets—I just want a nice big tree in the back yard. Well, fortunately we found a house with running water, toilets, bedrooms, and a tree! It was large, sprawling, even growing out over the surrounding yards. It had to be one of the largest trees in our neighborhood! It was wonderful! It provided privacy, shade, and unfortunately several years food supply for a pack of tree-eating beetles.

For several years, our news here in Southern California was reporting on a devastating beetle infestation. These beetles were literally eating and destroying trees all over Southern California, but, honestly, I never paid the reports much attention. After all, my tree looked fine. It was growing so fast that I had to have it trimmed nearly every year. It was healthy, budding, and sprawling. It was an awesome tree!

Well, recently, I called the tree trimmers out to cut my fast-growing monstrosity back because it was growing into the neighboring houses and yards. I feared the neighbors might start to get bothered by it. It was a sunny, summer afternoon as I arrived home from the church to find the tree-trimmer inspecting my tree in the backyard. The man was a very nice tree-trimmer who knew a lot more about trees than I did, but spoke somewhat broken English.

As soon as I saw him, I could tell there was a problem, but couldn't fully understand by his description what it was. After several moments of explaining that my tree was "muerte," he did something that I will never forget. He walked over to that tree, picked a spot on its trunk and poked his index finger straight through it! I'm talking this guy drove his finger four inches directly into the meaty trunk of my tree! This didn't make sense. Was this guy bionic or something? Who can do that to a solid tree?

> *The enemy always wants to enter our spiritual heart under the cover of something else!*

Then, he pulled his finger out, and with it, a large clump of dead trunk, right out of the core of that tree. Then he said the word "beetles" and I knew I was toast. My tree was a goner. In broken English, he proceeded to tell me that if I didn't remove the tree, it would fall down on its own within six months! This huge, beautifully budding and growing tree was literally going to fall down from rot! Though it looked fabulous on the outside, just below the surface it had been completely eaten by an unseen beetle army. A hidden enemy lurked just below the bark silently eating, corrupting, killing.

Your enemy is no different. He will try to do the same thing to your life that those beetles did to my tree. How does our enemy try to corrupt us? What is the process? It goes something like this five-step plan...

Step One—Attraction

The enemy always wants to enter your spiritual heart under the cover of something else! Remember we're dealing with bait—so it's always going to be something we like—something we enjoy—something that is very attractive to you. This attraction happens in a multitude of ways, but it's always a combination of appearance and desires. It would be impossible to fully describe every kind of bait in the world today, but remember, bait always appears fun, enjoyable, entertaining, funny. It appears harmless. It is attractive, cool, awesome, and exciting! This first glance usually catches us off guard, and draws you in for a closer look.

Hopefully, by now, you're discovering in this book that things are not always "as they appear" in the undersea world of the fish! Hopefully you're realizing you cannot trust what you see, especially not everything that attracts you. Just realize that the enemy will always disguise his voices with attractive physical devices.

Step Two—Adaptation

Especially to the Christian, this adaptation process is critical. You see, at first exposure, this corruption goes against the spiritual heart of the Christian. At first "listen," your spiritual heart will cry against it in shocked outrage, much like the lungs of a twelve-year-old would reject the first puffs of smoke from a cigarette. The violent convulsions of the respiratory system seem to say, "Get this out of me! I'm not made for this kind of pollution!"

In much the same way, at first the Holy Spirit of God within you will reject, resist, and warn you internally about this foreign substance entering your heart! Yet, God's Spirit is easily grieved. Ephesians 4:30, "And grieve not the holy Spirit of God...." His warnings are easily quenched. In 1 Thessalonians 5:19 God says, "Quench not the Spirit." This adaptation phase is when you resist God's warnings, and eventually His warnings are quenched and you become more comfortable with this new presence invading your spiritual heart! In fact, over a short time, the adaptation process is complete, and you feel quite at home with your newfound influences.

The Bible refers to this process in 1 Timothy 4:1–2, "Now the Spirit speaketh expressly, that in the latter times some shall depart from the faith, giving heed to seducing spirits, and doctrines of devils; Speaking lies in hypocrisy; having their conscience seared with a hot iron...." You see, these spirits seduce and sear the conscience. The searing process can be uncomfortable at first, but eventually the conscience stops feeling what it should!

Step Three—Addiction

Once you adapt to the new influence, you soon find yourself needing more and more! It's not addiction, you tell yourself, it's enjoyment. You want more, yet you fail to see this desire as an addiction. Yet, these influences that we speak of are truly addicting. They lodge themselves like hooks into the flesh of your spiritual heart. They snag and hang on—increasing their influence and strangle-hold on your inner man. It's all about increasing control. The more exposure you have, the more addicted you become, the more powerful this influence becomes in shaping or re-shaping you.

Like claws digging into your heart and mind, and tentacles wrapping around your spiritual throat, these influences wrap themselves intricately into the deepest part of your heart. Unknowingly, quite subtly, you find yourself increasingly needing, wanting, and depending on more of this influence. This addiction literally begins to take control. Every chance you get, you run to these influences and drink of their spiritual fluids. Amazingly, in our world, it has become increasingly more convenient to take these influences everywhere we go and to have them in a moment's notice, very much like a pack of cigarettes, a tiny liquor bottle, or even a pouch of narcotics. Yet this addiction is not a physical addiction! Far worse, it is a spiritual addiction of the heart.

Step Four—Alteration

This is where the real transformation begins to take place. Just as the goal of the Christian life is "to be conformed to the image of his Son..." (Romans 8:29), even so Satan wants to conform us to another image! He wants us to be conformed to the image of antichrist or the image of this world. Romans 12:2 says, "And be not conformed to this world: but be ye transformed by the renewing of your mind...." While God wants to transform our lives and renew our minds to conform us to the image of the Lord Jesus Christ, even so Satan wants to speak with his spirits through worldly voices to conform us to the image of the world!

And so it goes, alteration from within. The spiritual condition changes and the heart (your thoughts, emotions, desires) is transformed by this influence. Where there should be love, joy, peace, longsuffering, gentleness, goodness, faith, meekness, and temperance as fruits of the Holy Spirit, there is now bitterness, anger, immorality, and the seed of every evil work. This is the godless fruit of other spirits—spirits that are not of God, speaking things to the heart that are not from God, with voices that the world can clearly hear and understand.

Quite literally, a person who undergoes this process becomes a different person! The heart is reprogrammed! The spirit is radically reinvented from within. Joy gives way to anger. Love gives way to unfounded resentment and hatred. Peace gives way to trouble and frustration. Purity gives way to defilement and baseness. And when looking for some physical reason, some apparent explanation for the change, you won't find one! Unless you know about these spiritual influences and the vehicles they are using, it will all be a mystery to you.

You might sit in a room, stare this person in the face, and both of you attempt to find a cause, a reason, a physical source for the drastic change. You will both come up empty. "I don't know." This will be the only answer you get back when you ask "Why do you hate? Why are you angry? Why are you so troubled? Why are you so frustrated?" "I don't know. I really don't know." There will be no apparent reason, and to the best of his ability, this person will be telling the truth! That's what is so seductive and amazing about it all! It happens without our even realizing it.

Look deeper. Look below the surface. Ask a different question. "What is getting into your heart that is producing this condition? What devices are influencing you with the voices of spirits not of God to produce this heart alteration?" This is where you will find your answers. You see, the human heart—even the Christian heart—is capable of both good and evil—good, when under the control and influence of the Holy Spirit of God—evil, when under the influence of spirits of this world.

Is there ever a time when the human heart is neutral? I don't believe so. It is always under the influence of the spiritual realm—whether we realize it or not, whether we sense it or not. You cannot escape the spiritual realm and simply exist in a neutral spirituality. You are always either moving in the direction of good or in the direction of evil. This is not to say that evil is always some drastic or dastardly form of wickedness (though that might be the final destination). Evil can simply be a subtle direction away from God and away from His truth in your life.

Eventually, this alteration will find its way to the surface and with teenagers, it almost always shows up first in the countenance. The countenance is far more than a facial expression. In the Bible, the countenance is the spirit, the intent, and the condition of the heart coming through in your facial appearance. It's an amazing part of our being.

I remember as a teenager being told that an adult could look at a teenager's face and usually discern the condition of the heart. Well, that made me worry about my face! And if you saw my face, you'd know why! It wasn't that I had some secret in my heart. I was afraid of having the wrong countenance and not showing God's joy from within. So, I actually remember in tenth and eleventh grade, trying to physically concentrate on having a pleasant facial expression to protect my testimony.

I look back on that now and laugh, because your countenance stays on your face, regardless of the expression you wear! You can't erase it consciously because your heart places it there.

Look at what the Bible says in Proverbs 15:13, "A merry heart maketh a cheerful countenance: but by sorrow of the heart the spirit is broken." Again in Proverbs 27:17, "Iron sharpeneth iron; so a man sharpeneth the countenance of his friend."

Evil can simply be a subtle direction away from God and away from His truth in your life.

The influences of your heart produce a countenance that communicates your spiritual direction, and nothing you can do—short of yielding to God to transform your heart—will change the countenance. A healthy countenance—an innocent, pure, spiritual appearance—is the direct product of a healthy relationship with God! Here's how the Bible says it: "Why art thou cast down, O my soul? and why art thou disquieted within me? hope in God: for I shall yet praise him, who is the health of my countenance, and my God" (Psalm 43:5).

Over the years I have seen literally dozens and dozens of teenagers become trapped and altered by the influences I'm referring to in this chapter (which you're probably wondering about by now) and in every case, there was a dramatic change of countenance. For the parent, this countenance shift is the warning sign, the emergency broadcast network of the heart. Yet, somehow, we buy the lie that teenagers are just this way—it's normal.

Can I SHOUT something for a moment? It is never spiritually normal for any Christian to exist for great lengths of time with a downcast, moping, miserable heart and countenance! I don't care what age, maturity, or phase—it's not normal to be despairing and disconnected from a healthy heart. And the first step to correcting it is to stop accepting it as normal!

> *Your countenance stays on your face, regardless of the expression you wear! You can't erase it consciously because your heart places it there.*

We parents sure do buy the "it's just a phase" lie a lot! We can reason away any spiritual problem, any anomaly, any behavioral issue as a phase. Strangely, I cannot find this principle in Scripture. I cannot find a verse where God condones ungodly behavior as a normal phase. Perhaps predictable is a better word. It's never normal for a teen's countenance to fall or for a teen to consistently be estranged from his parents; yet these things are often predictable. Don't accept as normal what God would want you to act upon—to engage in. Rebellion, fragmentation, corruption—though these things are common, they are never normal!

What if on my vacation, my wife had just accepted my sinus infection as normal. "He'll grow out of it!" Perhaps I would have over time, but in the meantime, we surely would have missed some precious moments of our vacation. They would have been lost to my health struggle. Even so, why would you allow months and perhaps years of your brief family life together to be robbed by something that should be corrected and resolved? This is what happens when you relegate needed spiritual growth and transformation into a phase that is "probably normal."

Refuse to relegate the warning signs to the normal category. No, they are spiritual stoplights in the journey of your relationship! Stop the car, wait it out, resolve the issue, engage the heart, and then proceed forward. This is a good litmus test. When the devil tempts you to think, "It's just a phase"—you're probably staring a warning sign right in the face. The enemy wants non-action. God wants spiritual engagement.

Confusion is another warning sign of this inner alteration. For the teenager, not only do they not understand what is happening, they don't understand how either. Every time I've sat across a desk from a teenager in the grips of these voices—these influences—they can't seem to come up with a reason for their anger, their bitterness, their despair. It's just there! They can't say where it comes from or how it got there. A girl hates her parents, but just stares blankly when asked why. Finally, in confusion she just answers, "I don't know…" A young man is angry at God, but has no idea why. Time after time, I have looked into the frustrated countenance of some teenager and simply asked, "Are you confused?" The eyes reveal the response before the mouth speaks. "I'm more confused right now than I have ever been in my life."

Hmmm…1 Corinthians 14:33 says, "For God is not the author of confusion, but of peace…." Psalm 71:1 says, "In thee, O LORD, do I put my trust: let me never be put to confusion." Isaiah 26:3, "Thou wilt keep him in perfect peace, whose mind is stayed on thee…" I wonder whose voices we are listening to as the source of this confusion.

Teenager, are you confused right now? Parent, are you confused right now? Is there confusion in your relationship? One thing you can be sure, this confusion is not from God, which leaves only one other set of voices. Perhaps there are some spirits speaking and being heard in your heart that are not of God. Jeremiah 3:25, "We lie down in our shame, and our confusion covereth us: for we have sinned against the LORD our God, we and our fathers, from our youth even unto this day, and have not obeyed the voice of the LORD our God." This verse details the process—confusion covers us as a result of the sin of disobedience to God.

Step Five—Annihilation

This final step in the five-step corruption process is ultimate destruction. Again, we're talking spiritual destruction, not necessarily physical. This is not something you physically feel, but you do experience it spiritually—in your thoughts, emotions, and will. Once the enemy gains a stronghold through these spirit voices, once he reprograms the heart and reinvents your inner man, anything is possible. Usually this annihilation is the total destruction of any spiritual purpose and significance you should have in life, along with the total eradication of key relationships with family, godly mentors, spiritual friends, etc.

So just exactly how does this annihilation happen? First of all, it's all in the heart. I know at first that sounds less dangerous, but just the opposite is the case. By destroying your spiritual heart (the issues of life), literally anything could happen. Perhaps the enemy chooses emotions of depression and loneliness that drive you to utter despair, and ultimately suicide. Perhaps the enemy chooses strong desires of the will that drive you to vice, immorality, or bad decisions. Perhaps the enemy chooses destructive thoughts that translate into destructive actions. Perhaps it's less flagrant in your case and more of a distancing in your relationship with God that will lead you down the wrong road. In the end he wants to destroy you—to nullify your spiritual life.

Just look at our culture. Look at the destructive patterns that people all around you are engaged in, from the shooters at Columbine High School, to the Satan worshipping groups in every public high school, to the guy at work who just left his family for another woman, to the twenty-something college crowds who can't seem to get enough alcohol, illicit sex, and partying. We live in a culture where the destruction of the spiritual heart has become common—even among Christians! In fact, sometimes the person with a healthy countenance and a truly joyful heart seems to be abnormal! Someone who avoids these influences and who stops listening to the "spirits that speak to the world" appears to be extreme, holier than thou, pious, fanatical, or even cultic! At least that's what we tell ourselves to soothe the conscience. Perhaps they are just being uncorrupted (Daniel 1:8).

We live in a world of walking dead people, and among Christians, walking wounded. Psalm 91:7 refers to this, "A thousand shall fall at thy side, and ten thousand at thy right hand; but it shall not come nigh thee." So many hearts are influenced by the voices that we're referring to, that we've become accustomed to and tolerant of our wounds. We've accepted them as normal. In some cases, we do this ignorantly. In many cases we do it willfully, because, after all, we like these voices! They are indeed attractive.

We appear to be tall, strong, deeply rooted trees. On the surface of our lives everything looks healthy and productive. Yet underneath lurks a dangerous corruption process that threatens to eventually topple us.

My back yard is so bare now. I hate to even go out there. We replaced the tree with a new one, but it's going to take twenty years for it to be anything close to what the last one was. No shade, no privacy, no beauty—just a seedling tree that more closely resembles a long tent pole than a tree. And where the tree used to be, now there's just a big rotten hole. The beetles won.

Friend, that doesn't have to be your story.

*"Now the Spirit speaketh expressly, that in the latter times
some shall depart from the faith, giving heed to
seducing spirits, and doctrines of devils;"*
—1 Timothy 4:1

*"Pure religion and undefiled before God and the Father is this
... to keep himself unspotted from the world."*
—1 James 1:27

Twenty-Four

Unmasking the World's Voices

So, by now you're probably wondering what exactly these voices are. Perhaps you've figured it out. Honestly, you could answer the question in your own conscience before God. "God, what are the spirit voices of the world? How is the devil communicating to our world today?"

Rock music? Yes. Country music? Yes. Pop, R&B, Jazz, Hip Hop, Alternative? Yes, yes, yes. Rap? Yes. Top forty? Yes. New age? Yes. Christian Rock? Yes, even there. Christian pop? Yes. Christian alternative? Yes. What about TV, movies, talk radio, video games, newsstands, and the internet? Yes, to all of the above!

Now before you have a coronary or start defending your personal favorite music or entertainment form, and throw this book in the trash, I beg you to hear me out on this. More importantly, I dare you to let God pull back the cultural blinders that are on so many Christian eyes in today's world, and let His Holy Spirit guide you into all truth. If your heart is already resisting what I'm saying here, stop for a moment and ask yourself whose voice is speaking to your heart?

There are many voices that the devil is using today. The pages of this book do not allow me to discuss all of them, so I want to focus on what I believe to be the loudest voice. A careful study of culture will prove that music is the leading device that spirits not of God are using to communicate to the hearts of human beings today. I'm not saying that all music is evil. I'm saying it is a tool of communication that, for the most part has been distorted by the enemy to damage the heart. It has been twisted and shaped in a multitude of ways that negatively impact the human heart. I'm not even saying that all forms of secular music are wrong. I am saying that all music has spiritual significance—it is all either moral or immoral. It is never neutral. I realize I'm in the Christian minority to say this. I believe it can easily be proven that music in itself (especially without words) is spiritual in its very nature, and therefore has either good or evil effects upon the spiritual life. No, musical styles are not amoral (neither good nor bad). They cannot be.

Popular Christian thought states, "God likes all kinds of music. He made it all. It's all good." The problem with this ignorant, though well-intentioned, statement is that it completely removes the human influence from the equation. Yes, God made music. But then He placed it into the hands of men. In the most basic sense, a single note or musical tone might be considered amoral, before it reaches the creative process of a human touch. Yet, once it enters the hands of a man (a spiritual being) and that man shapes it into a musical message (even without words) that message most certainly takes on moral or immoral implications!

You cannot listen to music and merely be entertained. You are being molded.

Saying music is amoral would be like saying color is amoral. True, you can't point to red or blue or green or yellow as being intrinsically good or bad. Yet when placed into the creative hands of a man or woman—when painted onto a canvas, woven into a fabric, or placed into a magazine layout—those colors become a message, a photo, a work of art that can be either evil or good. Saying all styles of music are acceptable to God would be like saying all kinds of photographs, all kinds of paintings, all kinds of clothing, and all kinds of beverages are okay with Him too. This is a lie that Christendom has swallowed hook, line, and sinker!

What the Secular World Knows About Music

Yet, the secular world at large, understands quite clearly the power of music (alone, with no words) to shape emotion, thoughts, and desires! In other words, to shape the heart! Music affects behavior radically, because at its very core it is a spiritual form of communication, a language of the heart, that, when heard, translates into thoughts, desires, emotions, and choices. Do you get it? When you listen to music, your heart is affected. It's a law of the universe like breathing oxygen or being held down by gravity—music transforms the heart. You cannot escape it. You cannot listen to music and merely be entertained. You are being molded.

Now, the enemy wants you to believe that music and other forms of media are merely entertainment. Once you cross that bridge, anything goes, and anything goes for God too! In other words, we reason that we can take any musical style and make it Christian. Yet, not even Hollywood falls for this deception. You could never convince John Williams, famous Hollywood composer, that any style of music could be scary, or any style could be victorious, or any style could be seductive. In interviews that I have watched with Williams, the man ingeniously knows exactly what instruments, what chords, what rhythms to use if he wants to make you feel scared, creepy, happy, sad, or triumphant! In fact, music is very much the emotional interpretation of what you are experiencing in life at any given moment. When watching a movie, the composer of the score has literally implanted emotional responses, dictating to your heart how to feel. It all happens quite subconsciously, especially when you are wrapped up in the story line. Music communicates with your heart, telling you how to feel and how to respond to what you're experiencing.

> *When you listen to music, your heart is affected. It's a law of the universe.*

Why do we understand this in the context of a movie, but somehow we divorce the idea from our minds in regards to our car radio, our home stereo, our walkman, or our MP3 player? Why do we reason that the music of the world is acceptable so long as it has Christian lyrics, if indeed we understand that music alone communicates so loudly with the heart? If music always creates a heart response, then music is always either evil or good. Every musical style, every variation sends a different message to your heart.

Since this is not a book specifically about music, we won't spend much time on the philosophy of biblical music, but I would urge you to at least recognize the power of music and the influence that it has upon your heart. It is huge! The lyrics, of course, matter, but they are secondary to the style in their impact on your heart. The style creates the primary emotional heart response. Consider I Samuel 16, when David played his harp before Saul. The evil spirit that was troubling Saul fled away. What a powerful example of the spirits of this world responding to godly music! That's the kind of music I want! In fact, give me a truckload of it! Can you understand, this music actually caused the forces of the enemy to flee? Conversely, there must be a kind of music that makes him feel at home as well!

There are other voices speaking in the world today. Volumes could be written about them. There are a million ways that Satan is trying to get his message into your heart—movies, magazines, books, video games, TV—the list could be enormous! Each voice is a vehicle of communication with the heart, and if you stop and consider the big picture, you'll see that we live in a media-crazed culture. TV, entertainment, music is always on—always speaking—always being heard by the world. You cannot go to the mall without seeing music videos. You cannot go grocery shopping without the covers of magazines shouting the messages of the world. No matter where you turn, the voices never stop and are seemingly everywhere.

For instance, a recent study funded by the National Institute of Child Health and Human Development reported that teenagers who watched sexual content on television were twice as likely to be sexually active as those who didn't. The amazing fact of the study was that the TV shows that only talked about sex were just as influential as those that depicted it visually! Entire books could be written to verify that television and movies are huge contributors to the corruption of young lives.

The Power of Music is Everywhere!

Music is the "500-pound gorilla" of all the world's voices simply because it is so pervasive. Consider this, you can sit down and play a video game for thirty minutes—and the whole time be afflicted by spiritually harmful music, without even realizing it! You can watch a wonderful story line in a family film, yet hear rock music in the background during most of the story! Now that's subtle—that's pervasive! Parent and teen, beware of how the enemy tries to fill your heart with corruption while he attempts to get you to look the other way!

Also, music is now portable! For the first time in the history of mankind, our generation (roughly the last 80 years or so) has increasingly been able to take music with us—on a plane, in the car, in our pocket, and everywhere we go! Recent digital advances with music players enable a teenager to plug in some headphones, turn on a small device, and disconnect from any environment anywhere—or better yet, interpret that environment from within the confines of what the voices are saying. In other words, a walk in the country or down main street used to be just that, a walk, where your senses experienced and engaged in the world around you. Not any more, so long as we have headphones and a music player! Now a walk in the country can be a spiritual reprogramming event, and the world begins to be interpreted differently through those headphones.

There is a good side to the advances of our modern world. Now you can take good, biblically-sound music everywhere you go too! Now, no matter how mundane the surrounding, you can be communing with God in song and allowing godly music to transform your heart for good. It all depends on what spirits you're listening too—those not of God or the Spirit of God.

Let me be clear. Wordly music is certainly not the sole instigator of spiritual problems, but it is a huge agitator of them! Wordly music is to a pliable teen heart what a gallon of gasoline is to a small spark. Where the water of God's grace should have quenched a problem and healed the heart, wordly music explodes it into a raging inferno of destruction.

This is true with adults too, with the exception being that teens are so much more impressionable—like jello before it sets or concrete before it hardens. A ninth-grade heart is more quickly addicted to these influences, and the destruction is more thorough.

I'm singling out music among other corrupting voices, not because others aren't dangerous, but because, as a youth pastor, I have yet to deal with a struggling teenager where music isn't a major part of the picture. It's always there. Parent, it's always there! I've spoken with dozens of kids whose parents have unplugged the cable, emptied the house of other "voices," and still the teenager is secretly struggling with music. Let me say it again. It's always there!

Teenager and parent, here is my question to you as we press on in this study. Do you value the spiritual condition of your heart more than you value the entertainment of the world's voices?

"And be not drunk with wine, wherein is excess;
but be filled with the Spirit; Speaking to yourselves in
psalms and hymns and spiritual songs, singing and making
melody in your heart to the Lord;"
—Ephesians 5:18–19

"He that cometh from above is above all:
he that is of the earth is earthly, and speaketh
of the earth: he that cometh from heaven is above all."
—John 3:31

Twenty-Five

Whose Voice
Should I Listen To?

By now, you're probably wondering, "Okay, what styles are harmful and what styles are helpful?" The answer to that question is probably simpler than you realize.

A Heart of Submission to God

First, we must submit to God's Word in this area. Though God's Word is relatively silent on musical styles—especially those that exist today—we must rely on biblical principles to guide us.

Musical styles are like clothing styles—they are constantly changing from culture to culture. Music is a creative medium, always being discovered and rediscovered—designed and redesigned. Therefore, for God to try to pin down certain styles and detail them in the Scriptures would have been impractical for future generations as the devices of men created newer and newer styles. Let's face it, the most popular style of music today really hasn't been around very long! Similarly with clothing, God doesn't address specifics of dress, but rather principles.

God says when you dress, be modest, be distinct between a man and woman (e.g., 1 Timothy 2:9, "In like manner also, that women adorn themselves in modest apparel…")

Don't let the fact that God doesn't address styles in the Scriptures become a reason to abuse your Christian liberty. God gives principles that apply to our music very clearly. So what are they? Here are just a few.

1. Our music should reflect a new song after salvation. Psalm 40:3 says, "And he hath put a new song in my mouth, even praise unto our God: many shall see it, and fear, and shall trust in the LORD." A new song would be one that is different from those you sang before you met Christ.

When you came to Christ, He made you a new creature. Old things are passed away! You are no longer your own—you belong to God and everything from your life's purpose to the color of your toothbrush should be at God's discretion and for His glory. A Christian is not permitted to have an "I want my MTV" attitude. God clearly says in Scripture that you belong to Him and you should glorify Him in every detail of your life. First Corinthians 6:20 says, "For ye are bought with a price: therefore glorify God in your body, and in your spirit, which are God's." First Corinthians 10:31 says, "Whether therefore ye eat, or drink, or whatsoever ye do, do all to the glory of God."

2. Our music should be different from the world's. Romans 12:2 says, "And be not conformed to this world: but be ye transformed by the renewing of your mind…." This discounts most of the contemporary Christian music movement (CCM) right off the top, if you're honest. Most CCM artists are following, conforming in close step with the world when it comes to musical style and delivery!

The pop-Christian culture in America today is literally feeding off of the world like a nursing calf. Rather than being a "peculiar people" who are different from the world, we appear to actually envy the world— so much so that we are working over-time to make our Christianity just like it. MSNBC recently produced a story on "Christian Night Clubs" in America. The interview was a profoundly disappointing portrait of the current Christian youth culture! These clubs are exactly like the world in every way except a few of the more blatant issues like drugs, alcohol, and sex. The interviewees boldly stated that "we do not talk about God, and most of these teens don't even know this is a 'Christian club'!" One man was quoted as saying, "We're ready to talk about God when they are ready."

On the surface, that sounds noble, but it's rotten at the core. The Bible teaches that "There is none that understandeth, there is none that seeketh after God" (Romans 3:11). Apparently, the Christian nightclubs are willing to let someone spend eternity in Hell just because they were never ready to talk about God. Jesus didn't give His life for a "Christian nightclub." He did give His life for the church, and He commissioned the church to "go and teach"—to "preach the word"—whether or not the world is ready to hear.

This brand of Christianity that walks so closely in step with the world offers no difference except in the most basic moral concepts. To the news media and secularists of our day, Christianity appears to want exactly what the world has! In which case, why should the world want Christianity? Conforming to the world is no way to reach the world.

3. Our music should be songs, hymns, and spiritual songs. Ephesians 5:19, "Speaking to yourselves in psalms and hymns and spiritual songs, singing and making melody in your heart to the Lord." Colossians 3:16, "Let the word of Christ dwell in you richly in all wisdom; teaching and admonishing one another in psalms and hymns and spiritual songs, singing with grace in your hearts to the Lord." Spiritual songs speak to the heart about God, both in words and in styles. Remember, it's not just the words that do the speaking!

Every song without words has three distinct parts: melody, harmony, and rhythm. Most of the world's music speaks to the flesh with rhythms that vulgarize our human existence with sensuality. Putting Christian words to these rhythms doesn't change the spiritually carnal message of the rhythms themselves. These rhythms stir up anger, bitterness, hatred, despair, depression, sensuality, or lust.

The spiritual songs that the Scriptures speak of would never take your heart or your body in such a direction. Yet, most of our popular music today—even that which claims to be Christian—does exactly that.

4. Our music should be joyful. Psalm 98:4, "Make a joyful noise unto the LORD, all the earth: make a loud noise, and rejoice, and sing praise."

We could go on, but I truly believe that God's Holy Spirit will guide you if you will give Him total freedom and entrance into this area of your life. We've already read 1 John 4:6, "We are of God: he that knoweth God heareth us; he that is not of God heareth not us. Hereby know we the spirit of truth, and the spirit of error." If you have a seeking and submitted heart, God's Holy Spirit will guide you into truth and away from error.

Most Christians have a very self-centered "my-way" attitude when it comes to music. Our musical preferences and tastes become deeply entrenched in our lives like favorite pet areas of our heart. We are reluctant to let God get too close to our comfort zone! We would rather just convert our favorite style of music to Christianity than risk having God replace it with a new song.

Eyes that Understand What Music Produces

Second, we must look at the lifestyle that a musical style produces. Probably the greatest indictment against any particular style of secular or Christian music is the lifestyles of those who immerse themselves into the music. For any style of music, look closely at those who live with that music, perform that music, and yes, even worship that music. The lifestyle will always be a product of the music.

You cannot immerse yourself too heavily into a musical style without your life being reinvented and shaped by that style. It's another law of the universe. If you want to know what rap music produces, look at its worshippers. It produces violence, rage, anger, hatred, defilement, sexual perversion, and sexual violence of the worst kinds. It is no coincidence that this music requires warning labels to parents. It is unthinkable that we have even "Christianized" rap music! We might as well have "Christian rape"! There is no way that a musical style that produces such immoral and godless behavior can ever be "Christianized."

Other musical styles produce lust, immorality, loose living, sensuality, and adultery. Some styles produce despair, depression, and self-absorption. Some styles produce altered states of consciousness to assist with new age mysticism. Some styles contribute to Satan worship; some contribute to sensual romance; some contribute to carnal living. Just look at the product, and you will find your answer. Every style produces its own product within its worshippers, regardless of whether there are Christian lyrics or not.

You might argue that it is our flesh that produces these things and not the music. Truly, the flesh is where it begins, but I still contend that the music is a type of fuel that ignites the spark. Rather than transforming the heart into the image of Christ, carnal music enlarges and feeds the problems of the flesh until they are consuming!

Against the grain of culture, there are some styles that do not produce any of the above. Given careful study, you will not find greed, lust, anger, bitterness, or violence being produced by godly styles of music. You will find the fruit of the Spirit that is produced through psalms, hymns, and spiritual songs. You will not find confusion but rather peace! This kind of music may not be your favorite style—but it will not conform you to the world; it will not conform your heart to the world; and it will not warp your spiritual senses.

This kind of music may not taste the same as the world's music, but it will produce a joyful heart, a healthy countenance, and a peaceful life. Your fleshly taste buds will reject it at first, but not everything that tastes bad (at least at first) is bad for you, and not everything that tastes good is good for you—especially when you're dealing with bait! We'll get back to this point. Hang on. First, let's get a close-up glimpse of what wrong music and other similar voices do to our hearts.

"He brought me up also out of an horrible pit,
out of the miry clay, and set my feet upon a rock, and
established my goings. And he hath put a new song in
my mouth, even praise unto our God: many shall see it,
and fear, and shall trust in the LORD."
—PSALM 40:2–3

Twenty-Six

The Five Step Process In 3-D

Remember the process—attraction, adaptation, addiction, alteration, and annihilation. Remember that these voices are more dangerous than physical substances like alcohol and drugs. Have you ever been around somebody that is drunk on alcohol or high on drugs? They are two different people! Also, when your spiritual heart is in the grip, caught in the claw and tentacles of the aforementioned influences, you are a different person. And so I ask you, do you want to go through life being the incredible person God designed you to be, or being the product of some powerful ungodly force? Do you really want to be a puppet, under the control of a spiritually destructive hand? You have only one life! I challenge you to live it to the fullest extent of who God made you to be. Choose to be controlled by His Spirit rather than by the spirits of this world.

Hebrews 12:12–16 reveals the process in scriptural detail. "Wherefore lift up the hands which hang down, and the feeble knees; And make straight paths for your feet, lest that which is lame be turned out of the way; but let it rather be healed. Follow peace with all men, and holiness, without which no man shall see the Lord: Looking diligently lest any man fail of the grace of God; lest any root of bitterness springing up trouble you, and thereby many be defiled; Lest there be any fornicator, or profane person, as Esau, who for one morsel of meat sold his birthright."

Think about that passage. First, there is a wound, "hands which hang down, and the feeble knees." Then there is a turning out of the way—off of God's path. Because of this, there is no healing of the wound and a root of bitterness springs up. From that bitterness comes trouble (confusion, frustration, turmoil) and from trouble comes defilement. Once defiled, this person defiles others and begins to live a profane life of fornication. This is the exact path that these spirit voices want to take you down.

Eventually, what is in the heart finds its way to the surface, which leads to confrontation with somebody who cares— hopefully a godly parent.

I'm amazed at how, even through the course of writing this book, again and again God has led my path to these same issues in the lives of teens. It's almost as though He is reinforcing to me how critical this issue is and how duped we often are! In the past years, I have talked with dozens of young people about this subject, and here is how the appointment usually goes.

First, there is some issue that has arisen—a family fight, trouble at school, a surface revelator of a deeper problem. So, we sit down to talk. Always the countenance is fallen. Sometimes this young person outright admits that he is not happy and doesn't want to be happy. Often there is a defensive wall in place that seems impenetrable. The facial expression is always that of someone "under the influence" of something else. At this point, the Holy Spirit usually reminds me that this is a spiritual battle for the heart. Ironically, during this very writing, this happened twice in two days!

In every case, there is a spark of an issue at the root level—a broken home, a disconnected relationship, an abusive past, an argumentative marriage, a rebellious parent, a non-committal Christian home, or even some major tragedy or loss. The devil attempts to capitalize on that spark by pouring gasoline on it using the voices of the world—music, TV, certain video games, entertainment, and more music. He seeks to draw this young person away from resolution and into a sort of spiritual anesthesia. He implants imaginations through these voices that exalt themselves against God and His truth. This results in a life that withdraws and disconnects from key relationships. It's not long before this teen is out from under the protective hedge of authority and into the path of spiritual danger.

Eventually, what is in the heart finds its way to the surface, which leads to confrontation with somebody who cares—hopefully a godly parent. At this point, a spiritually-minded person will ask two questions —what is the spark issue, and what is fueling the fire and causing it to become a raging inferno? You see, the spirit voices that we've been talking about literally become strongholds in this young person's heart.

Second Corinthians 10:4 says, "For the weapons of our warfare are not carnal, but mighty through God to the pulling down of strong holds." God wants to pull down these strongholds through His power. The word "strongholds" here literally pictures a walled fortress or a castle. Imagine this. If you have been filling your life with these influences, you have literally allowed the enemy to quietly, carefully build a castle in your heart! Perhaps the enemy has set up a fortress within you and you don't even realize it.

Parent, as a side note to this thought of strongholds, please be aware that strongholds are never pulled down without a spiritual fight. These spiritual forces hold on tight, and when you try to interfere, there will be resistance. It may be a war—long, drawn out, even exhausting— but worth fighting. Be aware that as you take on this fortress, you are engaging in spiritual battle. You are not fighting your teen (flesh and blood) but you are fighting "other-world" forces on behalf of your teen.

If you have been filling your life with these influences, you have literally allowed the enemy to quietly, carefully build a castle in your heart!

There is nothing more victorious or wonderful than when the light of day first shines through the darkened fortress of the heart. I've seen this many times. Often it happens after several hours of meeting, talking, digging into the heart with the light of the Word. One young man in particular, who was tightly in the grasp of wrong music, sat stone faced for more than two hours. At first he was literally impenetrable. During the early part of this confrontation I felt as though I were talking with someone else, not really him. It was an exhausting two hours, with seemingly no progress, when suddenly a change in countenance—a window to the real issue briefly opened. The Holy Spirit seemed to jolt my consciousness to high alert status. Something seemed to be saying, "This is the root issue that we've been digging at all along."

Long story short, that young man's heart finally opened, and as we talked, the Lord shed some light on some amazingly dangerous issues. For one, a homosexual predator, posing as a friend, was targeting him and beginning to lead him astray. It would have been only a matter of time before he was pulled into this lifestyle, and he was oblivious to the danger. For another, he was dealing with bitterness towards disconnected parents, which made him run to his new friend as well as his new music for pain killer.

The stronghold had been exposed, and in a matter of another hour or so, this young man was on his knees in tears seeking God's help to pull it down completely.

You see, that's what these influences do. They numb the spiritual senses like Novocain so that spiritual problems can be enlarged to exalt themselves against God. Let's face it—this music is enjoyable (at least to those listening to it), and it does actually help in dealing with the crisis of our lives. It does make you "feel better" temporarily. There is a high that brings relief and escape from the pain of life. What a deceptive relief it is!

Listen to the story of another young man who recently gave me the following letter. This is his "five step process of corruption" in his own words.

One Young Man's Story

...A simple mistake...the truth is that it always begins in an innocent way. Just one song, or something simple, but the problem is, it never stops there!

I was in the ninth grade and I became very interested in poetry and literature, but especially poetry. In fact, I was enamored with it, I loved it. Never did I even think that not all poetry was good. As a result, I set no standard as to what type of poem I would read.

One day a friend gave me a copy of a poem. I was captivated by the lyrics—they were like nothing I had ever read. They were honest and they seemed to have captured exactly what I felt inside. I didn't ever realize that the poem was actually a song, and I would probably have never known if it hadn't been for the web address on the bottom of the page. I went to the website, having no idea or conviction about rock music. Oh, I knew it was wrong, but I didn't know why. I had just been told it was wrong and believed it. Because the song I had been given even named God, I assumed there was nothing wrong with the lyrics. That web site was something like a drug store, and I was a foolish kid…

I found myself reading more and more lyrics—the "good" and the bad. I would mark out the curse words, but it wasn't long until the power of music took control. I found myself purchasing the CD. At first, I only listened to a few tracks, the "good ones," but in a car, it wasn't long before I just listened to it all. Little by little, one CD at a time, I lost control.

On the outside I was perfect. I preached, I taught classes on Sunday, I went soulwinning, I even worked a summer at a Baptist camp. But my inside was full of dead men's bones. My life was quickly becoming an open sepulcher. My heart was corrupted by music and little by little, all the Christian principles I had been taught as a kid eroded away. And after time, the things that were within, crept without.

My senior year, I took off the mask, and the rebellion and hatred that I had buried inside, the hatred that was both created and fed by the rock music, finally came out. It was obvious, the change in public was blatant and without restraint. But the worst part was not the outward but rather the inward. I had forgotten my God, and life without Him is a lonely and depressing existence. My thoughts turned to suicide. I would stay up late and hold a knife to my wrist, making nooses, and every time I got in the car, I considered jerking the wheel into oncoming traffic.

I had no hope, but God gave me grace, and God remembered me. Through God's Word and loving authorities, I saw my music as it was, and I turned from it. One year ago, I burned hundreds of CDs and took a step toward freedom—a step, nothing more. You see, burning my music didn't immediately solve the problem. Quitting is against our nature, making it very hard to do. The struggle doesn't end with one decision, it will take all the strength you have, all the energy, and all the determination you can muster, but if you want it bad enough, through God's grace, you will rise above the power of Satan, and you will overcome the foe.

My story isn't over. I'm still just a kid, but I can promise that though the battle is hard and at times hopeless, it is worth it! I have never been so happy, so filled with joy. The pleasure that sin gave me was only for a season, but the joy God has given me is eternal. I no longer lie awake at night feeling angry and alone, because now I have a God who is right there with me. And all the (wrong music) in the world will never amount to anything more than trash and dung, in light of the joy that God offers to you. Can you overcome your addiction? Yes, because greater is He that is in you, than he that is in the world.

These stories are merely a few that barely scratch the surface of what this music does to a Christian teenager! It is horrid, destructive, addictive, and controlling. It poses as entertainment, but inside it is thoroughly mixing up and destroying the heart. It is, quite simply, public enemy #1!

When I speak on this to teenagers, I use a blender. In that blender I place a selection of fresh fruit and pure water, and then several cups of dirt. The fruit represents the good things that God wants to produce in your life through His Spirit. The dirt obviously represents the corruption that we're talking about. Once everything is neatly inside my blender, the lid goes on and the "high" button is pressed. Though everything on the outside of this blender appears the same, inside everything is getting mixed up. Inside, the dirt is corrupting every good and wholesome piece of fruit!

Friend, when you subject your heart to these corrupting influences, that is exactly what is happening to your spiritual life, whether you realize it or not.

"Put on the whole armour of God, that ye
may be able to stand against
the wiles of the devil."
—EPHESIANS 6:11

Twenty-Seven

Submitting to the Right Spirit

When Daniel was suddenly taken hostage against his will and taken to a foreign land, he made a choice while in that land. Daniel 1:8 says, "But Daniel purposed in his heart that he would not defile himself...." In spite of having to live among wickedness, Daniel purposed within that he would not defile himself. In much the same way, we are hostages in this foreign land called earth. God tells us to "Love not the world, neither the things that are in the world..." in 1 John 2:15. He tells us that "A double minded man is unstable in all his ways" in James 1:8. He teaches us that "No man can serve two masters..." in Matthew 6:24.

As you journey through this life, you must choose who will be your master, spiritually. You do not have the option of going through life without a spiritual master. This is another law of the universe. Aren't those laws wonderful things? You will have a master—either the spirits of the world or the Spirit of God.

Seeing music as more than entertainment—seeing entertainment as more than enjoyment—is pivotal to making the right choice. You see, poison can taste good, but that doesn't mean you would drink it. You would be more concerned with the result than with the enjoyment. So I ask you, when it comes to music and entertainment, what are you more concerned about—the taste or the result? Are you more interested in temporal enjoyment or in choosing the right master? The key question: Are you willing to submit your appetite to the will of God?

Daniel was. The young man was willing to go without good meat—kingly meat—in order to stay pure and right with God. He was willing to eat pulse (vegetables or fruit) and water, indefinitely, if that meant staying pure from corruption. What a fantastic choice—God first, appetites second!

With corrupting influences, the choice is the same. My carnal appetites might cry out for one thing, but I must choose what is right. This will be tough. Breaking free from the strongholds of wicked music and entertainment is very difficult. It tries to hold on, to stay embedded in your heart. It tries to return, again and again. And appetites seem to almost shout at us, "but I like this kind of music!"

In addition to this, when you start listening to right music, your carnal appetites will stage a revolt. Let me be brutally honest with you—you'll hate right music at first. Do you think these spirit voices will be quieted with no resistance? Do you think Daniel really wanted lima beans over a porterhouse steak with all the trimmings? I think not. Do you think he just had a natural aversion to meat and a craving for asparagus and water? Be serious here! He chose against the grain of his appetite and he discovered a wonderful truth. In the end, he was stronger, healthier, and more physically fit than those who had defiled themselves.

An appetite of the heart is a moldable thing in the hand of God. Appetites can be changed.

You see, an appetite of the heart is a moldable thing in the hand of God. Appetites can be changed. After all, you developed the appetite for that music at some point. You must yield your appetite to God to find out how He can change it from within by His power. It's only when you yield to God, submit to His control, that you discover He has the power to pull down these strongholds and to put up truth as the stronghold of your heart.

I'm literally saying, give God the music you know is wrong, and give Him time—and He will give you a new appetite for the right kind of music! In time you will not miss the old spirits, and in fact you will crave the new. Yes, God can change your tastes for music. He can actually conform them to the image of Christ. So how does He do it?

First, it requires obedience by faith. Oh no, there's that word again! Do what is right first. Get rid of the old. Break the CDs, burn the magazines, and clean out the house. Get rid of even the "Christian" rock and rap. Obey God from the heart by choosing and listening to the "psalms, hymns and spiritual songs" that the Bible speaks of, no matter how little you enjoy them at first.

> *It's only when you yield to God, submit to His control, that you discover He has the power to pull down these strongholds...*

Second, it requires patience. Appetites take time to change, and new ones take time to develop. Listen to conservative, Christ-centered music several hours a day for six months or more, with a pure heart before God and see what happens! This has happened to me—and hundreds of other Christians that I know personally. You will develop new taste buds. The Spirit of God within will lap up the fresh water of the right music like a drought-ridden landscape. He will come alive in your heart with a fresh appetite for that which is good to the use of edifying!

Think of it this way—you will always *like* what you *listen to*. Don't *listen to* what you *like*. *Listen* to what is *right*. Eventually, God will bless your obedience with a love for that which is right. Your appetites will either be conformed or transformed. Choose to be transformed!

Not long ago I shared these truths with a group of young people. Some days after that meeting, I received this letter. Listen to this young lady's experience in her own words.

> ...your message on music was one I've been trying to escape for months. I gave up my (wrong) music at Snow Camp in January. I even brought all my CDs to (my youth pastor). But then the devil crept up and I gave in. I didn't go out and buy new CDs, all it took was the push of a button, the radio. I went back on my decision, and it started to really affect me. Everything you

said was happening to me. My music took my joy. It was holding me down. I'd found myself bitter at authority, and I especially couldn't even talk to (my youth pastor).

My music was "choking" me. I found myself listening to it more often. It was like I was addicted to worldly music. I even did what most teens do, I threw in a little contemporary Christian, just to soothe my conscience. It was so bad that I couldn't stand to listen to good Christian music.

But I thank God in that service, the chains were broken, the choking stopped, and I GAVE UP the filthy music I had. I feel so free. It's still not easy, but it's better than before. I pray to God daily to give me a desire to listen to good music and to take the lyrics of the wrong music out of my head. Please pray I'll stick to this decision. Pride almost kept me in my seat, I felt stupid to give up music again. But thank God I put my pride aside and went to the altar…

Another young lady writes, in response to the same principles about wrong music…

I am writing to you today because I wanted to tell you that I finally did it, I got rid of all my (wrong) CDs. I know that it has been a week or so since the conference, but the devil didn't like the idea of losing another teen back to God, so as usual he did everything in his power to distract me from what was right.

Even though I knew what I had to do, the devil and the worldly lust inside of me told me that I didn't need to do it, that I could handle it. The truth is, I couldn't. I had gone right back to my old life, listening to music like (lengthy list of pop artists), which is only to name a few and it was all evil, it was tearing me apart and I didn't even see it. Of course my parents could see it, but they didn't know why or that I was listening to ungodly music until I decided to stop and I told them.

…I have never had this happen to me before. Even though the devil was still around, it seemed like the Holy Spirit was there pounding on my spiritual heart. He was telling me to stop with this sin and He kept running your sermon over and over in my head and I kept trying to block it out. Until one night I was lying there, and all I could hear was (the sermon) going over in my head.

I couldn't sleep, the conviction was unbearable, so I got out of bed at 2 AM, and I took a knife that was on my dresser, and I scratched up all my (wrong) CDs and threw them away. Praise God! The freedom I feel is great. I am back on track with God. I'm reading my Bible, and I couldn't be happier....

"He that handleth a matter wisely
shall find good: and whoso trusteth
in the LORD, *happy is he."*
—PROVERBS 16:20

Twenty-Eight

Standing In the Gap
for Young Hearts

Parent, before we leave this subject, might I ask, what spirit voices are you listening to? Perhaps God has revealed some "open gaps" in your family hedge. My first challenge to you is to let "your obedience come abroad unto all men" (Romans 16:19). Show your teenager that you are personally making changes to obey God. Submit to His Word in your life. Be willing to change music, TV habits, reading habits, or whatever else God has put on your heart to change. Be aware that a stronghold in your life will most likely result in a stronghold in your teenager's life.

My second challenge to you is, don't buy the lie of culture! Your teen needs good music! Recently a beer company has been using a billboard in our area that reveals Satan's lie in this area. The billboard pictures the head and shoulders of the teenager with headphones on. The words on the billboard say, "Music? Probably not. But you *can* influence your teenager's choices about drinking." I shudder when I see that billboard. Parents all over the world are buying the lie that "this is just the kind of music teens listen to...there's nothing I can do to change it." If I could shout this—YES, THERE IS!

This issue requires that you stand in your gap! Teens are rarely strong enough to stand alone on this one, and they rarely understand what is at stake. Yet, every Christian teenager I know, no matter how protected, has been hit by this temptation. Most strong Christian teens won't fall to drugs or alcohol, but all of them are susceptible to this bait! Set up proper guidelines, enforce them with love, and expect the devil to dig a hole under the hedge and still attempt to get at your family cargo. I've spoken with many godly parents over the years who were surprised that their son or daughter was secretly into the world's music. In fact, *so many* that I'm expecting this particular lie to sneak up in my family at some point. Suspect the enemy! Take preemptive action now. Here are some ways you can do so…

Protecting Your Teen from Corruption

1. Submit your own will to God. Without expounding the submission to God issue again, suffice to say, you must be willing to make changes first in your own entertainment habits. This is the starting point. I know you may have a pet music style or a pet TV series but in the end, your tiny allowances personally could become the trickle that opens the floodgates into your teenager's life. No personal preferences or enjoyment is worth that.

2. Expect that the enemy will tempt your teenager, no matter how sheltered he has been. I have seen the best of Christian homes be infiltrated by this temptation. In fact, this is one sin that I believe every Christian teenager is tempted with, so you must anticipate it. Don't think your fortress is impenetrable. I've seen the best of parents shocked by the presence of wrong music in the life of their child. Expect it and teach your teen, preemptively, how to handle it when it arrives!

3. Suspect the enemy constantly. The devil has many ways of hooking a teenager with these forms of corruption. There are many outlets, many ways your teen could be exposed. He loves it when you drop your guard as a parent. He would love nothing more than for you to think everything is fine in Dodge. Don't drop your guard on this issue. As soon as you do, the enemy will be there.

4. Look for warning signs, and don't ignore the Holy Spirit's promptings in your heart. Oftentimes God will pinpoint a warning sign—a fallen countenance, a behavioral shift, and change in attitude. Other times, the promptings will be in your heart with that gentle, still, small voice of the Holy Spirit giving you uneasiness. Don't ignore this spiritual intuition. It's the worst thing you could do. If God is prompting your heart, ever, about an issue, you must respond! Don't doubt His prompting, don't reason it away…FOLLOW IT!

5. Set up a watch-guard over your teenager. Boy, the teens are loving this right now, I'm sure. I don't mean like a prison compound; I mean like a carefully guarded, private, resort-residence! Ask your teen about temptations in these areas. Unplug or get rid of the TV if you need to. Disconnect the cable. Use alarm clocks with no radios. Don't allow extended hours at home alone. Do what it takes to be a guardian over the young hearts in your family.

6. Fill your house with that which is good. Replace bad music and bad entertainment with good. Get some great Christian music and play that throughout the house regularly. Buy some great family games and sit down at the kitchen table to play them frequently. Get some wholesome books and read them out loud during family time together. These are just as enjoyable as a good movie, and a whole lot healthier!

We have done this on a few occasions, and I hope to do a lot more of it as my kids grow older. Honestly, my children get more excited about me reading a good book to them than they do about any movie, TV show, or video game. Give it a try and see how your clan gets in to it!

7. Look for backdoors that the enemy might use to gain entrance into your teen's heart. I mentioned a few of these above. Look for ways that the enemy can feed your teen without your knowledge. Clock radios are a huge temptation for a kid who is struggling with this. Internet connections, headphones, closed bedroom doors, and video games are all potential hazards.

Also, don't always buy the "label" on a particular recording that your teenager is listening to. It's easy to record another kind of music over a cassette with a different label or to burn a CD with wrong music but then label it with a different title. This is common practice in the music underworld for Christian teens. Check it out.

Look for ways that music sneaks in through other forms of "innocent" entertainment. For instance, don't allow your son or daughter to sit for hours listening to rock music in the background of a video game or in the sound track of a movie. Most games have the option of turning off the music portion of the track and most TV's have a mute button. More importantly, train your teenager what this music does to the heart and how to respond, so that she will respond properly when you aren't in the room!

My first exposure to really rotten music was in seventh grade as a Boy Scout. Yes, I was a Boy Scout for a grand total of about six months. Yet in that six months, we took a couple of trips during which time I was exposed to some pretty rotten material in the forms of jokes and music. Something that seemed so good, healthy, and even growth-oriented was actually just a back door for the enemy in my young life.

On one trip we were placed into the car of an "Eagle Scout"—one of our country's finest! He was barely eighteen and shouldn't really have been driving us anywhere. I was thirteen and just doing what I was told. That three-hour trip with that Eagle Scout was one of the worst three-hour periods in my entire life. That guy blared his music loud and long—and asking him to turn it off only worsened the situation.

Then he started on the jokes. For an hour or more that guy was nothing less than an emissary of my enemy sent to corrupt me as much as possible in the short time we were together. Needless to say, my family lost interest in that particular Boy Scout troop at that point.

Parent, the enemy will sneak attack. You must be prepared for the inevitable.

Restoring a Corrupted Heart by God's Grace

Hook #3—Pollute and Plunder! The enemy wants to fill your heart with any and all kinds of corruption. Beware of the bait! Once it's swallowed, it makes you a different person. Music is the biggest destroyer in a world of others. Beware of "mere entertainment"—there may be a hook buried there.

Back to the Z-pack! Remember the atomic bomb of antibiotics? It cured me quickly and completely—because it was greater than the infection within! It was awesome! Here's the great news. If your heart has been in the stronghold of wrong entertainment for some time—if you know the corruption has already taken place, God's grace is GREATER than the power of that stronghold! ("For the weapons of our warfare are not carnal, but mighty through God to the pulling down of strong holds…"—2 Corinthians 10:4). Looking back to 1 John 4:4, right in the middle of talking about ungodly spirits, God says, "Ye are of God, little children, and have overcome them: because greater is he that is in you, than he that is in the world."

Not long ago, my wife's cousin Randy trusted Christ as his personal Saviour. Randy had basically grown up surrounded by the influences we've been talking about. He had not lived one day of his life apart from the world's music and other devices. Through the prayers of some faithful family members and the witness of a godly pastor, this young man was saved by God's grace. My wife and I rejoiced when we heard the news, and we were recently able to visit with Randy and his family at a family gathering. It was a wonderful experience to see what God's Spirit had done in his heart. Any other time I had seen Randy he was withdrawn, reclusive, and obviously under the oppression of "the spirits of this world."

Now, for the first time, when he spoke to me his eyes were wide with joy, his countenance was healthy and happy, and his spirit was obviously "made new" in Christ! It was AWESOME!! I was sitting at the kitchen table when he came in. He immediately pulled up a chair, and said, "Hey, Brother Cary, this was the best decision I've ever made in my life!" It was surprising to hear him refer to me at all, much less with the word "Brother"!

"What decision was that Randy?" I knew where he was going, but wanted to make sure.

"Getting saved!" he answered with excitement, "My whole life is different. I've never experienced this before. I've never felt so clean!"

As we talked, my heart was overjoyed at God's work in Randy's heart. He had entered into a new life that he had never even imagined! It was as though his whole life he had been a hostage, and now he was free. It was awesome to see him relish in his newly found salvation, when so many Christians take it for granted. It reminded me of the power of God and of how wonderful it is to know Him personally. After several moments of rejoicing together, he made a statement I'll never forget.

"Brother Cary, my testimony is short and simple—from tie-dies to tithing!"

We had a great laugh out of that one, but the depth of the statement impacted me more than Randy realized! "From tie-dies to tithing!" WOW! From the drug, rock music culture to new life in Christ that produces joyful and willing obedience to God! What a wonderful snapshot of the transforming power of God! What an awesome God we have, who so powerfully pulls down the satanic strongholds in our lives and restores us to full, abundant, and eternal life!

Claim God's Grace as Your Own

Millions of teens and their parents are under the same bondage that Randy was under. They are corrupted in their heart and that corruption is like a prison. Yet, God offers you an atomic bomb of grace to restore your heart, cleanse your life, and restore your joy. That "Z-pack" of grace is available at any moment—all of the time! That doesn't mean you should take it for granted, as Paul warns us in Romans 6:1. It does mean that God is ready and waiting to break down the strongholds in your life. God is eager to lift you up out of the miry pit of corruption, and to make you clean. He will cleanse your heart and restore you to the new creature He created you to be in Christ! In that moment when you let go of the music, the movies, the media forms that have a strong hold on you, you will feel truly clean!

Take a moment as you close this chapter and do business with God. Teenager, come clean with your parents regarding the music you have been listening to. Parent, come clean with God about changes He wants to make in your life, and stand in the gap for your teenager in this area. You may be the last line of defense for your teenager. Then, together, lock arms against the enemy. Recognize the spirit influences that are found in modern day media forms, and then carefully stand guard over your heart. The temporary discomfort of letting go of a favorite CD or a favorite TV program will be greatly overshadowed by a clean life and renewed joy. Let God have His way in your heart, and let the real life that God intends for you begin today!

Look at Psalm 51 and make it your own prayer from a sincere heart…

Psalm 51:1–13, "Have mercy upon me, O God, according to thy lovingkindness: according unto the multitude of thy tender mercies blot out my transgressions. Wash me throughly from mine iniquity, and cleanse me from my sin. For I acknowledge my transgressions: and my sin is ever before me. Against thee, thee only, have I sinned, and done this evil in thy sight: that thou mightest be justified when thou speakest, and be clear when thou judgest. Behold, I was shapen in iniquity; and in sin did my mother conceive me. Behold, thou desirest truth in the inward parts: and in the hidden part thou shalt make me to know wisdom. Purge me with hyssop, and I shall be clean: wash me, and I shall be whiter than snow. Make me to hear joy and gladness; that the bones which thou hast broken may rejoice. Hide thy face from my sins, and blot out all mine iniquities. Create in me a clean heart, O God; and renew a right spirit within me. Cast me not away from thy presence; and take not thy holy spirit from me. Restore unto me the joy of thy salvation; and uphold me with thy free spirit. Then will I teach transgressors thy ways; and sinners shall be converted unto thee."

"He brought me up also out of an horrible pit,
out of the miry clay, and set my feet upon a rock,
and established my goings. And he hath put a new
song in my mouth…"
—Psalm 40:2–3

Part Five

Hook #4
Befriend
and Bewilder

Overcoming Wrong Companions

The enemy's lie to a teenager...

"I must have friends, and I must be friends with whoever accepts me. I'm willing to do whatever I have to do to have friends…"

"My parents don't understand my friends and don't care about my friends. I feel more at home with my friends than with anyone else!"

"I would never do all the things that my friends do. I can be friends with somebody without being like them…"

"If I don't rescue my rebellious friends, nobody will…"

The enemy's lie to a parent...

"At least my kid's friends are 'Christian'—that must mean their parents have rules for them and that they will be good for my teenager…"

"It's not my responsibility to know my kid's friends—who could possibly have time for that?"

"The peer pressure of drugs, alcohol, worldly music, illicit sex, and other forms of vice are aimed at other people's kids."

"I can't dictate my teen's friends. That's not my responsibility as a parent. Who am I to tell my teen who they can or cannot be friends with?!"

"My teen doesn't care to be friends with me!"

Twenty-Nine

"Gray Matter"
The Curse of the Teen Brain

The devil wants to bewilder your life by befriending you with the wrong people. He wants to rob your purity through a wrong dating relationship; destroy your good name through wrong companions; break up your family through rebellious influences, and rewrite your future by conforming you to the world's crowd. Beware of this hook!

The December 7, 2002 cover of *Newsweek* magazine simply said "Teen Depression—3 Million Teens Suffer From It." The article proceeded to explain the rise of teen depression in recent years and the increase in related problems. It was in reading this article that I finally discovered the real problem with all teenagers! It's called gray matter. The news story explained that the teen years are a transition time between childhood and adulthood when the brain is changing. During this change, the brain has cells that are dying and being replaced with more mature cells for adult life, and these dead cells that are being cleared out are called gray matter!

So, there you have it! Teenager, you suffer from too much gray matter! Has anyone ever told you that "you are brain dead"?! I tease teenagers in our youth group all the time by saying things like, "Hey, the hospital called and left you a message during class. Your brain is ready, and you can stop by and pick it up any time"! Have your parents ever said something to you like, "You would forget your head if it wasn't attached!"? Amazingly, yes, it's true. You don't have a brain between the time you are 12 and 20. You just have gray matter! It *was* at one point, a brain, sometime way back in your childhood—and it will eventually *become* a brain again after years of clearing out the gunk—but for now it's just "gray matter"! Your brain has gone into non-operational status while it clears out the gunk,

You don't have a brain between the time you are 12 and 20. You just have gray matter!

so you must depend upon those whose brains are actually functioning to help you survive these years—and I have the medical world backing me on this. Don't mess with gray matter!

I recently discovered a wonderful phrase. Being in youth work, I have become quite familiar with the phrase "young people." Teens don't really like to be called kids or children. Yet they aren't quite ready to be called men or women (that would require actual acceptance of responsibility like paying their own rent)—and so adults who actually *care,* try to find some middle ground. "Teens" is okay, but it still sounds juvenile in public, and tends to be overused. "Young adults" is okay but sounds so formal. So, many of us have landed on the phrase "young people" when speaking to teenagers.

After I read that article about gray matter I discovered how "young people" and "dumb people" sound exactly the same if they are spoken at a high rate of speed! So, for a period of several weeks I began to say "dumb people" every time I addressed a group of "young people." I'll never forget the first time I said this. I expected the group to respond, but they completely missed it! It flew right over the heads of the entire crowd, workers included! "Wow, this could be fun!" I thought. So, I continued. A second time, no one caught on, but this time I found the ignorance of the crowd too enjoyable, and I actually burst into a quick flurry of laughter. The group just looked at me like I was on some kind of psychotic trip or something. It was great.

Here I was calling an entire room of teenagers "dumb people" and they weren't catching it! In fact, it was absolutely hilarious. This was incredibly FUN!! The problem was, by the third and fourth time, I was so caught up in the amusement that I couldn't say it with a straight face. As soon as "dumb people" would come out, I would crack up! "Dumb people, let's all stand for Scripture reading!" "Dumb people, it's time to quiet down and listen to the lesson!" "Dumb people, give God His way in your life!" This was like a little party I was having all by myself—and it was *wonderful*!

By about the fifth time, the teens started figuring out that something was up. Eventually my laughter gave me away. The senior class students were the first to catch on, but they didn't tell the others. So, indeed the party continued with a few more in on the secret! They were enjoying the joke too! We would all laugh at every mention of "dumb people." Eventually they figured out that the phrase was an insult to them as well, and so they stopped laughing. They got that look on their face that seemed to say, "Okay, this isn't funny any more." By that time, I started to feel convicted that I was being disrespectful to a group of people that I love very deeply—no matter how fun it was! So, the fun had to go away before I inadvertently offended someone. It was good while it lasted. Try it, you might enjoy it as much as I did!

You know, the fact of the matter is, we're all "dumb people" when it comes to fully knowing and understanding our spiritual warfare and the strategy of our enemy. That's why Paul prayed that "the eyes of your understanding" would be enlightened. The sooner we admit that we are dumb to the spiritual world, the sooner we can depend upon God's wisdom and Word to enlighten and empower us to victory in our lives. I hope by now you are seeing through some of the bait—the lies that your enemy is using against you. I hope you are willing to accept the fact that we are dumb people who need desperately to depend upon God.

All kidding aside, the *Newsweek* article I referred to actually presented some very disturbing facts about teen life in America. It explained that millions of teenagers in America exhibit symptoms of depression and listed suicide as the third leading cause of death among 10–24 year olds. The writer detailed how doctors are treating depression with drugs whose long-term effects are relatively unknown. He also detailed how the causes of depression and the radical increase of teen depression and suicide in our culture are relatively unexplainable.

Culture points with considerable uncertainty to broken homes, social pressure, and chemical changes in the brain (no doubt all of these play a role). Then society attempts to solve the problem with drugs and therapy.

Often, depression is more than a mental illness. It is a spiritual problem as well, and the effects of the spiritual traps that we are talking about can certainly induce and greatly amplify this depression in the lives of teens.

Quite often spiritual and emotional problems like depression or despair are the result of the matters we've talked about up to this point. These surface problems lead to a root problem—loneliness—which leads to our final hook of destruction. We will explore in the coming chapters—wrong companions.

"...in thy presence is fulness of joy; at thy right hand there are pleasures for evermore."
—PSALM 16:11

Thirty

Never Alone—
Our Heart's Desire,
Our Saviour's Promise

If you aren't seeing it by now, these lies weave together, working together to become a multifaceted attack in the life of a teenager! First, a fragmented family breeds a rebellious spirit, which feeds off of cankerous entertainment influences, which creates a confused, depressed teenager! This pattern leads to utter loneliness and despair (no hope), which leads us to the following chapters of this book. You see, the devil's traps and lies always lead you to despair and loneliness, a place of self-destruction. His goal is to isolate you utterly and completely from the only thing that can make you whole and give you real HOPE—a real, dynamic, personal relationship with the one true God, who wants to be your loving Heavenly Father!

In breaking down our family relationships, he robs us of knowing and loving those that should model and ultimately lead us into a heavenly relationship with God. He robs us of the closest thing on earth to God's love, the love that should be exhibited in a true family. In breeding rebellion, he isolates us in a desert land where we are blinded to his attacks and open to his devices. In corrupting our hearts with music and godless entertainment, he numbs the pain of the deep needs of our heart while rewriting our thoughts, emotions, and desires.

We emerge a confused, despairing, hopeless shadow of what true life is really supposed to be. From there, he attempts to lead us on a false journey into destructive behavior and relationships. He teases us with tiny tidbits of pleasure, mere echoes of momentary happiness, and fleeting follies that only *appear* to be the love we're really looking for! He lures us on this never-ending journey through a life of surviving and searching for true meaning and deep inner happiness. And then we come to the end of our lives, still empty, still searching—but better at coping, surviving, and (at best) numb to the spiritual needs of our hearts that we buried long, long ago. And then we die.

Friend, is that the way you want to live your life? Is that the way you want to spend your brief existence on this planet—experiencing not even a figment of what God planned for you in eternity past? In all of this, I truly pray that God is enlightening your understanding and showing you that it is He that you crave. If you have never trusted Jesus Christ as your personal Saviour and entered into that personal relationship with your Heavenly Father, I would urge you to make that decision.

Jesus Christ gave His life to purchase your salvation. You can literally be born into God's family the moment you pray and ask Jesus Christ to come into your heart as your personal Saviour. The moment you confess to Him that you need His forgiveness and call upon Him to save you, you will truly be alive for the first time—spiritually alive! For the first time your heart will taste the only love that can fill the deep search and longing of your heart. Romans 10:10 and 13 say, "For with the heart man believeth unto righteousness; and with the mouth confession is made unto salvation…For whosoever shall call upon the name of the Lord shall be saved."

If you already know the Lord personally, then this fourth hook and the resulting solution will truly make sense to you. The fourth hook that is ruining the lives of teens and parents is simply evil companions. By evil companions, I'm referring to the fact that your enemy desires, through various strategic ways, to connect you with friends who will magnify your spiritual desolation and lead you down the wrong path. He is only too happy to bring to you false friends who will influence you away from your True Friend—Jesus Christ, and your true friendships—God's people and the spiritual authorities that God has given to you. His primary way of doing this is by toying with you—manipulating you through "loneliness"! Let's talk about it.

My First Experience with Being Alone

Have you ever been left alone? There is never a more terrifying experience than the feeling of being left completely and utterly alone.

My earliest memory of being left alone was when I was five. Though I have a loving family and a loving extended family, I was nevertheless subjected to a harrowing experience at this delicate and frail young age that probably had a defining, indelible impact upon my tender toddler psyche.

I was left alone. Left to die. Left to wander the cities and streets of Severna Park, Maryland. Left to find shelter under a freeway overpass, to beg for bread, and to be raised by a pack of wild dogs. Left alone, simply because I was small, quiet, and easily missed. Left alone—because, at a mere five years old, I had to use the potty at an inopportune time. Yes, the scars run deep into my psyche, and even now, it is difficult to recall this experience (repressed memories)—but for the need of the hour, I will persist, that you might gain from my tragedy.

It all began on a beautiful summer day at my grandmother's house with all eight of my cousins and my aunt and grandmother. The day promised to be filled with adventure and fun, and most of all good food! You see, we were going to McDonald's for lunch, and to any elementary child, a day that includes McDonald's is going to be a great day!

We were not disappointed! McDonald's in Severna Park, Maryland on this particular day was perfect! What could possibly be better than being five years old, sitting in a McDonald's plastic swivel chair, swinging your legs (bonking the center pole of the table) and eating food fit for kings—a cheeseburger, French-fries, and a small Coke?

Nay, I say—nothing could be grander!

As a side note, somewhere amid the feeding frenzy, I had noticed, almost subconsciously, that a police officer had entered the restaurant and was waiting in line to purchase his lunch. I remember seeing him, being intrigued with his uniform (like any five-year-old boy) and thinking, "Policeman…yeah, he is a good guy. If I was ever in trouble, my teacher said I could get help from guys like him…." It was merely a fleeting, wisp of a thought, amid a flurry of chaotic laughter and exchanges within our family party—seemingly nothing at the time.

I remember the moment as if it were yesterday. There we were, eleven of us, nine kids, two adults. Everyone was family, and everyone was having a wonderful time. It was about this time that nature called. So, amid the frolicking and fun, I quietly slipped out of my swivel chair and told Mamom that I needed to "go." After being told to hurry, but granted permission—I dismissed myself to the restroom, where I, unfortunately became amused with other fun things like splashing water in the sink and playing with the paper towel dispenser. (Give me a break here—I was only five!)

Well, several moments of fun passed, when it occurred to me that Mamom had told me to hurry. So, leaving the water running and the sink area rather cluttered with water-soaked paper towels, I proceeded into the restaurant where I intended to reunite with my family and rejoin the frolicking fun.

When I arrived back at my seat, to my utter dismay there was some weird four-year-old kid sitting on my throne—and he didn't even closely resemble one of my cousins! "What's this kid doing here?" I thought to myself, "He needs a good pounding for just coming out of nowhere and taking my plastic swivel chair!"

It was only then that I looked up and around. The sight before me sent my tiny heart into convulsions that nearly sent me to the closest ICU. These people…my eyes darted from face to face in panicked searching, needing someone familiar. These people…none of them…I… (eyes still darting)…I don't see any of my people! None of these faces belong to my tribe! Where did my people go? At this point, amid the fast-paced breathing, the blood pounding through my entire body, I had the fleeting thought that perhaps I was disoriented and had gone to the wrong table—or perhaps my grandmother and cohorts were playing some sick practical joke on me and they were about to jump out from their hiding places at any moment.

So, again, my eyes searched, as my body rotated to view every last table in that entire restaurant! No…no…not there…not there either…

no, those people aren't mine…not in line…not bounding out of their hiding places…I'm alone on a foreign planet, and my earthling friends are not here!

The cars! Aha! They must have gone to the cars and they are waiting outside for me. I should have known. So, in a quick-flash motion reminiscent of a Bugs Bunny cartoon, I dashed for the exit. As I landed outside on the sidewalk, I could see the answer to my question, and my heart sunk even further than before. There, before me, were the parking places…as empty and desolate as any I had ever seen in my life. These weren't just a vacant spots; they were the most deserted, wasteland of forsaken parking places that my five-year-old heart could ever imagine. I stood in stunned disbelief for several seconds as the enormity of the situation enveloped me.

My mind raced with panicked pressure…"What do I do? I'm here alone, in trouble…and if I don't do something fast, I will never catch my family. I will never see them again! I will be doomed forever to live as an orphan." Curiously, it never occurred to me that I would eventually be missed and someone would return for me. No, I had to brave this one myself. So, as quickly as I could, I switched into self-preservation mode! I'm in trouble…I must get help…get help…my brain raced…get help from who?

My thoughts were frantic and fragmented. Trouble…help… trouble…POLICEMAN!!! I knew I had noticed him for a reason! POLICEMAN can HELP!!! I ran back into the restaurant…searching… looking…frantic…find policeman…policeman isn't here…anywhere. Mad dash back outside…searching parking lot…eyes frantic…breathing heavy…heart pounding! POLICE CAR!!! Yes…POLICEMAN, closing his car door…must hurry…must run…must catch him before he leaves!!! Yes, I was merely seconds from being stranded at McDonald's forever, but with a final sprint that harnessed all the raw fear and superhuman energy I had ever imagined having, I made a break for the police car.

As I arrived at the driver's side door, I was breathing heavily, heart in my throat, and just about to break into a tear-storm like you have never seen. I think I startled the officer, but he quickly opened his door and offered help.

I don't remember the entire conversation; I just remember that I didn't remember my grandmother's phone number, her address, or even her or my grandfather's first name. I also remember that the officer kindly told me he would take me home. Then he showed me to the front seat of his squad car. This was getting better all the time!

Well, ten minutes and one "front-seat-ride-in-a-real-police-car" later I found myself pulling up in front of my grandmother's house—a true hero! Yes, all eight of my other cousins came running out of the house when they saw the police car. I was a star! I got to ride in a real police car with a real policeman! It was awesome!

My grandmother came running out of the house, white as a ghost, but relieved that I was all right. You see, a few moments earlier they had discovered my absence and my aunt had returned to McDonald's at a high rate of speed only to discover that I wasn't there! Fortunately, I was home by the time she called in terror to tell my grandmother I was gone for good.

So a really scary, "alone" experience became one of the greatest memories of my young life—riding with a policeman, being famous with my older cousins—it was too cool! Yet, to this day, when I visit my grandmother and drive by that McDonald's, I still twitch a little with flashbacks. The emotional damage lingers.

You know, many of us go through life like that McDonalds' experience—looking for food, friends, and fun. Our greatest fear is that at any moment we might look around our life only to find out that we are alone—no friends, no fun. So, in an effort to feed our need, we become willing to do anything, say anything, or dress in any way we have to in order to get friends. "Having acceptance and fearing rejection" becomes the driving force of our lives.

As we'll see by the end of this section, when you know the Lord, you are never truly alone, no matter who "left you standing in McDonald's." The real issue is seeing Him, running to Him, and finding in Him all the acceptance and friendship we really need. In the matter of a few seconds I went from being out-of-control with panic, to being the honorary "partner" of one of America's finest law enforcement officers! I found acceptance, safety, and care in the police officer, and in turn had my heart delighted beyond imagination.

In the same way, if you find your total acceptance and security in Jesus Christ—if you make Him your best friend—you will escape this hook of wrong friendships and you will be a survivor. Your Best Friend will provide other friends who will sharpen you, strengthen you, and influence towards righteousness.

Your life—your entire future—will be dramatically impacted by how you handle your need for acceptance and friendship. God has a plan for meeting that need and the devil wants to thwart that plan. The devil wants you to panic in fear and run to all the wrong places for friends. Approach the coming chapters with an open heart and ask God to show you the hook instead of the bait.

"...for he hath said, I will never
leave thee, nor forsake thee."
—HEBREWS 13:5

Thirty-One

Our Deepest Fear
"Chum Rejection"

Chum (n.)—a close friend.

Chum (v.)—to be friends with somebody, or behave in a friendly way toward someone.

Chummy (adj.)—friendly or close (informal).

Chum (n.)—an angler's bait, especially chopped fish, scattered on the water.

Chumming (v.)—the act of scattering bait, especially chopped up fish, on the water to attract other fish.

Chump (n.)—somebody who is unwise or easily deceived (informal).

Before you read on, think about those definitions again. We'll get to them in a minute!

Teenagers seem to crave two things, fun and friends. Sort of like kids and candy, teenagers crave fun and they crave acceptance from friends. Adults are much the same, only the words might be "pleasure and companionship." Now, there's nothing wrong with having friends or fun, but this fourth hook of wrong friends plays on our craving for acceptance in a major way. Just as I feared "being alone" at that McDonald's, every teenager fears "being alone" without friends in life. The fear of being alone, the fear of being a freak—not being acceptable to a perceived "in crowd" becomes a major driving force somewhere between seventh and ninth grade. Why?

First, because you are growing up. This is a time when you are naturally trying to build a little independence from your family. This isn't always bad, but the devil wants to greatly exaggerate it. He tried to convince you that you don't want or need your parents. He wants you to believe that you must have friends or you cannot be happy! He will play on this particular craving to chum you right into the boat!

Second, because you are self-conscious of the fact that you are changing physically. Never is a teenager more insecure than between seventh and tenth grades. Your body is no longer that of a child. It is becoming an adult—which means, some part of you probably feels "out of whack"! Your feet, your height, your teeth—something! This makes you hypersensitive to being accepted—in spite of the fact that everyone else your age is "out of whack" too!

My son Larry, going into fifth grade, would gladly go to school without touching his hair or his teeth in the morning. He doesn't care whether his clothes match and isn't concerned with impressing anybody. Yet, my son Lance, going into eighth grade, not only touches his hair and his teeth, but is considerably concerned with even the "folds" of his tucked-in shirt. Why? Partially because he's a neat freak and wants to look nice, but primarily because he wants to be acceptable to his friends.

Parents, be aware that your teenager will be incredibly sensitive to personal insecurities during this time of life. The slightest word from you or from a friend can wreak emotional havoc! A teenager's worst nightmare is the thought of being made fun of in a belittling way by supposed friends.

Third, because we all have a deep heart-level need to be loved and accepted. The devil will work overtime to bring imaginations and experiences into your life during your teen years that cause you to feel unlovable, unlikable, and uncool! The amazing thing is, he does this to everybody! Every teenager experiences this, and yet every teenager is convinced that they are the only one experiencing it! You would think we could figure this out and start being everybody's friend. We all crave and need acceptance. God made you with that craving and has a way of filling that need, but the devil wants to use it to snare you.

Fourth, because we all fear rejection and loneliness. Again, the enemy wants to isolate you from true friends and true safety. Then he wants to partner you with chums (or perhaps chumps is a better word). No one wants to be lonely and no one wants to be rejected. If you allow him to, the enemy will prey upon your need for acceptance and your fear of rejection by bringing false friendships into your life. You must understand, these are not true friends—they are bait.

Chumming

I know I said I'm not much of a fisherman at the beginning of this book, but I took my boys out on a "deep sea" fishing trip with some friends recently. We had a great time! While on the trip, I learned a word I've never heard—"chumming." It's defined at the beginning of this chapter as "the act of scattering bait, especially chopped up fish, on the water to attract other fish."

All through the day, the deck hands on the boat kept throwing fists-full of bait (small fish and minnows) over board on the surface of the Pacific Ocean. They called it "chumming"! The idea was that this bait would draw the fish out and up toward the water's surface where they could be hooked. Think about it! The fisherman threw in real, live bait—no hooks—just the real thing, to lure in the fish. A few moments later, all fifty of the fishermen on the boat would drop baited hooks into the water—and boy, did the fish start biting!

I thought about that word all day long—in light of this section. Chumming. Chums. Chumps. There is an interesting connection here. For years I've watched the devil go "chumming" before he goes fishing!

I've watched him throw bait overboard with no hooks attached. The plan is not to catch the entire school of fish, but just to get one to follow the crowd—right to his hook! While on that trip, I didn't catch the whole school of fish. Plenty of fish ate real bait, with no hooks, and probably swam away happy with full stomachs. Yet, I was hoping that my fish would be drawn out among them and follow the crowd, right to my hook! I only wanted one...and then another one...and then another one. Yes, the destruction happened one at a time, while the whole crowd was swimming and eating!

Sending in the Chums

This is what I've seen teenagers do time and time again—follow the crowd, swim with the entire school—right to the hook. I've watched teens—teens with good homes, strong parents, loving pastors—follow their hunger for friends and acceptance right into the wrong crowd and right into the angler's baited hook!

This tactic of "chumming" does some fairly brutal damage to young lives. At nearly every commencement service for our Christian school, right on the verge of a Christian teenager's launch out into adulthood and into God's will, the devil sends in the chums—past friends who will influence this young person to the wrong path, the wrong life, and the wrong destiny. It's now so common that it couldn't be more blatant (at least to my eyes and to our pastor's). Yet, to the graduate, the danger is never that apparent. It's amazing to me that these friends only come around at critical times of decision (like graduation) and then they linger, reconnect, and try to endear this person to themselves.

These friends rarely do these things consciously—usually they are just the unwitting tool of their master (whom they fail to see or understand). And, these friends always have an amazingly powerful persuasive ability. They prey upon those who are weak and hungry for acceptance or friendship, and they choose a time when vulnerability is at an all time high—school is out, school is OVER for the graduate, summer provides more free time, and many graduates are "high" on being eighteen and a legal adult at last! Amazing! What a great time to do some "chumming"!

Often, the weaker teenager feels endeared to these friends, sees them as being more "cool," more "free," and having more "fun"! Often the weaker teenager craves the acceptance of this "cool" crowd, and their presence at commencement is like a doorway that leads to another life. The devil tells the graduate, "Now that you are out of high school, you can finally walk through that doorway. You can finally be

> *I've seen teenagers time and time again—follow the crowd, swim with the entire school—right to the hook.*

free, live the life you want, have the fun you want, and have the friends you want. You're done with school. You are your own person now!"

The enemy also brings these chums at another time of high vulnerability between seventh and tenth grade. When you are the most insecure as a teenager (probably your ninth grade year), you can expect that the enemy will try to connect you with wrong friends and ungodly influences. He will send in the "chums" to influence your behavior, your attitude, your speech, and your dress. He will try to make you so hungry for friends and acceptance that you are willing to do anything! He will tempt you to make "friends" your idol and their acceptance the thing you worship and love more than God. He will try to partner you with someone else who is struggling spiritually so that together you can influence each other towards the traps. Truthfully, these are not true friendships They are nothing more than mutual insecurity dependencies.

Wrong Friendships Destroy Lives

Be mindful, I'm not attacking these "false friends." In truth, I love them too! I hope and pray that each and every one of these individuals will come to or return to God with their whole hearts and love Him with the rest of their lives! I would do anything within my power to bring them back to God and to rescue them from the snares. I'm not against them, except when it comes to protecting another from their influence. In this case, I can be down right "fight-ish" in the sense of spiritual battle—and you should be too, parent!

In all honesty, chum on a fishing boat is just other fish that have been caught previously to use as bait! These friends are the same. They are simply teenagers or young adults who were snagged in the same hooks and traps, and in their search for friends, they are unwittingly being used as bait (chum) to snag another!

Teenager, wrong friendships are in the top four ways that the enemy is destroying the lives of young people in this generation! Parent, I'm including you in on the discussion because we've already pointed out how vital you are to the process of guidance, protection, and even this issue of acceptance.

Folks, this is no light, laughing matter! All over the world, teenagers are destroying their lives with the help of their friends. We are so hungry and starving for friends and acceptance that we follow blindly in groups—large schools—to our own destruction!

Yet, our need for friends and for acceptance is real, and our desire to be loved and to have companions on our journey is genuine. So, what should we know about friendships? What is God's better way of meeting these needs in our hearts? You can be sure that God wants to meet your needs—to give you great friends who will help you truly become what God wants you to become. God wants to fill that craving for love and companionship, and He never uses bait or hooks! He's not trying to snag you, He's trying to "Father" you! Let's look closer at this issue and God's answer.

"Henceforth I call you not servants;
for the servant knoweth not what his lord doeth:
but I have called you friends…"
—JOHN 15:15

Thirty-Two

Our Most Common Friendship Mistake

Dear _____,

I like you. Do you like me? Circle one.

    Yes   No

Love, _____

The names above have been withheld, to protect the innocent. Does it look familiar? You're probably wondering if your parents slipped me one of those embarrassing "love notes" you used to pass around during your "swingin' elementary years"! Remember those days? For the most part girls had "cootees" and boys were made of "snakes and snails and puppy dog tails." Yet, every now and then, some hint of attraction would show up in the strangest of places—the playground, the lunchroom, the restroom line—in the form of a "do-you-like-me" note.

When it comes to friends, from our earliest days of understanding we tend to think this way. Who do I like? Who likes me? We work at being likeable, and we work at becoming friends with people we like. And herein is our big friendship choosing mistake. We choose to be friends with people we like and people that like us! If I'm confusing you, hang in there.

From our childhood we learn to walk, talk, dress, act, and live in ways that will cause people to like us. We usually like the people who like us, and the people who don't are always "stupid jerks." It's like driving—anyone who's driving slower than you is an idiot—anyone who's driving faster than you is a raving lunatic!

This natural phenomenon really kicks into gear when you hit ninth or tenth grade! Suddenly your need to like and be liked hits about 14.2 on the Richter scale. Kaboom! Now, the only thing that matters in life is "who likes me"—and Mom and Dad don't count! Many teenagers become completely consumed with needing to be "liked" or accepted by a certain crowd. If they make it into the "cool crowd," life is suddenly happy and wonderful. If they don't, life might even be considered "not worth living" in their own mind.

This is a mistake of grand proportions! Rather than choosing friends based upon who likes us and who we like, we should choose our friends based upon who we want to be like! We'll get back to this thought, but for now, it leads to this critical point…

Universal Law #1
You Will Always Befriend People Like You.

I know I'm getting carried away with the word "like"—but what teenager doesn't understand that word?! So…like…stay with me.

If you are focused on being likeable in life, you're missing a foundational truth. You won't only befriend someone you like—you'll befriend someone you are like! It's true. You will have a natural bonding friendship to someone who is very much like you.

I'm not referring to personality. In many cases people with opposite personalities do indeed attract each other. I'm referring to the you that is underneath the personality. I'm talking about your true character— your spiritual life. You will normally, naturally, and subconsciously befriend a person whose life character and spiritual condition is very much like your own. Regardless of how you try to cover up your own issues, or how your friend does the same, your heart will be drawn to someone whose heart is similar in character, desires, and integrity. It's another one of those laws of the universe that you cannot escape.

The Bible says it this way in Amos 3:3, "Can two walk together, except they be agreed?" Again in Proverbs 13:20 we're told, "He that walketh with wise men shall be wise: but a companion of fools shall be destroyed." Wise men attract men who want to be wise, and fools generally find each other as well. Malachi 3:16 says, "Then they that feared the LORD spake often one to another...." People who fear God find each other and speak with each other.

Every year, a good portion of my life is spent with teenagers or young adults—in classes, at fellowships, during activities, and often on a retreat or trip. Several times a year, our student groups mix and mingle with other student groups of like-minded churches, whether at camp or at a conference. For more than a decade, I've witnessed an amazing phenomenon. When any two groups of kids come together for more than a few moments, students of like character and background instinctively find each other and begin friendships! It never fails; it never changes—it's as predictable as the sunrise.

Students with a heart-level commitment to Christ quickly identify with those in other groups of the same character. Students who are dealing with serious personal trials instinctively seek out those who identify with their lot in life. Sadly, students who are rebellious quickly entrench themselves with the same crowd as well. Now, you might argue that rebels are more easily spotted by potential friends because they sit in the back, wear scornful faces, and show out a rebellious message. True, but the instinctive attraction I've witnessed goes far deeper than that.

You won't only befriend someone you like—you'll befriend someone you are like!

How do you explain two girls with separate histories of being victimized by sexual abuse—who are strangers to each other—instinctively finding each other in a crowd of 400 teenagers? I've seen this several times, and every time these girls instantly become fast friends—neither one having any idea why they connect.

How do you explain two complete strangers in a large crowd—a promiscuous girl and a promiscuous boy—never having seen each other before, and both struggling with exactly the same broken family relationships, finding each other so they can sneak off somewhere to make-out? Chance? No way! I've seen these connections made dozens of times. It's an instinctive connection that happens between people of "like character" and "like struggles."

Try this one: two boys from separate youth groups meet at the orientation meeting of teen camp. They come from families who are faithful to their individual churches, but in both cases these families spend more of their time criticizing the church and the pastor than they do bringing their children up in the nurture of the Lord. As a result, both young men harbor deeply resentful and critical spirits. They have no clue as to each other's upbringing, but within moments, they click as friends. They have no idea as to why they become such good friends so quickly, but to a pastor who knows "the rest of the story," it's painfully clear.

The list could go endlessly on! I've seen people as different as night and day on the surface (in their personalities) suddenly find an emotional connection for reasons unseen outwardly. These are the kinds of friendships you would never "imagine" happening. It's only when you know that both of these people resent spiritual authority, or both of them come from broken homes, or both of them were abused by a loved one, or both of them have been involved in promiscuous pasts, or both of them are estranged from their fathers—that you understand why they connect.

Students with a heart-level commitment to Christ quickly find each other...

By the way, I'm not saying this connection with like character is always a bad thing. It certainly can be, but don't miss my point. I'm just stating the fact that it happens with all of us.

This principle is true in your life! Again, I remind you that the Bible says in Amos 3:3, "Can two walk together, except they be agreed?" You will naturally connect with people of like character—people you identify as being like you or those you want to be like. Let me say it another way. Your core character and life experiences are what create that intangible connection between you and your friends.

When my wife and I were in high school and college, there were certain types of people we simply avoided. Not only did we not connect with their character, we didn't want to become like them!

Just as a major earthquake has fore-shocks—slight tremors that sometimes warn of a much larger and more damaging quake coming in the future—the weak youthful character of these people provided a fore-shock to the devastation that would one day come. Their stories tell of prison, divorce, custody battles, immorality, homosexuality, substance abuse, loneliness, brokenness, and spiritual desolation.

> *Your core character and life experiences are what create that intangible connection between you and your friends.*

Please understand, I'm not saying our friends were better than the others or that their lives have been without mistakes. It's only by God's wonderful grace that any of us have experienced His blessings. I'm simply saying the character choices we made many years ago drew us together with others of similar character, which in turn had a sharpening effect on all of us.

Birds of a Feather...

In Acts 6, the New Testament Church was facing a minor crisis. Some needs were being neglected and some good men were needed to fill the void. The apostles' solution is found in Acts 6:3–5, "Wherefore, brethren, look ye out among you seven men of honest report, full of the Holy Ghost and wisdom, whom we may appoint over this business. But we will give ourselves continually to prayer, and to the ministry of the word. And the saying pleased the whole multitude: and they chose Stephen, a man full of faith and of the Holy Ghost, and Philip, and Prochorus, and Nicanor, and Timon, and Parmenas, and Nicolas a proselyte of Antioch."

I find it interesting that the whole multitude seemed to settle on these seven men so quickly, and I don't think it's stretching it to use this passage to prove my point. I believe these men were all friends—godly friends—who were commonly found together in fellowship, worship, leadership, and service. When the church began to look for seven good men, I believe they found them all in the same place! Strong character always finds companions with strong character. Similar hearts knit together with common passion, common commitment, and common purpose!

Friend, you cannot escape this law. You will naturally be attracted—as a friend—to someone with similar character to your own. It only makes sense that you should carefully take inventory in your own heart and seek to understand what "connects" you with a certain crowd. If you are bent on your own destruction—if you are swallowing the hooks of fragmentation, rebellion, and corruption—then you will find friends who are swallowing the same hooks. You will wallow together in each other's misery. Scary thought.

On the other hand, if you desire to love God more, live for Him purely, and follow Him unreservedly—then you will, in time, find others with those same heart desires. Your friendship will sharpen those desires and your time together will deepen your devotion and your commitment to Jesus Christ. This kind of true friendship is something that the world cannot comprehend. It's truly awesome!

There are two more "universal laws of friendship"—let's see what they are...

"Iron sharpeneth iron; so a man
sharpeneth the countenance of his friend."
—Proverbs 27:17

Thirty-Three

More Laws of Friendship

I really love these "universal laws"! God's principles always apply to everybody in the human race, and no one can escape them or beat them—no matter how hard they try! They really are wonderful things—like those Ginsu knives sold on TV—they can cut through anything, and nothing can dull them—not even old truck tires! You can never beat these laws, no matter how hard you try. Friendship law #1 was: "You will always befriend people like you," and remember we're talking heart level here, not just surface behavior or personality.

Here are the other two unbeatable laws of friendship:

Universal Law #2
You Will Always Become Like Your Friends.

You may not like or believe what I'm about to say, but it's true nonetheless. You will always, always without exception become like your friends! It is physically and spiritually impossible to be exposed to the companionship of another person for any length of time without that influence shaping and changing who you are. The Bible says in Proverbs 27:17, "Iron sharpeneth iron; so a man sharpeneth the countenance of his friend."

In 2 Samuel 13, the Word of God recounts a tragic story of Amnon, David's son who secretly desired to have an immoral relationship with his half-sister Tamar. Amnon struggled with his lust, and couldn't bring himself to act on his desire, knowing it was wrong. His conscience would not allow him to dishonor his sister. The Bible says in verse three, "But Amnon had a friend, whose name was Jonadab, the son of Shimeah David's brother: and Jonadab was a very subtil man." Perhaps you know the story. Jonadab was Amnon's friend—his chum—and the enemy knew exactly when to send him in. Jonadab saw Amnon's frustration and depression, and so he encouraged him to sin. Jonadab, being subtle and intelligently cunning, devised a plan so that Amnon could literally rape his sister.

The story that unfolded and the destruction that the enemy caused in David's household was tragic, and it all began with a friend. Now, we might say, at first, that Amnon was the better of the two young men. We might conclude that Amnon would have never acted so wickedly on his own. I'm certainly not excusing Amnon's lust and sin, yet it took a friend's influence to actually bring about the action. And through the influence of a friend, he became exactly like his friend.

I have seen this principle lived out in young lives for years. I've seen this principle lived out in my own life! We always take on the qualities, attitudes, and character traits of those we spend time with. I've had teenagers argue with me over it, debate me on it, and tell me it isn't true. You can reason the truth away, you can resent the messenger, but you cannot escape the law! You are, right now, becoming like the very people you associate with. And here's the final clincher...

Universal Law #3
People Will Always Judge You by Your Friends.

This is the part that all teenagers hate! No matter what you say, where you go, or what you do, people will always judge you by your friends, and they will be judging correctly!

Heavy? You bet! Hard-hitting? I sure hope so. True? Inescapably so!

Dozens of times a rebellious teenager has said to me, "It doesn't matter if I change, because everybody already thinks I'm a bad kid!" Dozens of times a teen with a bad reputation has said to me, "Everybody thinks I'm bad just because I hang around _____, and that's not fair!" What are these statements saying? I want to have bad friends, have a bad past, but not deal with keeping a bad reputation. Sorry, pal—no can do! They all go together!

The Bible says in Proverbs 22:1, "A good name is rather to be chosen than great riches, and loving favour rather than silver and gold." Did you catch that word—chosen? That's you—you do the "choosing" part of that verse. You have the right to choose your name—then you have to live with the name you choose. Make your choice, but recognize that you have to live with the consequences. I'm simply saying, when you choose your friends, you choose your name! Quite simply, you get your friend's name!

"Not fair!" you might argue. Who said it was fair? That's what they always say, "It's not fair that people judge me by my friends or by my past!!" Well, what should they judge you by—your height? People always look on the exterior to judge you—your appearance, your friends, your past, the way you walk, talk, chew gum, the expression on your face. The Bible teaches this, 1 Samuel 16:7, "…for the LORD seeth not as man seeth; for man looketh on the outward appearance, but the LORD looketh on the heart." Man always looks on the outward appearance to make a judgment call—it's all he can see! Yes, God looks on the heart, but nobody on this planet can see your heart, so we have to work with whatever you give us. So far, all you've given us is your past, your appearance, and your friends. So, we will work with that and take it as an accurate representation of who you really are—until you give us enough material to change our opinion.

Man, sometimes those choices just really get you, don't they? And you know what, since your heart is the decider of your choices, your friends, and your appearance—we're generally going to be right on target when we make these judgment calls. Since people befriend people who are like them, and then they will become even more like them, it's pretty safe to judge someone by the crowd they hang out with.

I know what you mean when you say, "Unfair!" You're referring to the time when you sense the terrible misery of being away from God, and you make your heart right to come back to Him. In that moment people should be like God and give you a clean slate, right? People should just "forgive and forget"—cut you some slack—and immediately trust you as if you were perfect. In some ways, yes, people should grant you the same love and forgiveness that God does, but trust—a good name—will still take time to establish.

You can't live rebelliously for four years and then expect one tearful prayer at an altar to restore the trust and confidence of the whole world in your good name. No matter how sincere you are at the time of repentance, you still have a bad name to deal with. True repentance will always lead you to courageously accept this truth—accept the fact that people still judge you by your past—and persist on, allowing time for the good name to be built. Fair? Maybe not. Reasonable? Sure it is.

Would you want your daughter to date a repentant serial killer? Probably not. But, hey, that's not fair… God has forgiven him, and so should you. It's not about forgiveness, it's about trust and a good name. These things take years to build—or rebuild, yet they are always worth the journey. Ecclesiastes 7:1, "A good name is better than precious ointment; and the day of death than the day of one's birth."

It's pretty safe to judge someone by the crowd they hang out with.

Perhaps you have some authority figure harping on you about your friendships. Perhaps you have been struggling with people pre-judging you by the friends you keep. I'm sorry to break it to you, but this goes with the territory of wrong friends, and only you can change the course of public opinion.

The kind of person you are drawn to says "a whole bunch" about what kind of person you are. If you truly love the Lord out of a pure heart, you will have a strong desire to be around people who share that heart, and they will desire to be around you as well! If you despise godly Christians, then you will be attracted to people with those same feelings, and that's a terrible fore-shock of events to come later in your life!

So, don't get bent out of shape because people judge you by your friends. It's a fact, because your close friends reveal your true spiritual condition and course. I hope you get so bent out of shape that you'll start choosing better friends—that's truly the only solution.

> "A good name is rather to be chosen than great riches,
> and loving favour rather than silver and gold."
> —Proverbs 22:1

Thirty-Four

God's Good Plan for Right Companions

Okay. Enough harping on wrong friends. Let's get to the solution. Are you tired of not being yourself? Are you sick of knowing your friends will reject you if you do something "uncool" like "get spiritual"? Are you tired of having to put up a front—an act—just so someone will be your friend? If so, God has a better plan for providing you with friends. It's not always easier, but it's well worth the effort and the faith! Let's discover the best path to true friendships.

A few days ago, I was sitting on the swing in our back yard—now treeless—with my four-year-old daughter Haylee. The evening was calm, the breeze was just right, and the stars were just becoming visible in the night sky. As we sat, holding each other, she said the most profound thing, completely out of nowhere.

"I can't hear Jesus with my ears..." and then she was quiet. My curiosity was aroused, and I thought I would pursue this line of thinking with this four-year-old theologian.

"Of course not," I stated flatly.

"But why?" she asked innocently, inquisitively.

"Because Jesus doesn't speak to your ears. He speaks to your heart!"

"But why?" she continued.

"Because everybody else speaks to your ears, and He doesn't want to be like everybody else. He wants to be special to you. He wants to speak to you in a place where no one else can! He wants to speak only to your heart where only you can hear Him because you are special to Him, and He wants to be special to you!"

"Okay…" and with that we went on to talk about important things like why moths aren't dangerous. But that conversation stuck with me because it taught me something about my friendship with Christ. He doesn't speak to our ears. He speaks to the heart, and that's why many Christians never make Him their best friend. We are so busy looking for outward, physical, audible signs of significance and affirmation, that we rarely take time to find it from Christ within.

As we journey into this chapter, let's start right here…

First, choose the friendship of Christ. I know this sounds hyper-spiritual, but get beyond that for a moment. The Bible says in Proverbs 18:24, "A man that hath friends must shew himself friendly: and there is a friend that sticketh closer than a brother." Jesus said in John 15:13–15, "Greater love hath no man than this, that a man lay down his life for his friends. Ye are my friends, if ye do whatsoever I command you. Henceforth I call you not servants; for the servant knoweth not what his lord doeth: but I have called you friends; for all things that I have heard of my Father I have made known unto you."

Jesus literally calls Himself "your friend" and calls you "His friend"! Do you get it? God Himself wants to have a friendship with you.

If this concept is new to you, it might sound a little weird—but it's still true, and very real. God desires to be your close friend, and for you to be His close friend. He wants to talk to you, and you with Him. He cares about the most mundane details of your day, and there isn't a moment that you don't have His attention. He is always waiting to hear from you and He always gives you the first move in this friendship. He calls you to "seek Him" in Hebrews 11:6 or to "open the door" to Him in Revelation 3:20, and though He will pursue you, He will not force you to love Him or respond to Him.

No one knows you more intimately or loves you more passionately than God. In our minds, these two don't go together. In human relationships, usually, the more someone truly knows us, the less they love us. That's why we often go to such great lengths to create facades—fake covers to disguise who we really are. But with God, it's just the opposite. He knows everything there is to know about you, and still He loves you with an everlasting love.

No one knows you more intimately than God, and no one loves you more passionately than God.

Think about this statement. God accepts you. I'm sure, even now, your enemy is throwing lies into your mind about your past failures. If you are a Christian, the fact—the truth—the knowledge of God on this matter is that He truly does accept you just as you are because of what Christ has done. Romans 8:1 teaches that you have "no condemnation" in Christ as you choose to walk in His Spirit! His offer of friendship to you is not the product of your good behavior. His friendship to you is the product of His powerful, unconditional love—and it is, in fact, the very power that will change your imperfections! His friendship—His daily transforming power—is the solution to what's wrong with us! Without a personal, dynamic, daily relationship with Him, we're bound to our imperfections, and we will probably journey this life trying to compensate for them and cover them up. Yet, with God's awesome friendship and powerful grace, He wants to transform us into the image of His Son.

There is nothing you could tell God that would surprise Him. There is no secret that He doesn't already know. There is no pretending with God. He knows everything you think and feel! Yet, He fully accepts you and wants your friendship.

You know that craving for acceptance and friendship that we talked about earlier? Well, this is the only answer. Jesus Christ is the only one who can truly and fully meet that need, because He is the one who created it. You have a God-shaped hole in your heart, and no one else can ever fill it.

Yet, when you accept God's invitation—when you run to Jesus Christ like I ran to that police officer—you find that He is more wonderful, welcoming, and awesome than you could have ever imagined.

He will fill the need for friendship in your life, and truly He will become your BEST FRIEND! From this solid ground of a whole heart that is filled with God's perfect love, you won't find yourself running to and from earthly friendships craving approval and needing friendships so desperately. You won't act like a starving refugee dying for another taste of acceptance. You won't find yourself stooping to new lows in human behavior just to be acceptable to a certain crowd! When God fills your heart with His friendship, He truly is all you need!

Recently, I interviewed a couple in our church who had gone through some considerable trials in their lives. This man, for years, suffered with a bad kidney and had to spend many hours each week on dialysis. Since then, the Lord has provided a kidney transplant that spared his life. Yet, during that time, he shared with me how real his friendship with the Lord became. He said with tears, "Jesus Christ truly is my best friend." His statement seemed to say, "No matter what happens, as long as I have Jesus, I know everything is going to be fine."

Contrast that with a man whose daughter was facing a terrible health trial who said to me over lunch, "I'm so angry at God! Curse God! How can He do this to my daughter?"

That statement ignited a fire in my soul like few things ever have! As controlled as I could be, I locked eyes with that man's and said, "Look here, sir…Jesus Christ died the cruelest death imaginable on a cross to redeem you and your daughter to Himself so that you could spend all of eternity together in Heaven where nothing could ever separate you! Now, He may choose to take your daughter to Heaven sooner than you, or He may choose to answer prayers and heal your daughter—but in light of the CROSS and His promise to you for ETERNITY…whatever He chooses is just fine!" Silence.

When you run to Jesus Christ—you find that He is more wonderful, welcoming, and awesome than you could have ever imagined.

I proceeded to try to offer comfort and an understanding of God's hand in this man's situation. I didn't know if I had said the right thing, but I do know this. I was looking at a man who had searched in all the wrong places for his security, acceptance, and friendship. I was looking at a man who had no friendship with God—at a time when he needed it the most!

God wants to be your friend. You must respond to Him. All you've ever longed for, you will find in Him, and your enemy will do everything within his power to keep you from that friendship. See the truth. Don't bite that hook. Song of Solomon 5:16 says, "…he is altogether lovely. This is my beloved, and this is my friend…"

In choosing Christ as a friend, you must be ready to stand alone. You must be willing to make Him your only friend if need be. He may require you to lose your friends for the love of Him—to leave those who would influence you wrongly. Down the road, He will always give you better friends, but you must be willing to stand alone!

Second, choose the friendship of your authorities. The lie of the enemy will always say, "You could never be friends with your parents, your teachers, your pastors, or other godly influences." He will do anything he can to divide those relationships. Yet, I can say, having experienced both sides of this equation—the teen side and now the authority side—these authorities want your friendship, need your friendship, and even enjoy your friendship!

One thing I know to be true—adults intimidate teenagers, and teenagers intimidate adults! Did you get that? It's not that one group doesn't like the other. Both groups, adults and teens, are greatly intimidated by each other! Teenagers think that adults don't like them—that adults think they always have bad attitudes—that adults think they are nothing but problems. I'll never forget sitting in a library at my Christian school as a teenager. In the middle of class, a book on the shelf caught my eye. This book must have been at least 600 pages in length, appeared to be slightly smaller than an encyclopedia volume, and the title was simply "TEENAGERS"! I sat there as a sixteen-year-old, thinking, "My goodness… are we really that big of a problem?! Am I so complex a blot on society that I require a volume of information that size for adults to be able to deal with me?!" I was a little bothered by that.

On the flip side, adults are uncomfortable around teens! Adults think that teens think all adults are old, stupid, not-funny, and out of touch with reality. Adults feel that teens don't like them, don't respect them, and would rather spit on them than talk to them. Adults always feel "on trial" with teens—a very intimidating, uncomfortable feeling. I know because I feel this way every time I stand in front of a group of teens to teach or preach!

Teens and adults intimidate each other! Maybe this would be a good time for family-sharing! Yes, teens often intimidate their parents—and parents intimidate their teens. This natural intimidation usually drives the two groups apart. Because of this intimidation factor, one misunderstanding leads to another, and eventually both sides shut-down and stop communicating! It's tragic.

Teenager, because of this intimidation, I promise you, you are missing out on some of your closest and best friendships! You have friends you have never discovered! Your teachers could use a good teenage friend encouraging and sharpening them. Your parents could really use your encouragement and acceptance, especially when they fail. Your pastor surely would love to have you as a friend and encourager! These relationships should be the most rewarding of your young life. Don't let your enemy cheat you out of these special bonds!

When I was a teenager, some of my best friends were my authorities. I don't mean in a "teacher's pet" sort of way. Sure you might be teased or made fun of by other teens, but who cares! Decide now to go against the grain—to break the intimidation barrier and start befriending those godly authorities that God has placed in your life. You won't believe what great friends they will become in your life! When I fell in love with Dana, all of our double dates were with parents, teachers, and other authorities. We wanted it that way. We needed those friendships, and we cherish them to this day.

As a youth pastor, I can honestly say it's a joy to befriend a teenager who actually makes an effort at being friendly! I am the friend of every teen in our youth group, but there are always some who just go out of their way to become friends—they exert the energy it takes to be friendly, and those relationships have proved to last many years!

Parent, decide now that you will break through the intimidation factor! Someone has to! Interestingly, when an adult takes the risk to break through that barrier—when an adult places personal acceptance on the shelf, and really invests in a teenager's life—teenagers usually respond with incredible respect and acceptance! It requires that you risk your whole acceptance issue and be willing to be laughed at, rejected, and even scorned. And teens may actually put you to the test! It's no fun, but in time, God will give you the heart of a teenager who really appreciates your transparency.

This thought comes back to fragmentation. The enemy does everything he can to separate us from these key relationships. Realize, you need the friendship of your authorities more now than you ever have. Don't let insecurity rob you from these wonderful treasures!

Third, choose the friends of Christ. I've heard all the excuses. "I don't fit in with that crowd." "They don't like me." "That's just not who I am." "I don't want to be hyper-spiritual." Blah, Blah, Blah. In every student group there's a good crowd and a bad crowd. Usually, in the good crowd there are a few who are arrogant, a few who are fake, and a few who are truly sincere. In every bad crowd there are a few who play both sides of the fence, a few who blame the good crowd for "the way they are," and a few who just don't give a rip at all. Those who blame the good crowd always point to the fakers or the arrogant and say, "I don't want to be like that!" I always say, "Great, you just be sincere then!" How we reason that a phony or a boaster gives us an excuse to be rebellious against God is beyond me!

It's time that you choose friends who you want to be like! Choose the crowd that loves Christ sincerely and earnestly. Choose to associate yourself with those who truly have a good name. Only you have the choice! Use it. Choose friends who are willing to wound you when you are doing wrong. The Bible says it this way in Proverbs 27:6, "Faithful are the wounds of a friend, but the kisses of an enemy are deceitful." Choose friends who will provoke you to do right. Hebrews 10:24, "And let us consider one another to provoke unto love and to good works." Choose friends who will strengthen your relationship with God.

First Samuel 23:16, "And Jonathan Saul's son arose and went to David into the wood, and strengthened his hand in God."

Think about Psalm 119:63 where God's Word says, "I am a companion of all them that fear thee, and of them that keep thy precepts." Can that be said of you? Are you a companion of "all them" that fear the Lord and keep His commandments? If so, then you are well on your way to establishing a good name. If not, there's no time to lose.

Look at Psalm 1:1–3, "Blessed is the man that walketh not in the counsel of the ungodly, nor standeth in the way of sinners, nor sitteth in the seat of the scornful. But his delight is in the law of the LORD; and in his law doth he meditate day and night. And he shall be like a tree planted by the rivers of water, that bringeth forth his fruit in his season; his leaf also shall not wither; and whatsoever he doeth shall prosper."

So, the question is not "who likes me"? The question is "who am I like? What kind of person am I, and who should I become friends with so that my character can be sharpened into the image of Christ?"

Are you courageous enough to make the right choice? Teenagers by the millions are falling prey to this hook. They are following the school of other fish—they are following the chumps right into the chum! But you could be different. You could defy the odds. You could see through the bait and escape the hook, if you are courageous enough to choose the right friendships.

By the way, that tree mentioned above in Psalm 1? That, I'm sure, is a beetle-free tree!

"A man that hath friends must shew himself friendly: and there is a friend that sticketh closer than a brother."
—PROVERBS 18:24

Thirty-Five

What's Worse than Cutting Off Your Own Arm?

To act upon this section of this book will possibly require you to make some major, earth-shaking changes in your life! You may have to sever some close ties. The Bible is very clear about this choice, and for you it will come down to obedience. God cuts right to the heart of this matter in Romans 16:17–19, "Now I beseech you, brethren, mark them which cause divisions and offences contrary to the doctrine which ye have learned; and avoid them. For they that are such serve not our Lord Jesus Christ, but their own belly; and by good words and fair speeches deceive the hearts of the simple. For your obedience is come abroad unto all men. I am glad therefore on your behalf: but yet I would have you wise unto that which is good, and simple concerning evil."

Think about that. God says first MARK them! Wow! That's pretty tough language! Mark them—point them out, spray paint a big red X on their forehead, make sure you establish who they are! Then He says AVOID them! Stay away from them, walk away, and deliberately avoid their presence! This borders on being rude! Yet, in the case of protecting yourself from the wrong crowd, God grants you the right to "avoid." He does not give you the right to mistreat them. He simply says mark them and avoid them!

Teenager, parent—let me be pointed here. When it comes to the wrong crowd, God leaves no margin for diplomacy! He says straight out—mark 'em, avoid 'em, and get away from 'em! He commands you to do everything within your power to stay away from those who would influence you contrary to Him. Don't sit at the same lunch table; don't walk on the same sidewalk; don't share a pew in church; don't hang around by the water cooler at work! Walk the other way!

Now, you might be thinking, "I can't do that; it's rude!" Let me be clear here. You have two choices—you can either completely avoid the wrong crowd, or you can disobey your God. Which would you rather do? Standing right, staying right, and having right friendships requires that you have the courage and the will to obey God and deliberately avoid the wrong crowd! You must value your obedience to God and your spiritual health more than you value the respect or acceptance of the wrong crowd!

God says that these people "deceive the hearts of the simple." They are there for your destruction! These are not friends; they are chum. No matter how good their words or how fair their speech—you'd better get a clue—God says, "get away from them!" Then, God says, "For your obedience is come abroad unto all men. I am glad therefore on your behalf: but yet I would have you wise unto that which is good, and simple concerning evil." Hey, obey God and let that obedience be seen openly by all men! Be glad to be simple concerning evil! Be openly obedient and be glad to be a good kid!

Look at God's command in 2 Thessalonians 3:6, "Now we command you, brethren, in the name of our Lord Jesus Christ, that ye withdraw yourselves from every brother that walketh disorderly, and not after the tradition which he received of us." Withdraw! Get away from these people. Leave them. Sever the ties. Disconnect from their influence. Tell them straight up that you cannot and will not be hanging with them any more. Make it clear. Draw the line in the sand and stand your ground!

This is tough to do, but those who take this kind of stand always end up with true friends! God always honors this kind of blatant obedience.

In May of 2003, Aron Ralston was hiking alone in a canyon in eastern Utah. As he was making his way through a narrow, three-foot-wide slot in the canyon, an 800-pound boulder shook loose and fell onto his forearm. The boulder pinned his arm literally "between a rock and a hard place"—trapping Aron for five days. In panic, Aron spent many futile hours during those days throwing and heaving himself against the boulder, trying to break it loose. He tried in vain to chip away at the rock with his cheap, multi-tool knife. By the fifth day, Aron's water and food supply was gone, and he knew there was no chance of breaking free. He knew if he stayed in the canyon, he would not survive. He had exhausted all other options. He was in a drastic situation that called for drastic measures.

So, with his one free arm, he prepared some ropes and tackle with which he would rappel out of the canyon to meet help. Then, he prepared a tourniquet and some crude first aid. What he did next made news stories all over the world. Using only a small pocket-knife, he began to amputate his own arm just below the elbow. For about an hour, Aron cut through skin, muscles, blood vessels, and finally bone. This man literally severed his own arm with no pain medication—in order to preserve his own life. Several hours and six miles later, he walked out of the canyon with one less "forearm"—but very much alive—very much a survivor!

Severing your wrong friendships may actually seem to be more difficult and more painful than Aron's experience! I know many teens who would rather lose an arm than lose their wrong friends. Friendship can be that powerful with teenagers—especially when a fragmented family has left a young heart starving for acceptance and validation. Yet, you must see that these wrong friendships are holding you hostage. You are literally pinned between a rock and a hard place. The enemy will soon devour your life and your future if you don't take drastic measures. It's time to sever something most precious to you. It's time to do what is necessary to preserve your future

Those who take this kind of stand always end up with true friends! God always honors this kind of blatant obedience.

destiny! Act now! Take courage! Sever those friendships, and walk away a survivor to live the life God has planned for you!

May I warn you? They won't let you go easily. They will try to convince you to stay. If you stand strong, they will get angry and reject you. (Some great friends you must have…) Then they will get down right mean! They will mock you, make fun of you, stab you in the back, and maybe worse. It will hurt. You might cry yourself to sleep. You might go a while with no friends. You might be totally rejected. But you will have your BEST FRIEND. He will never leave you, never forsake you, and always be with you. And He really is all you need.

You must decide what kind of person you want to become—what kind of character you want to have—and then choose to befriend people with that kind of character. Ask the Lord to give you those kinds of true friendships. Proverbs 13:20 tells us, "He that walketh with wise men shall be wise…." Over time, God will create within you a more stable, mature, and spiritual inner man—first through your strong friendship with Jesus Christ, and then through the godly influence of parents, authorities, and other strong friends. God will always meet your need for acceptance and friendship, but only if you trust Him to do so. Psalm 37:25 says, "I have been young, and now am old; yet have I not seen the righteous forsaken, nor his seed begging bread."

How Can I Reach My Old Friends?

There are two types of old friends—saved and unsaved. In this section I want to primarily address those who profess salvation but who are living contrary to the Word of God in their lives. I'm not necessarily referring to unsaved friends who need the Gospel. You should always try to courageously share Christ with those who need Him, yet even then, any connection with old friends can be devastating if you don't take the right steps to protect and safeguard yourself from temptation.

Many times a teenager has approached me with a statement. "I know my friends are living wrong—I know they are headed the wrong direction—but if I don't help them, nobody will." This is a smoke-screen 99% of the time. Usually this statement is simply a cover up for a disobedient heart. Most teenagers are not so concerned with reaching and changing their friends as they are with keeping their friends.

So, let's say you are honestly and sincerely in the 1% minority. Let's say you are genuinely concerned for your friends and their wrong direction. You are in a very precarious (dangerous and unstable) position. As a teenager, you are extremely vulnerable to wrong influences, yet you have also been given the command to "love your neighbor." How can you blend the two? How can you sever your wrong friendships and yet still attempt to influence your old friends in the right direction? Here are some thoughts.

1. Recognize your responsibility to obey God first. No matter how strong your burden for another person, God never gives you permission to do wrong in order to do right. In other words, you cannot hang with this person, participate in his lifestyle, and disobey God simply to reach him. This isn't the way God works. Your primary responsibility is to take heed unto yourself before God.

2. Understand God's way of reaching your rebellious friend. In 1 Timothy 4:16 Paul warned Timothy to, "Take heed unto thyself, and unto the doctrine; continue in them: for in doing this thou shalt both save thyself, and them that hear thee." Look at the last part of that verse—"thou shalt both save thyself, and them that hear thee." You see, God's way of reaching your friend will be as you first take heed to yourself—your own relationship with God. You will never reach your friend if you don't first take a strong stand. God will use your stand to convict your friends. Your example will have a far greater impact than your meager attempts to convince them of their errors.

3. Recognize your limited role in your friend's life. You must realize, even as a close friend, you are not the primary influence or authority in this person's life. God can use you, but it must be on His terms and in His time. Don't place your own walk with Christ in jeopardy simply because you elevate yourself into the position of spiritual authority that God didn't intend. I've seen young people become so burdened for a friend, that they short-cut God's sovereignty and they appoint themselves as the savior of this friend.

Most often, they are not strong enough and don't have the spiritual preparation needed to keep this friend from drowning. Instead, the friend pulls them under as well. Your role as a friend is first to protect yourself, to take the right stand, and to consistently point your former friends to God and to spiritual influences who can truly help them. Until they are willing to submit to God, your influence only serves to place you in jeopardy.

Teenager, you must recognize that you are not the hedge of protection in your friend's life. Others are. In fact, I've watched many teens leave their own hedge of protection, under the guise of trying to "help a friend." You cannot do this and win. You cannot escape God's authority in your life and hope to help your friend. In this case, you will simply expose yourself to greater destruction, and lose your friend in the process.

4. Determine to be the stronger Christian influencer. In every friendship, both friends are influencers, but one always carries a heavier influence. One always pulls the other. If you are weaker—usually finding yourself being pulled by your friend—then stay away from this situation completely. If you find it impossible to "speak up" and to "take a stand"—then just walk away.

The Bible pattern for restoring a friend is that it must be done with great meekness and spiritual commitment. Galatians 6:1 says, "Brethren, if a man be overtaken in a fault, ye which are spiritual, restore such an one in the spirit of meekness; considering thyself, lest thou also be tempted." Paul expresses here that restoration can work if the restoring Christian is first, spiritual; Second, meek; third, considering the protection of self; and fourthly, prepared to withstand the resulting temptation. That's big stuff, and few teens are equipped or ready for such spiritual engagement.

5. Recognize that silence is an endorsement. If you sit silently by while your friend smokes dope, loses her purity, fills his life with corrupt influences—you are aiding in the process. Your silence makes you an accessory to the sin. You're actually helping in the destruction.

Someone who is truly burdened for a friend will not stay silent. True love is tough love, and when someone is about to be hooked and reeled in, true love would never sit by and watch it happen. Friends don't let friends bite hooks!

6. Be willing to leave this person in God's hands. If you desire to live godly in Christ Jesus, you're simply going to have to leave some harmful associations behind. There's no other way around it. You should never be mean, harsh, arrogant, or judgmental to these people. You should always express genuine concern, prayer, and love for them. You should always be open and hopeful that this person will come back to Christ. Yet, in the end, you're going to have to love your God more than your friends. You must be willing to walk away if you will ever discover God's best blessings in your life!

7. Trust your parents' insight and guidance. When choosing friends, there's no safer place to be than within God's protective hedge! God has given you parents who can see the spiritual world—the spiritual battle for your life—more clearly than you can. You may find a friend that your parents immediately decide they don't like. Before you reason that they are just harsh, unfair, or judgmental—realize that they are probably seeing something that you cannot see! They probably see character issues, heart problems, and bad influences that will harm you.

Don't be a dumb fish. If your parents are trying to break up a friendship or relationship—if they are uncomfortable with a certain crowd—you'd better realize that they see a hook! You see the bait—they see the boat. Let them be the authorities that God commands them to be. No matter how bad you want friends, trust your parents' insight, and ask God to help you find friends that they are comfortable with.

This brings us to our final thought in this section…

"Blessed is the man that walketh not
in the counsel of the ungodly…"
—Psalm 1:1

Thirty-Six

Bringing Dad and Mom In On the Quest

Dad and Mom, you may not have realized it, but this section was directed at you and your teenager. Yes, adults struggle with this friendship thing, too—being that adults are just "grown-up teenagers." Every single truth we've talked about applies to adult life as well as teen life.

The most disturbing thing about the "Christian nightclubs" that I mentioned in the last section of this book, was the response of the parents! I wouldn't expect teens to always know and understand the difference between what is godly and what is ungodly. Yet, Christian parents were interviewed in the same news story, and they swallowed the whole thing, hook, line, and sinker.

These parents were so glad their teens could skate, dance, rock-for-Jesus in a club where there was no drinking and drugs! Amazing! They were willing to let their teens surround themselves with corrupting music and wrong friendships, all under the guise of a "drug-free, alcohol-free environment." How foolish we have become! How dulled in our sensitivity to spiritual dangers! How blinded! Truly, we need the Holy Spirit of God to enlighten our spiritual eyes once again. Please know I'm not trying to question the sincerity or motives of the people running these organizations. I just believe they've swallowed the lies of a culture far from God.

Parent, perhaps you have been blinded or disengaged in your teenager's life. Perhaps you have inadvertently "left your child at McDonald's." You were busy and you became fragmented somehow. Perhaps you've just now realized that your friendship with your teenager is not what it should be. There is little chance that your teenager will singularly run to the Saviour to fill the void. Usually he will run to the wrong crowd. What should you do?

From One Confused Parent to Another

Sometime ago, I was able to listen to the audio book "She Said Yes," written by Misti Bernal, the mother of Cassie Bernal—the young lady who was shot and killed in the Columbine High School shooting. In that book, Mrs. Bernal details their fight, as parents, to get Cassie out from under the influence of satanic music and wrong friends. The process happened in Cassie's life much like what I have explained in the pages of this book. At one point, Cassie was in a state of utter depression and misery—even plotting to kill her own parents—and the Bernals felt that their home-life was literally being torn apart.

At this point, the Bernals chose to "enter the fight" for their daughter. They chose to engage. Little did they know what they were up against. Fortunately, they had some Christians in their lives who helped them understand the spiritual battle. They did some things that seemed pretty extreme at the time. First, they completely emptied Cassie's bedroom and sorted through every item piece by piece. They destroyed music, trashed ungodly influences, and completely "cleaned house." As you can imagine, Cassie blew a gasket (as will your teen). She was enraged with them and threatened all sorts of things. Yet, the Bernals persisted with tough love.

Second, they withdrew Cassie from public school and prohibited her from even talking to any of her friends. This seemed extreme, but these were desperate parents fighting a desperate force for the life of their daughter. Cassie did everything she possibly could to stay connected with her friends—sneaking phone calls, leaving the house late at night, etc. She defied her parents in every way possible. Her friends refused to let go as well. They threatened Mrs. Bernal, vandalized the home, and generally wreaked havoc on this family.

Third, her parents restricted Cassie to the home except for church and youth group activities. In other words, other than home and Christian school, Cassie could only go to church and youth group. This further enraged Cassie. She resisted and believed that she was literally a prisoner in her own home. No, she was a much-loved teenage girl who needed to be free from the bonds of a spiritual enemy. The hooks were deep.

Rather than give in, the Bernals stood strong in battle for their daughter. They sold their home and moved! When things didn't get any better with Cassie's old friends, they literally relocated their family to protect their daughter.

It wasn't until a teen camp when Cassie trusted Christ as her personal Saviour that things began to change. When Cassie returned from that retreat, her Mom said she was a completely different person. She reconciled her life with her parents and from that point forward, she was a joyful young lady. A look into her diary and writings revealed that over the coming months, Cassie truly did develop a personal friendship with Jesus Christ that became the foundation of her life. It is an amazing story.

The relocation and Cassie's life transformation is what ultimately led the Bernals to allow Cassie to attend Columbine High, where several months later, she was killed in cold blood for her faith in God. When the killers pointed the gun at Cassie, they asked her, "Do you believe in God?" Her answer was simply, "Yes, and so should you." With that, the killer pulled the trigger.

Cassie is in Heaven today, because of her personal relationship with Jesus Christ. Yet, I ask you, why did she come to Christ? What was the key factor in her salvation? I submit to you, it was the fact that her parents refused to give up. They entered the fight, engaged the enemy, and fought the battle for her spiritual life. I'm not sure they even completely understood what they were fighting for. I only know if they hadn't fought, she probably wouldn't be in Heaven today.

What is it, in relation to your teenager's friends that you haven't been willing to engage in? Are you fearful of offending someone? Are you feeling that you can't really control your teen's friendships? Are you just too busy to enter the fight and to be aware of who your teen's friends are? I challenge you—I urge you—I plead with you to enter that arena! Be the hedge around your teenager that will protect him from wrong friendships. Endure the rejection of your own son or daughter if that's what it takes. Be loving, be gentle, be kind—but be strong. Don't give in. Surround your teenager with loving influences—be the friend that you should be in his life—and then stand your ground against the forces of darkness on this issue.

Be loving, be gentle, be kind—but be strong. Don't give in.

Perhaps most importantly, guide your son or daughter in this area. Help them see what you see! Do more than lecture or force your will. Nurture spiritual growth in this area. Help your teenagers understand the truths of this chapter. Help them know that when they choose a friend, they are giving another human being the power of influence in their lives! Help them see character issues and warning signs. Help them develop the spiritual discernment and wisdom to choose right friendships. Help them have the courage to stand alone when necessary. Help them by being their friend. Break through that intimidation barrier and develop a sincere teen-parent friendship that provides a healthy emotional foundation for other friendships.

Best Friends

Some time ago, about mid-way through Lance's seventh grade year, he gave me, quite unintentionally, the greatest compliment he could have ever given me as a dad. We had been through a busy season of life. I had been away from home a little more than I usually was, and we hadn't had the time together that we normally do. In addition to this, often the little time we did have was spent working on math homework—a subject that Lance was struggling with at that time.

On one particular night, trying to encourage Lance before a math test, I said, "Lance, we've studied so hard on this, I know you're going to get an 'A' or a 'B.' When you do, I'm going to take you to Circuit City and we're going to get a Playstation 2 game, just to celebrate."

Well, the next day, I asked Lance's math teacher to give me the test grade as soon as he knew it. Suffice to say, it wasn't what we had hoped for. I didn't want to break the news to Lance, because I knew how hard he had worked preparing for that test! He was so sure he had done well, and when the news hit, it hit hard. Really hard. Long, and hard.

Somewhere amid the disappointment, I tried to console him by saying, "It's okay, son, there will be other tests and we'll get that Playstation game the next time." Fathers say stupid things when they don't know what to say, just give us a break. I'll admit, I was fumbling for some words of comfort—and ended up sounding like geek of the year instead.

In that moment, he dried his eyes, wiped his face, and looked sternly into my eyes, "Dad, don't you understand! I didn't work so hard on that test to get a dumb Playstation game! I worked hard on that test just so you would be proud! That's the only thing I care about. Don't you understand Dad, you're like my BEST FRIEND..." and with that he started to cry again and buried his head on my chest.

"Don't you understand, Dad...you're like my best friend!" I will never forget those words. I hope and pray that they will remain true throughout our lives. It was the greatest thing Lance could have said to me. That's truly how it should be! Parents and teens should be the best of friends!

So, what will you do with the hook of wrong friendships? Teenager? Parent? Will you allow the devil's crowd to befriend and bewilder you? Think about it. Choose wisely. Choose Jesus Christ. Choose each other. Choose those who will help you become more like your Saviour. Mark the wrong crowd. Avoid the wrong crowd. Sever them from your life so you can survive the hike! When you find yourself "alone and left to die at McDonald's," run as fast as you can to the acceptance of Jesus Christ. Find in Him all you need.

Stay away from the chum—the chumps that the devil will send your way as bait. Don't give them the power of influence in your life.

Decide not to "need" their acceptance. Don't give up the friendships that God will bring into your life for the devil's cheap substitutes.

Most importantly, don't forget—the BEST FRIENDS you could ever ask for are always pretty close. One resides in your heart, and the others sleep in the bedroom just down the hall...

"My son, hear the instruction of thy father, and
forsake not the law of thy mother:"
—PROVERBS 1:8

"Whoso curseth his father or his mother,
his lamp shall be put out in obscure darkness."
—PROVERBS 20:20

Conclusion

Surviving
the Slaughter

*Overcoming the Enemy
by God's Grace*

Thirty-Seven

Escaping the Prison Camp of the Enemy

In 1941, our country entered World War II. This conflict brought engagement on two fronts—the Pacific Rim and the European Continent. In Asia, we were fighting the advancement of a maniacal dictator leading the Japanese empire, and in Europe we were fighting the maniacal advancement of Adolph Hitler and his Nazi Germany.

In the course of this conflict, the islands of the Philippines were in great danger of being completely taken over by Japanese forces. Tens of thousands of Americans, under the command of General Douglas MacArthur, fought in the Philippines and especially on the Bataan Peninsula, along the northern edge of Manila Bay. Yet, by early 1942, due to the fact that most of our energies and resources were needed in the European theatre, the American soldiers fighting on the Bataan Peninsula began to be outnumbered. Through a series of tragic developments, the forces on Bataan were forced to surrender to the Japanese.

General Edward King was forced to either surrender or allow the slaughter of tens of thousands of American soldiers. The surrender took place on April 9, 1942. At that time, over 98,000 American and Filipino fighters were fighting under his command. General King was quoted as saying, "If I do not surrender to the Japanese, Bataan will become known as the greatest slaughter in history."

The Japanese only anticipated 25,000 men surrendering and being placed into POW camps, and therefore planned food rations, prison space, and slight medical care for about that many. They were only off by about 75,000—as nearly 100,000 soldiers (American and Filipino) emerged from the jungles in surrender.

These captives were then forced to begin what history has called "the Bataan Death March"—a foot-walk into the northern regions of the Bataan Peninsula where these soldiers would be placed into ill-prepared prison camps. It is estimated that through the course of the march, which took an average soldier a week, 750 Americans and 5,000 Filipinos died from exhaustion, disease, neglect, and outright slaughter. This march is recorded as one of the most brutal and bloody acts of atrocity ever committed against American forces.

Most of these prisoners were taken to Prison Camp O'Donnell—a camp designed to imprison only 9,000 that immediately filled with more than 50,000 POWs. Camp O'Donnell, in these conditions, was appalling. It was a breeding ground for parasites, disease, and pestilence and it became the sight where literally thousands of American lives were lost to unimaginable diseases, and unthinkable cruelty. The ensuing cruelty of the Japanese troops was harsh and bloody. Thousands of Americans were slaughtered in the most heinous of ways for the slightest of reasons, and sometimes with no apparent reason at all!

Due to the overcrowded conditions, the Japanese were forced to scramble for other arrangements. Most prisoners only stayed at O'Donnell for fifty days, until they were sent to other POW camps in Japan and elsewhere. In these other camps, many thousands suffered unspeakable atrocities and slaughter.

In a short time, O'Donnell housed just over 9,000 POWs. One out of ten prisoners who passed through O'Donnell perished there! In two months 1,500 Americans and 15,000 Filipinos were buried in mass, unmarked graves just outside the camp.

In June of 1942, many of these POWs were moved to another camp named Cabanatuan. About 500 died at Cabanatuan in June alone, and another 786 perished in July. Of the 9,000 men originally moved to Cabanatuan, nearly 3,000 would be buried there in the coming few years. In addition to this, due to death and the transfer of the prisoners, Cabantuan eventually dwindled to just over 2,000 prisoners.

At this point, these valiant soldiers began a three-year stay at this indescribable place of horror. During that time they suffered disease, starvation, torture, and unbearable cruelties. Over time they began to feel forgotten.

Yet, they weren't. In January of 1945, the United Stated re-invaded the Philippines with adequate forces and quickly closed in on the Japanese Imperial army. In the face of this rapid aggression, the Japanese army began to gradually slaughter thousands of American POWs held in camps all over southeast Asia. As the United States proceeded towards the Bataan Peninsula in the Philippines, it was feared that these prisoners in Cabanatuan would be executed and disposed of before American forces could reach them.

To avoid this massacre and hopefully spare over 1,500 POWs, a secret rescue plan was devised. It is the least known and perhaps the most incredible rescue effort of any American conflict of all time. In January of 1945, Colonel Henry Mucci and Captain Robert Prince led a group of 121 Army Rangers, 280 Filipino guerillas and a small band of Alamo Scouts into a rescue mission that had little chance of succeeding. The hope of these rescuers was to free the POWs and deliver them to safety before the Japanese massacred them.

From the launch of the mission these soldiers were required to journey across 30 miles of no-man's land—a twelve-hour march across Japanese patrolled roads, across Japanese-held bridges, through open country infested with Japanese pillboxes, and through villages that would potentially hold Japanese spies. Once they arrived in the area of the camp they were required to scout the entire camp layout without being detected by the hundreds of Japanese soldiers that were stationed there. Then they were required, in the middle of the night, to prison-break over 1,500 men, 500 of which were probably incapable of leaving the camp of their own power.

The Alamo Scouts spent the better part of two days silently and stealthily studying the prison camp without detection. That, in itself, was a miracle since the camp lay in a flatland hundreds of acres across in which it was literally impossible to hide.

Then, with the help of Filipino guerillas, at the strategic moment, as the guerillas blocked bridges leading into the camp, and as literally thousands of Japanese forces camped just a few miles away, these 121 Army Rangers overtook more than 200 Japanese guards and led over 1,500 suffering POWs out of Cabanatuan, unharmed. In all of the massive assault, only two men of the rescue team were lost.

In the ensuing hours, under cover of darkness, 1,500 prisoners walked several miles, many of them being carried or assisted by Rangers and by other prisoners. Wounded prisoners were then loaded into 71 oxcarts—supplied by friendly Filipino villagers—and they commenced what would become known as the Cabanatuan Life March. This march was approximately 20 miles to American lines where the prisoners and rescuers were welcomed, cared for, fed, nursed, and later transferred to safety and ultimately home! The press made only slight mention of their rescue, and then their story faded into history in the shadow of the atomic bomb and the war's conclusion.

These POWs were rescued by a group of soldiers who were truly courageous, who were captivated by a cause greater than themselves! These men were willing to engage, to fight, and even to die if necessary to rescue those held hostage in enemy territory. They were joined together with unity of heart, purpose and spirit to preserve the lives of thousands against a ruthless and merciless enemy. And they won!

It's Time for a Prison-Camp Rescue

Friend, today we live in a generation held hostage to a different kind of ruthless enemy. This enemy is on a rampage—destroying thousands of young lives and families with four primary lies. Teenager, you are the POW! You have been lied to, captured, and held hostage to a brutal enemy. You have been fragmented from those you need, divided against protective authorities, corrupted through the voices of the world, and befriended by the worst kind of chums. Now that the enemy has you on his hook, he will do everything he can to finish you off. The clock is ticking, and with every passing day your enemy becomes more and more desperate and blood thirsty.

Parent, you are the Secret Ranger force that God has assembled to send on a covert rescue mission. You cannot rescue your teenager if you are a POW. You must be trained, fit, and ready for the mission—and you must be fully briefed on these lies! Your teenager is depending on you. Future generations in your lineage are depending upon you. There is no time to lose. If you do not act fast, if you do not engage in the fight, you will lose your teenager. The mission ahead poses great threat to your spiritual life. There may be tears. There may be blood shed. There will be warfare against spiritual wickedness in high places.

One incredible observation about the Cabanatuan rescue mission—you'll never believe what happened when the Rangers invaded the camp and began telling the prisoners to get up and walk out. The prisoners didn't believe them! They thought it was a trap. Many of them were so delirious and confused that they hid in corners, refused to follow orders, and some even considered suicide! Many didn't get it at all! For several minutes the Rangers had to work at proving the reality of the rescue attempt. Many had to be physically picked up and carried out of the camp—not because of weakness, but because of delirium. Being held hostage for so long, they didn't recognize freedom when it came!

In order for that mission to succeed, the Rangers had to force the POWs to follow them out of camp amidst a hail of gunfire and explosions. Ultimately, the truth became clear, the gunfire faded, and freedom settled in like a long lost friend! Eventually the hearts of those prisoners brought reality back into clear focus and they understood what wonderful thing had been done for them.

Parents and teens, don't forget the gray matter. Sometimes teenagers can't see reality as clearly as they should and parents must spiritually and sometimes physically carry them to safety—even against their own will. That gray matter can do terrible damage!

Please remember, teenager—your parents are not the enemy! They are not the ones who hold you hostage. They are here for your freedom—your long-term freedom! They may enter your camp under cover of darkness. They may return fire upon an invisible enemy. You may feel that they are threatening the last bit of security and sanity that you have. That's what it's like in a prison camp—even when you're being rescued. Yet, with all of their fervor and activity in your life, do not buy the final dying lie of the enemy. Don't fight them. They are not the enemy. They are your rescuers and they are putting their lives on the line to defeat the strongholds of the enemy in your life.

Parent, remember as you launch into this mission, that you are dealing with a subtle and invisible enemy. Your teenager is not the enemy, although Satan would have you think so. You are engaging the forces of darkness. You are resisting an enemy that resides in a world you cannot see. Your teenager may not understand. He may not respond at first. She may think you are a threat. There may be a fog of spiritual delirium hanging over the prison camp that holds your teenager. Regardless, it is up to you to carry out the mission, engage in the fight, and rescue your teenager from the strongholds of the enemy.

Four Prison Camps of the Enemy

Much like Camp O'Donnell, Camp Cabanatuan, and others, the devil has four major prison camps for young lives.

Prison Camp Fragmentation is where a young person and his family are divided either by the unnatural busyness of cultural demands or by the choice of their own hearts through anger or bitterness.

Prison Camp Rebellion is where young lives are held hostage by their own resistance against all rescue attempts. This camp is one of the most miserable because it turns the heart against all its rescuers, and this camp specializes in torture techniques of the soul.

Prison Camp Corruption is where the enemy fills the heart with the infectious, defiling influences of worldly music, harmful entertainment, and cultural indoctrination. It is here where the prisoners are brainwashed and indoctrinated into the world and where the heart is conformed to the spirits of the world.

Finally, Prison Camp Evil-Companions is where the enemy, disguised as good friends, holds prisoners hostage to insecurity, fake love, and artificial acceptance. In this camp, a prisoner is disconnected completely from God's great love, from true friends, and from a deep inner feeling of acceptance. At this camp, prisoners destroy themselves in groups.

Perhaps you've been imprisoned so long by these four lies, that you've forgotten what freedom feels like. Well, it's time to wake up!

It's time to prepare for escape! It's time to organize a covert operation and to prison-break the POWs. Romans 13:11 says, "And that, knowing the time, that now it is high time to awake out of sleep...." Again God commands us to "Awake to righteousness, and sin not; for some have not the knowledge of God..." in 1 Corinthians 15:34. It's literally time to wake up to the life God intended for us. Too long we have given the enemy ground in our homes—teenagers by falling prey to the lies, and parents by ignoring the warning signals and failing to enter the fight. Too long have we slumbered under the drunken influences of fragmentation, rebellion, corruption, and wrong companions. It's time to make a break for freedom before the enemy finishes us off!

> *"Wherefore he saith, Awake thou that sleepest,*
> *and arise from the dead, and Christ shall give thee light."*
> —EPHESIANS 5:14

Thirty-Eight

Sail On—Losing No One!

When the children of Israel were about to enter the Promised Land, they were entering a battle zone. The story is an amazing paradox. On one hand the people have been promised a land flowing with milk and honey. On the other hand, they cannot have it unless they fight for it.

My first question to God would have been, "Why make them fight? If you've already given them the land, why make them engage in bloody, life-threatening combat?" When you read the first few chapters of Joshua, the dual promise of God is clear—fight and you will win, claim and you will possess. Losing the battle was not a possibility. God repeatedly says that the battles are already won and the land is already given to them, so long as they take courage and follow Him in faith. Amazing.

Friend, the story is much the same for you and me. God has promised us an abundant life to be found in Him—the Christian life, if you will. It is a life of eternal hope, eternal significance, and eternal blessings. Yet it is also a life of warfare, of physical and spiritual engagement. The two cannot be separated, and God's promises are true for both sides of this existence. If we fight, we will win. If we claim, we will possess. God's command is to fight, and His promise is victory. God's command is to enter in and claim His blessings, and His promise is possession. We can experience the life that God intends for us if we will brave the battle and claim the promises.

We live in a day when Christians neither want to battle nor to claim. We want what the children of Gad and Reuben wanted in Numbers 32. In this chapter, the descendants of Gad and Reuben are considering their options before crossing over the Jordan into the land of battles and promises.

The Bible says that they have a "great multitude of cattle" and that they really like the good land where they are! In other words, they are considering staying put! Across the river is a war, but right here is good land for the cattle. These people were making a sensible decision. They had enough. They were comfortable on the east side of Jordan. Why bother entering the fight and risking so much? Why put everything on the line to trust God when this land would make a fine home?

This chapter is a powerful picture of the twenty-first century Christian family. We have more than we've ever had. Our garages are filled with stuff, our land is good, and our bellies are satisfied. We're comfortable right where we are. Why fight? Why tire ourselves? We're already busy getting and caring for all of our things. We like it where we are!

When Dr. J. Frank Norris was voted into his first pastorate at the First Baptist Church of Fort Worth, Texas in the early 1900's, he was already known as a fighting, fiery preacher. The church family that accepted him knew that he would come to pastor their church with a fighting, visionary spirit to do something great for God. Three hundred people voted *on* him and 299 voted *for* him. The one dissenting voter wrote this explanation on his ballot. "If he comes here, there will be the most allfiredest explosion that any church has ever seen. We are at peace with the world, the flesh, the devil and each other... I'm warning you."

"We are at peace with the world, the flesh, the devil..." What an accurate picture of modern day Christianity and most Christian families. Recent research shows that there is little to no difference between the lifestyles of the lost world and the lifestyles of professing Christians— we listen to the same music, attend the same movies, drink the same alcohol, smoke the same cigarettes, watch the same TV shows, dress in the same clothes, and engage in the same behavior. We truly are at peace with the world, the flesh, and the devil. And so were the children of Gad and Reuben. They didn't want to fight; they didn't want to change; they wanted to stay right where they were!

In Numbers 32:20–27, Moses said, "If ye will do this thing, if ye will go armed before the LORD to war, And will go all of you armed over Jordan before the LORD, until he hath driven out his enemies from before him, And the land be subdued before the LORD: then afterward ye shall return, and be guiltless before the LORD, and before Israel; and this land shall be your possession before the LORD. But if ye will not do so, behold, ye have sinned against the LORD: and be sure your sin will find you out. Build you cities for your little ones, and folds for your sheep; and do that which hath proceeded out of your mouth. And the children of Gad and the children of Reuben spake unto Moses, saying, Thy servants will do as my lord commandeth. Our little ones, our wives, our flocks, and all our cattle, shall be there in the cities of Gilead: But thy servants will pass over, every man armed for war, before the LORD to battle, as my lord saith."

What an amazing passage! God said, "If you follow in faith, cross the Jordan, and fight, then you can return to this land and care for your future. Yet, if you stay here and refuse to fight, you will be sinning and be sure 'your sin will find you out.'" Wow! God commanded them to resist the enemy! Even though the battle was already won, even though He didn't need their help in winning it, even though to human eyes it seemed pointless, God still expected obedience.

Parent, teenager—now that your enemy is exposed and his lies have been uncovered—he would like nothing more than for you to "stay still." His nightmare is that you actually might fight—resist. What you know about the enemy doesn't matter unless you use it in the fight. At this point he will try to keep you from fighting back. He will try to render you AWOL in the fight, make you comfortable on your side of the Jordan. The last thing he wants is for you to cross the Jordan and engage in this fight for your family.

God's command is to fight and His promise is victory.

Yet, if you do not, you can't know the abundant life of promise and hope as a family that God has for you. The fight must be fought. One preacher recently preached to our men and boys, "If you lose your fight, you lose!" He must have said that 200 times during his message as he compelled our men and boys to engage the enemy. Then he said, "But if you fight, you always win!" How true! What a great promise. God's instructions to the children of Israel were quite simple—"Be courageous and fight—and you will win. Yet, if you choose not to fight, you lose!"

Paul challenged Timothy in 1 Timothy 6:12, "Fight the good fight of faith…." God tells you to resist in James 4:7, "Submit yourselves therefore to God. Resist the devil, and he will flee from you." Again in 1 Peter 5:6–9, "Humble yourselves therefore under the mighty hand of God, that he may exalt you in due time: Casting all your care upon him; for he careth for you. Be sober, be vigilant; because your adversary the devil, as a roaring lion, walketh about, seeking whom he may devour: Whom resist stedfast in the faith…"

When you fight, you win! Every time! This is a guarantee from God—fighting is winning and disengaging is losing. First Corinthians 15:57, "But thanks be to God, which giveth us the victory through our Lord Jesus Christ." First John 5:4, "For whatsoever is born of God overcometh the world: and this is the victory that overcometh the world, even our faith."

So, parents, teens, it's time to engage in the fight and claim the promises of God for your future. Your enemy is fighting, but he cannot win so long as you engage against him. And his ultimate loss is unavoidable. Revelation 20:1–3 says, "And I saw an angel come down from heaven, having the key of the bottomless pit and a great chain in his hand. And he laid hold on the dragon, that old serpent, which is the Devil, and Satan, and bound him a thousand years, And cast him into the bottomless pit…" What an awesome sight that will be! One angel dragging Satan to the bottomless pit—I hope it's the smallest angel in Heaven!

> *It's time to engage in the fight and claim the promises of God for your future.*

As we come to the end of our time together, I challenge you to always remember that you live in a dual world—one that you can see, and one that you cannot see. Usually when the one you can see becomes almost unbearable—it's because something very important is happening in the one you cannot see! The world you cannot see contains an enemy that is warring against you in very real and physical ways—ways that impact your physical and spiritual life immensely—ways that impact your family and your future. Remember how he operates and seek God's enlightening—ask Him to constantly open the eyes of your understanding.

Then beware of these four lies—the devil's bait: fragmentation of your family, rebellion against authority, corruption in your heart, and companions of the world. These are the ways that young lives are being snagged and reeled into the boat in record numbers.

Then engage in the fight and endure 'til the end. Enlighten, engage, endure—three words that capture the true essence of the Christian life and the Christian home.

Surviving the Storm By God's Grace

In Acts 27, the Apostle Paul is being taken as a prisoner to Rome. He is on a ship and headed into a terrible storm, which will ultimately lead to a terrible shipwreck. He knows this because God has revealed it to him. The storm, the wreck, the suffering, and the attempts to survive had dramatically less of a fear factor on Paul than on the others, for one simple reason.

Beginning in verse 21, here is what Paul says, "But after long abstinence Paul stood forth in the midst of them, and said, Sirs, ye should have hearkened unto me, and not have loosed from Crete, and to have gained this harm and loss. And now I exhort you to be of good cheer: for there shall be no loss of any man's life among you, but of the ship. For there stood by me this night the angel of God, whose I am, and whom I serve, Saying, Fear not, Paul; thou must be brought before Caesar: and, lo, God hath given thee all them that sail with thee. Wherefore, sirs, be of good cheer: for I believe God, that it shall be even as it was told me."

Can you imagine a deck hand on the Titanic giving this speech to the people on board, "Sirs, be of good cheer, we're about to hit an iceberg and sink in this unsinkable vessel. The water will be freezing, the ship will be lost...but be of good cheer!" Yeah right...

Yet, Paul had enlightenment into "the rest of the story." You see, when you know the truth of God, you have reason to be of good cheer, no matter what is happening in your physical world! So Paul says, "Sure, we're going to lose the ship, we're going to have to swim for it, the raging waters could kill us, but I know a greater truth, a higher revelation. I understand reality as it truly is and not how it simply appears in this storm."

What reality? What promise did Paul know? He knew that God had promised him that no one would perish in this shipwreck. Paul believed God. He believed the Word of God, the message of God from the angel that stood by him! In my mind I can see the waves tossing the vessel, the spray blinding the panicked, scrambling men on deck. I can see the fear, the chaos, the tossing to and fro, the throwing overboard of gear and possessions to lighten the ship. I can hear the screams of the men as they face death and fear the worst, as all hope of survival is taken away. I can hear them shouting orders at one another above the roar of the storm and I can see the fear in their eyes as they wonder and dare to hope that Paul was telling the truth.

Then I can see the Apostle Paul literally take charge and pastor that group of rough seamen through death-defying waters. You can read the story. He kept them from jumping overboard, he prayed and broke bread with them, he comforted and helped them—at one point the Bible says they were truly "of good cheer." Then at the right time—one man after another jumped overboard to swim for land.

Guess what? Every one of them arrived safely on shore just as God promised.

Even so, parent, you are in the midst of a storm called "child-rearing." In the teen years, your ship enters the most dangerous waters on the journey. At times you will feel like either jumping ship or throwing someone else overboard! At other times you will feel like sharing a meal and being of good cheer! The storm will rage stronger and stronger, and your enemy will wage war against your spirit and the spirits of those in your vessel. Yet I believe you can truly be of good cheer! I believe that the Angel of God will truly stand by you. Don't jump ship, don't fall to your fear, and worst of all, don't disengage from the battle. Stay afloat, stay the course, fight the storm, and in time God's promise will prove true. You can be of good cheer.

Consider Lance's letter that I used in the introduction of this book:

"You're my friend, no matter what tries to get in the way…"

Friend, you can be sure, there *is* an enemy trying to get in the way.

"…what I'm trying to get across to you is there is nobody ever in this universe that can replace you…"

Dad, Mom, nothing ever can!

"I'm with you all the way!"

Parent, can you say that to your teen? Teen, can you say that to your parents? By God's grace, may you be *with* each other…all the way!

May God truly give you the hearts of "all them" that sail with you!

"…*God hath given thee all them*
that sail with thee…"
—ACTS 27:24

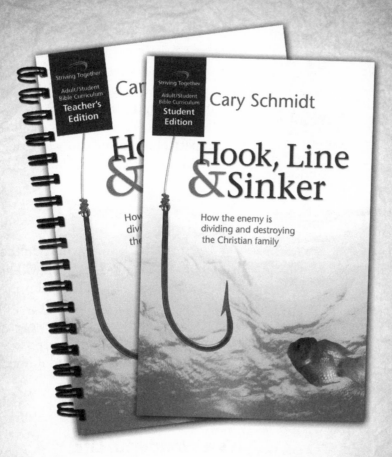

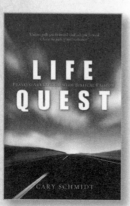

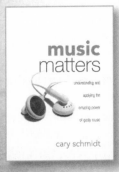

Fruit Grows Where the Stream Flows
Adult Sunday School Curriculum
The only way to truly live the Christian life is to allow the "stream" of the Holy Spirit to flow freely through your life, so He can bear the fruit of spiritual maturity. In this thirteen-lesson study, you will be rejuvenated as you discover what the Holy Spirit wants to produce through you.

Discover Your Destiny
Teen Sunday School Curriculum
Discover what every young adult needs to know about making right choices in a world full of wrong. This seventeen lesson series will equip students to discover the perfect will of God for their lives. The teacher's guide contains lesson outlines, teaching ideas, and Scripture helps.

Jonah: A Whale of a Lesson on Obedience
Adult/Teen Sunday School Curriculum
Dr. John Goetsch brings to life a powerful study in this new Sunday school curriculum. These thirteen lessons will take your students verse by verse through the book of Jonah. This study is perfect for adult Bible classes as well as young adults and teens.

Visit us online

strivingtogether.com

dailyintheword.org

wcbc.edu

lancasterbaptist.org

paulchappell.com